Tony Pastor,
Father of Vaudeville

Tony Pastor, Father of Vaudeville

ARMOND FIELDS

McFarland & Company, Inc., Publishers
Jefferson, North Carolina, and London

ALSO BY ARMOND FIELDS AND FROM MCFARLAND: *Women Vaudeville Stars: Eighty Biograpical Profiles* (2006; paperback 2012); *Maude Adams: Idol of American Theater, 1872–1953* (2004); *Sophie Tucker: First Lady of Show Business* (2003); *Fred Stone: Circus Performer and Musical Comedy Star* (2002); *James J. Corbett: A Biography of the Heavyweight Boxing Champion and Popular Theater Headliner* (2001); *Eddie Foy: A Biography of the Early Popular Stage Comedian* (1999; paperback 2009); *Lillian Russell: A Biography of "America's Beauty"* (1999; paperback 2008)

Frontispiece: This portrait was prepared in 1885 for a colorful poster commemorating Tony Pastor's 20th year as a theatrical manager. No sooner were the posters mounted than they were removed by loyal patrons and admirers (Harry Ransom Humanities Research Center).

The present work is a reprint of the illustrated case bound edition of Tony Pastor, Father of Vaudeville, *first published in 2007 by McFarland.*

LIBRARY OF CONGRESS CATALOGUING-IN-PUBLICATION DATA

Fields, Armond, 1930–2008.
Tony Pastor, father of vaudeville / Armond Fields.
p.   cm.
Includes bibliographical references and index.

ISBN 978-0-7864-6424-1
softcover : acid free paper ∞

1. Pastor, Tony, 1837–1908. 2. Lyricists—New York (State)—New York—Biography. 3. Entertainers—New York (State)—New York—Biography. 4. Vaudeville—New York (State)—New York—History.
I. Title.
ML429.P34F54   2012   792.7092—dc22   [B]   2007017398

BRITISH LIBRARY CATALOGUING DATA ARE AVAILABLE

©2007 Armond Fields. All rights reserved

No part of this book may be reproduced or transmitted in any form or by any means, electronic or mechanical, including photocopying or recording, or by any information storage and retrieval system, without permission in writing from the publisher.

Cover art: Tony Pastor
(Harvard Theatre Collection, Houghton Library)

Manufactured in the United States of America

*McFarland & Company, Inc., Publishers
Box 611, Jefferson, North Carolina 28640
www.mcfarlandpub.com*

Contents

Acknowledgments	vi
Introduction	1
1. Family Heritage	3
2. Circus Days	11
3. "444"	19
4. "Greatest Comic Singer of the Age"	29
5. Tony Pastor's Opera House	41
6. The Elks, John Poole and Touring Success	54
7. Variety's Triumph	66
8. New Talent and Crowded Houses	82
9. The Emergence of Vaudeville	100
10. The 14th Street Theater	115
11. "The Most Popular Theater in Town"	127
12. Business Challenges and Changing Audiences	136
13. Continuous Vaudeville and Shrinking Profits	151
14. Tony Retires from the Stage	166
15. Struggling to Stay Open	178
16. The Venerable Showman's Decline	190
Epilogue	194
Chapter Notes	197
Bibliography	201
Index	205

Acknowledgments

Three outstanding libraries and archives supplied me with most of my research material for this book.

The Harry Ransom Humanities Research Center at the University of Texas, Austin, provided examples of Pastor's lyrics and songs, a wide assortment of photographs of Pastor and his performers, articles, reviews and other pieces of information from years of touring, programs, posters, correspondence, financial journals, sheet music and miscellaneous scrapbooks of Tony's career from 1861 to 1908. Rick Watson of the HRC was of considerable assistance in making the materials available and understandable.

The New York Public Library, Billy Rose Theater Collection gave me access to scripts, songs, programs, articles and clippings, photographs and Pastor's personal papers.

The Houghton Library at Harvard University made available song lyrics, scripts, programs, photographs and Pastor's correspondence.

Also of substantial assistance were:

The Circus World Museum, Baraboo, Wisconsin
The Circus Historical Society
The University of Southern California, Special Collections
The Museum of the City of New York
The New York Historical Society
Library of Congress.

My particular thanks go to Claude Zachary of USC's Special Collections; Mary Jane McIntire, the intrepid genealogist; and Kathryn Perez, a loyal and hard-working researcher, for their extraordinary contributions to this project.

To Sara, wife, friend, lover and editor, my deepest gratitude for her years of enduring and accepting my obsession with American popular theater.

Introduction

When Tammany Hall fell into the hands of wreckers in 1928, the famous old theater that was once Tony Pastor's was no more. For the previous twenty years, it had not been Pastor's in name, but to New Yorkers it would always be Tony Pastor's theater.

For sixty-four years, the old theater had been a place of amusement. It was not Pastor's originally. Dan Bryant ran his minstrels there for some years and it was a German theater right before Tony moved in.

Tony had owned a theater down on lower Broadway. He observed that business was moving uptown. In 1881, he grabbed the house on what was then an uptown street full of high-class shops and customers, next to the Academy of Music, located in the magnificent new Tammany Hall.

In the quarter of a century from 1881 to 1908, hundreds of artists who became celebrated headliners had graduated from Tony's theater. They went to the legitimate theaters, to vaudeville and to musical comedy. Many of them, like Edward Harrigan, Lillian Russell and May Irwin, became theater legends.

The performers who passed through Tony's stage door included America's favorites in the late nineteenth and early twentieth century. Pastor's was the show house of father and grandfather. They liked it, and when mother and the children went but once, they returned because the show was entertaining and clean.

The ambition of young performers was to obtain an engagement at Tony's. If Tony put the stamp of approval on them, they were booked across the country. If they worked a week at Tony's theater, they were good. If they were booked for a return engagement the same season, they were of class. If they became favorites of the audience, they appeared at Tony's for years.

The audience at Tony's was composed of people who generally attended the theater every week and they wanted the bill to change. Tony gave them what they wanted. He learned that during his early circus days and his variety beginnings at 444 Broadway.

In one night, Gus Williams became famous with a song that swept the country. He had been playing in beer halls and got his first engagement as a professional with Tony. His Dutch act was one of the first on the variety stage.

Tony gave pretty Helen Louise Leonard her stage name of Lillian Russell and launched her on a career as "America's Beauty" and a magnificent actress.

Annie Yeamans came out of the circus, did a turn on Tony's stage and became a varieties regular. Two decades later, Tony introduced her daughter, Lydia, to Broadway's bright lights. He also introduced Lottie Gilson, Ella Wesner, Lillie Western, Anita Summerville, Blanche Ring and Irene Franklin.

No manager was able to duplicate Tony's success with foreign stars. Bessie Bonehill and Bessie Bellwood, Jennie Hill, Vesta Tilley, Cissie Loftus and Vesta Victoria delighted packed houses with their songs and dances.

Weber & Fields were at their funniest at Tony's. Maggie Cline sang "Throw Him Down, McClosky," and the stage boards rattled. Nat C. Goodwin, who later became America's foremost actor, was introduced by Tony doing a song and dance routine. Francis Wilson was part of a team of comedians when he appeared at Pastor's; in a few years, he was a star in musical comedy. Dan Sully did his stuff first for Tony's audience. Billy Barry, a versatile blackface comedian, came back repeatedly to Pastor's and went on to operate a farce comedy company. Kelly and Ryan, Irish two-act specialists, sang and danced "Good Bye, Jack, Till You Get Back," and appealed to the Irish in every patron. McIntyre and Heath, Fields and Hanson and other blackface comedians found a comfortable place on Tony's bill. Denman Thompson showed Tony's audiences what melodrama was all about.

Harry and John Kernell, Charles "Honey Boy" Evans, Nat Wills, James F. Hoey and Pat Rooney were favorites at Pastor's. When the circus season was over, Tony featured high wire artists, club swingers, acrobats, magicians, contortionists, bicycle riders, ventriloquists and card manipulators, introducing them each week to excited patrons.

Tony was raised in poverty, the first boy and third child of six. He had little education and was apprenticed to a circus man at the age of fourteen. Ten years in the traveling circus as acrobat, tumbler, clown and ringmaster taught him the rudiments of performance. He entered variety at twenty-four, already a veteran with a unique specialty, singing comic songs. He was a poet and a consummate businessman and had a keen eye for talent. At thirty-two, he owned, operated and performed at his own theater. Tony managed a theater for forty-three years, the longest of anyone in New York.

Tony's strategy was to offer audiences only the best in popular entertainment. Every act that went on had its rehearsal; no matter how good the performers were, Tony kept them motivated and fresh. He challenged them, he counseled them, and he promoted them vigorously. Loyalty to Tony among both performers and audiences was unbounded.

When Tony's theater closed, Tony died with it. His theater in Tammany Hall was as a training ground for actors and the model for vaudeville entertainment.

1

Family Heritage

Antonio Pastor and Cornelia Buckley met briefly at the neighborhood Catholic church. She knew immediately that she would marry the handsome young Spaniard.

Antonio had arrived in America in 1823.[1] Born in 1800, the twenty-three-year-old had left Seville, Spain, to seek his future in New York City. Cornelia was born in New Haven, Connecticut, in 1811 and came to New York to seek employment and a husband.[2] Antonio had already opened a barbershop in a well-to-do section of the city and offered a comfortable life style for Cornelia.[3] On March 29, 1826, but a few months after they had met, they were married. Antony (he had assumed the Americanized version of his name) was twenty-six years old. Cornelia was fifteen.

Antony had a skill, a business and a respectable life style while living in Seville, and had probably been brought up in a bourgeois family. When he decided to travel to the United States, he made his way to Algeciras to seek passage on a ship to New York. There he became a passenger on a packet. Packet ships were 140 to 160 feet long, three-masted, six-sailed, and with a reputation for being very fast. They were the first ships to be called liners. Their captains were known to drive the ships for speed no matter the weather. While primarily freighters carrying olive oil and fortified wines, they also offered a few comfortable cabins for paying passengers. Only recently had sailing ships between Europe and America developed specific schedules and destinations, significantly improving trade relations between the various countries. Depending on the weather, the trip took from five to six weeks.

The ships were unloaded at wharves in the lower Bowery, where Battery Park would later be located. Their cargo was carried by wagons to factories and manufacturers located nearby. Passengers stepped off the boat with their baggage free to go where they wished, after a brief, almost cursory stop at Customs.

New York had no immigrant processing center in 1823. A customs office greeted each newcomer and recorded his name, age and reason for visiting the U.S. Customs officially designated Antony as "a gentleman," which meant he had paid his own way, was cultivated, and had a profession. In his deposition, Antony unequivocally renounced his allegiance to the king of Spain. Why?

It is likely that Antony wished to immediately establish himself as a potential citizen and express his loyalty to his new country. Judging by the Customs declaration that he was "a gentleman," he probably had some knowledge of English. The fact that he opened his business in an upscale part of the city almost immediately after arriving in the U.S. would also suggest at least a moderate fluency in English. People living in this section of New York, near Park Row, had strong prejudices against obvious foreigners.

Another possible reason for Antony's departure from Spain and renouncement of the king may have been religious. The Holy Office of the Catholic Church of Spain had identified the surname Pastor as a Sephardic (Jewish) name.[4] While Antony had to have been familiar with his family heritage, when he entered the U.S. he claimed to be Catholic.

The Spanish Inquisition was in full force from the late 1400s until Napoleon's invasion and defeat of Spain in the early 1800s. During this disastrous period, most Jews had escaped the country. Those remaining had two choices: convert to Catholicism or face being burned at the stake. Many Jews who publicly converted continued to practice their traditional rituals in secret. They were called conversos.

After the Spanish defeat, the 1812 Cortes of Cadiz declared the Inquisition abolished. Jews could openly practice their religion, operate businesses and hold property. At the time, most Jews were living in Madrid, Cordoba and Seville. Still, Jews were wary of the new law and many maintained a strained relationship between Catholicism and Judaism. Antony was brought up during this period in which suppression was followed by religious freedom.

When the Spanish monarchy was reestablished in 1823, one of the first laws reinstated was the Inquisition. Antony left Spain that same year. Why Antony chose to be identified with the Catholic church is unknown, but he may have felt that belonging to the church in his new country would allow him to make his way more easily.

Antony located his barber and hairdressing shop at 147 Fulton Street, within two blocks of Park Row, one of the more elite residential neighborhoods of the city. At the time, male fashions demanded impeccable grooming; female hair care required the skill of a hairdresser. Antony and Cornelia lived in a house he purchased in 1828 at 68 Reade, in a quiet residential section north of "The Collect" (a pond that had served as a colonial reservoir, had become a swamp and was being converted into a park) and Park Row, with its large homes and mansions. The house had been purchased from an old Dutch family who had owned the property since early colonial times.[5] The Pastor home was a two-story, brick-fronted wooden house with a backyard outhouse. Antony paid $780 in "lawful money" for the property.

During the late 1820s and early 1830s, New York City was rapidly changing from a colonial town to a bustling, commercial city, enjoying a galloping prosperity. From the Battery, the burgeoning metropolis was growing in three directions. Up the west side along the Hudson River, the area was made up mostly of docks, factories and housing for transients. Along Greenwich Street, it was made up of residential neighborhoods and small entrepreneurs.

The middle of the island featured Broadway, Orange and Bowery Streets as the main arterials for commercial enterprise, while nice-appearing residences were found on the side streets off these primary thoroughfares.

Up the east side was Water Street which paralleled the city's docks, the neighborhoods a few blocks inland housing the poor, with significant pockets of slums.

In 1806, a plan for the growth of the city had been developed, but it took more than four years to begin implementation. A rectilinear grid was laid out, with the exception of Broadway and Bowery. The rationale was for economic purposes; to provide regular shaped plots, right-angled intersections, corner lots, and straight streets. By 1828, Broadway extended as far north as 10th Street. It had quickly become the city's main business street, and was one of the first to be fully paved and the first with gas lighting.

By the late 1820s, with the opening of the Erie Canal and regular sailings to and from foreign countries around the world, New York had become an important commercial center. The establishment of a large shipping company, the Black Ball Line, solidified the city's close involvement with international trade. But due to its haphazard expansion, the city was marked by extremes in neighborhoods, from dock areas to customer-driven business streets, from elite mansions around Park Row to the slums of the East Bowery. Accompanying these dramatic differences in living and working conditions came fires, epidemics, riots and financial panics. Still, the city grew and prospered.

New York's population in 1820 was slightly more than 152,000; by 1830, it had grown to 242,000, and in 1840, it was 391,000.[6] To complement the better class section of the city, in 1816 the City Hall was built in the Park Row area. In 1825, the first gas pipes led along Broadway to Canal Street. Four years later, they were extended to Houston Street. By 1830, the first horse drawn minibuses were operating on Broadway, helping to open the street to more distant customers. By 1833, thirty minibus operators had been granted licenses to serve customers. During this period, three and four story buildings were built to hold commercial businesses like department stores, hotels and theaters. Within this expanding milieu, Antony prospered.

Still, New York remained a walking city. Almost everything in lower Manhattan could be reached by human locomotion. Carriages belonged to rich families. Hackneys (coaches) were available for hire, but were expensive. Even with all the new transportation available, it was faster to walk.

Two railroad lines were begun in the early 1830s, the New York and Harlem, serving the East Side and the Hudson River Railroad Company serving the West Side. One could travel from City Hall to Harlem (out of the city), but for the six-cent fare, which prevented the working class from using the train. Steamboats began to cross the rivers, to Brooklyn and Hoboken.

The penny press, introduced by the publication of the *New York Herald* in 1835, swept the city, and other newspapers rushed to duplicate the *Herald*'s success. Advertisements for goods and services became an important feature of the newspaper.

Antony and Cornelia's first child, Delores, was born in 1828, almost two years after their marriage.[7] A second daughter, Caroline, was born in 1830. Antony maintained his shop through 1829 and moved to larger quarters at 155 Fulton in 1830. But the house on Reade Street was getting crowded. Housing for the Pastors became particularly significant when Cornelia was again pregnant in late 1832. Antony sold the property for slightly less than he had paid for it, likely due to the recent decline in property values. The family moved to larger quarters at 400 Greenwich Street, at the time an attractive neighborhood, although quite a walk from Antony's shop. The house was quite comfortable, containing a coal stove, gas lighting and an icebox, as well as bedsteads, clocks and prints on the wall.

The first major calamity to strike the city was the cholera epidemic in June 1832. The city's water supply had been badly neglected, the sewer system overloaded, and debris pickup from the streets was infrequent. When cholera made its way to the U.S. from Europe, it gradually crept into New York. Although the city fathers were warned of the threat, little was done to prevent it. Threatened by the predicted invasion of the disease, the better classes of people left the city. The Pastor family joined them. Close to 100,000, nearly half of the city's population, departed to more healthy climes.

By the end of August, the city council declared the city safe and the people returned to their homes. But thousands had died in the interim. Most people were out of work, businesses and manufacturing plants had closed, and food was scarce. Not surprisingly, the epidemic hit the poorer areas the hardest because the people living there were unable to leave the city and the city government did little to extend itself to help them. But Antony was able to reestablish himself quickly when the well to do reopened their businesses and returned to their personal necessities and amusements.

Whether Antony and Cornelia attended the theater is unknown. Certainly their home was close to those theaters that featured dramatic plays and operas, but such venues were primarily for the enjoyment of the city's elite. With the Pastors' life style and the demands of a growing family, attending the theater had to have been an infrequent luxury.

As the city grew, so did people's interest in theatrical entertainment. At the turn of the century, only the Park Theater (called the New Theater when it was opened in 1798) served all the city.[8] The most famous actors and actresses appeared at the Park, along with the best in English plays. In 1825, the Park introduced Italian opera. The theater was located in a strategic area, close to Park Row, the City Hall and lower Broadway. It had no real competition until the 1820s.

In 1825, the Lafayette Theater opened, designed to compete against the Park. The goal never materialized and, when the theater burned down in 1829, it was not rebuilt. In 1826, the New York Theater opened, with hyperbole that claimed it was the handsomest theater in America. After several seasons, it closed as audiences returned to the venerable confines of the Park Theater.

In the 1830s, neighborhoods were in transition, the rich moving uptown, the poor invading what had been pretty residential areas. Irish and Germans moved into lower Manhattan and the Bowery attracted a different set of patrons. The change reflected rapidly growing immigration. By 1835, one-fifth of the city's inhabitants were immigrants. The Irish alone accounted for 30,000 new arrivals a year during the 1830s.

The New York Theater became the Bowery Theater and offered popular entertainment to its neighborhood clientele. As the theater's ownership turned over many times, the theater changed its name often, finally reverting back to its original name. It also changed its types of entertainment depending on the tastes of the audience. It was destroyed by fire six times, a common occurrence among early theaters, in 1828, 1836, 1838, 1845, 1923, and 1929. The theater became the main attraction for new types of popular entertainment, introducing melodrama, minstrelsy and variety amusements as each passed through its vogue.

In 1835, the Bowery Amphitheater opened across the street from the Bowery Theater. It was declared the largest theater in America, large enough to offer circuses, spectacles and large minstrel companies. The same year, the Franklin Theater opened on Chatham Street and thrived for two years, closing, like most theaters, due to the financial panic of 1837.

Antony Pastor was born April 26, 1833, at the family home on 400 Greenwich, the first son, named after his father.[9] Past biographies have claimed various dates for Tony's birth, from 1832 to 1837. These dates were suggested by Tony himself who, when interviewed, mentioned a date that seemed to meet his current theatrical status. He was not born in Brooklyn, as some historians claimed.

Tony's early years were defined by the events that impacted on his family, particularly his father. December 1835 saw the most disastrous fire in New York's history. The year 1836 was filled with worker strikes against management because of poor salaries and working conditions. The devastating Panic of 1837 closed down banks and created almost total unemployment in the city. The depression that followed lasted almost six years.

While the 1835 fire occurred in the lower Bowery and was not close to Antony's shop, the impact on his business was severe, as owners of major businesses saw their property destroyed and viewers of the destruction were shocked by the loss of life and the inability of the city to fight the conflagration. It was several months before Antony could depend on his regular clientele to return.

Sporadic riots broke out during 1836, some of them quite close to Antony's shop, and home, at 165 Greenwich Street. Living separately from work had become impossible due to the rapidly rising cost of housing, the overcrowding of neighborhoods and the lack of a sustainable income. Workers took to the streets and destroyed property while complaining about unsafe working conditions, long hours and unsatisfactory wages. At the same time, their bosses were reaping large profits, thanks to the city's rapid growth. People were afraid to walk the streets, and the police could not be depended upon to protect private citizens.

It was the Panic of 1837, however, that devastated Antony and the Pastor family's comfortable life style. The Panic of 1837 was an economic depression, one of the most severe financial crises in U.S. history. It was caused by the inflationary boom of the 1830s and a failure of confidence in bank notes. The bubble burst on May 10 in New York City, when every bank stopped payment in gold and silver coinage. The depression caused many bank failures and record unemployment levels.

The Jackson administration preferred the secured value of gold and silver to bank notes from banks. When the administration published a Special Circular declaring that the government would stop accepting bank notes, it was a "no confidence" vote in paper money. Most banks did not have specie (coinage) to back their paper. The result was a major decline in land sales. Companies paid their employees in scrip, IOUs were circulated, and specie payments halted. The demand for coin became critical in New York City. During April 1837, 250 business houses failed. Laborers, who normally worked for a dollar a day, were out of a job. Small entrepreneurs, who earned about twenty-five dollars a week, had no customers. Their income usually came from coins. Antony saw his hairdressing business decline precipitously. He was unable to pay his bills. No banks would offer loans. By June, one-third of New York was out of work; 200,000 were without adequate means of support. Only the neighborhood church was available to assist its parishioners with food and clothing.

St. Mary's was the first Catholic church in New York. Its initial congregation during colonial times was made up of Spanish and French immigrants who were escaping religious prosecution. Its members were mostly from the merchant and trade class. Catholics were a minority religion in the 1820s. In the late 1820s and early 1930s, the rapid influx of Irish — mainly males, young, unskilled and poor — Catholicism became a threat to the native population. Clashes between Protestants and Catholics were common, particularly in the poorer areas. And the era became one of ethnic and religious bitterness. At the same time, new Catholic churches were opening to accommodate the immigrant working class and, now more Irish according to the better classes, less respectable.

St. Mary's was a few blocks away from the Pastors' residence. The church assisted the needy with food and clothing until it was overwhelmed with demands. In 1833, the Church of the Transfiguration (later called the "Little Church Around the Corner" due to its proximity to the theaters and actors' attendance) opened and attracted families like the Pastors. Tony was baptized there.

It was unfortunate that Cornelia was pregnant at the time of the panic. Frank, the fourth child, was born on November 13, 1837. Antony struggled to maintain his shop and home even though the income was barely enough to pay for the necessities. The neighborhood of 165 Greenwich consisted mainly of manual workers and factories. The Pastors now made do with candles, oil lamps and wood.

Antony now called himself a "haircutter."[10] He spent the next five years attempting to eke out enough to provide for his family. William, the Pastors' fifth child and third son, was born August 6, 1840. Antony and Cornelia worked heroically to keep the family together in these hard times.

In spite of their hardships, the Pastors were a warm, loving family. Cornelia provided the care of an affectionate and protective parent while Antony did his best to support his growing household. The older sisters looked after the younger brothers. The brothers were inseparable, as their later life confirmed.

At the age of six, Tony entered the Thames Street elementary school. Delores had some elementary education but left school when Cornelia needed her to help with the family. Caroline had begun school in 1836 and was still there when Tony began his education. A common practice for families in poverty was to send out their six and seven year olds to earn a few pennies a week selling newspapers. Since the church strongly frowned on such activity, it is likely the Pastor children were saved from such humiliating and dangerous work.

In recalling his early life, Tony talked about singing with a sidewalk temperance group from the Dey Street Catholic Church at the age of six, for two years.[11] If he actually did participate in this activity, it more likely occurred when he was ten or eleven. He claimed to be a singer.

In 1829, the first temperance societies were formed in New York. They were heavily supported and financed by factory and manufacturing owners in order to prevent workers from drinking on the job and coming to work drunk. By 1832, ward groups had been established to reach neighborhood families. Temperance groups were now affiliated with local churches with three support groups: religious associations, politicians and anti-union organizations. The Panic of 1837 curtailed most of the temperance activities; the movement did not flourish again until the early 1840s when the New York Temperance Society set up street-corner pulpits. After 1843, temperance's greatest appeal was to lower classes, strongly backed by the churches. The Washingtonian temperance group became the largest popular movement in New York history.

Tony also recalled that in his temperance days he appeared with Christian B. Woodruff, who later became a state senator from the 4th district in New York City. At the time Tony said he appeared with Woodruff, the man was twenty years old, employed and had been arrested for selling lottery tickets, an unlikely time to be singing with street corner temperance groups. However, Woodruff was a friend from Tony's association with Tammany Hall politicians.

In May 1840, P.T. Barnum leased Vauxhall Gardens as a venue for entertainment, bringing in performers by the night. Barnum's American Museum opened in 1841, at the corner of Broadway and Ann Street. For a small admission, visitors viewed hundreds of oddities, from a "real" mermaid to the bullet that killed Lincoln. The museum also displayed natural history menageries, taxidermy exhibits and wax figures. Its Lecture Room, or theater, featured live entertainment, offering a wide variety of the latest amusements. Tony claimed that his first paying job was performing at Barnum's with a minstrel group.[12] Tony said he played the tambourine and sang as a "child prodigy." The date of his appearance there was said to be the fall of 1846, when he was thirteen years old. He said that his colleagues in the minstrel group were Charley White, Billy Whitlock and Hall Robinson, all on their way to becoming famous minstrel performers. However, at the time, all three performers were appearing with other minstrel companies outside of New York. While Tony may have performed at Barnum's, it was not with the aforementioned actors. Tony made these claims about his personal accomplishments as a child performer in the first published biography found in his 1862 songster. They were repeated in biographical sketches in later press and theatrical newspaper articles. The information may be suspect, as Tony probably romanticized his childhood performance experiences. Recounting a history of acting accomplishments would help to substantiate his later success in the circus and in variety.

The Pastor family's sixth child, and fourth boy, Fernando, was born in 1842. In 1843, at the same address, 165 Greenwich, Antony became a fruit seller.[13] He continued as a fruit seller for four years, although at different addresses each year. This may have indicated that the family moved as well, from Greenwich to Canal to Grand Streets. Antony's ability to support the family was now problematic. The future was anything but promising.

John Nathans, a circus man, married Amelia Pastor, from Philadelphia, Pennsylvania, in 1840. She had already been married and divorced from a Pastor (unspecified relative) and had a small daughter. As a cousin-in-law, she was familiar with the challenges facing Antony and Cornelia. At Amelia's suggestion, Nathans proposed to the Pastors that he take on eight-year-old Frank as an apprentice.

John Jay Nathans was born in 1814.[14] As a boy he became a circus equestrian. By the time he was a young adult, Nathans had the reputation for being one of the best equestrians in the business, the first showman to ride a four-horse while carrying a child above his head. Between 1829 and 1840, he was associated with ten different circuses (they started up and died with frequency) as their star equestrian performer. In 1839, Nathans turned to management along with performing, with Hall, Nathans and Tufts Circus. After marrying Amelia, he began teaching his stepdaughter, Emma, to be an equestrienne. (She first appeared in Welch and Nathans Circus in 1851 and performed through 1866.) With the Welch and Nathans show in 1841, Nathans managed the company and, with various partners, continued to manage through the 1860s.

The Pastors were persuaded that Frank would be taken care of and, at the same time, would learn a skill that would make him a good wage earner. Frank left with Nathans to embark on a circus career that would make him a famous equestran who performed around the world. It was also one less family member to care for.

A year later, after positive reports about Frank's progress and initial performance success, William, age six, was apprenticed to Nathans, also to be trained as an equestrian. William now joined his brother and Emma as members of a traveling circus company. Although relieved of two children, the Pastor family remained in poverty. Delores had a suitor; Caroline worked as a housekeeper; and Tony had an unspecified job that paid a few dollars a week, still not enough to adequately support the family as Antony struggled to make a living. The economic depression was easing and profitable commerce returning to New York, but its benefits were initially reflected in the manufacturing, banking and real estate sector, among those people who had already represented the better classes of the city. Common workers still suffered, many still out of work or paid low wages. Small entrepreneurs, like Antony, earned a meager income since few customers in their neighborhood had enough money to partake of their wares. In fact, the times were so hard, women took on jobs that not only reflected their perceived roles in society, like doing laundry, child care and seamstress work, but also those that questioned their virtue and were dangerous, like prostitution and running shops in poorer areas.

The Panic of 1837 and the depression that followed devastated city theaters. Many closed; some staggered on with frequent shutdowns and reopenings; some reduced prices and promoted extravagant bills to entice patrons. The Bowery came into its own during the depression as a plebian recreation zone. Saloons provided free entertainment to attract and hold drinkers. Concert halls did the same with the addition of "waiter girls" who served customers with a broader variety of services. A succession of variety theaters opened, primarily catering to those people needing a diversion from the trials of daily life. People were searching for inexpensive pleasures. Sharp businessmen recognized that profit could be made by providing cheap amusements.

Among the theatrical innovations that took place in the early 1840s, two became outstanding public successes. Audiences witnessed the birth of minstrelsy in New York, where white performers in blackface entertained enthusiastic audiences by emulating Negro dialects, songs and dances. The emergence of minstrelsy as a pleasing and enjoyable amusement helped to reshape American popular entetrtainment for half a century. When P.T. Barnum added variety entertainment to his museum, he helped to legitimatize the form that spurred new growth in theaters and the acting profession. By promoting his shows with printed posters, billboards and through newspapers, Barnum initiated an industry of public advertisements that reached all classes.

In 1847, the Pastor family consisted of Delores, Caroline, Tony and Fernando, now five years old, along with their parents. Delores married Junius Alexander Fuller on July 9. Born in 1821, he was the first of nine children, and now a member of the brewing firm of Howard and Fuller.

He was also a descendent of Edward Fuller, who arrived on the *Mayflower*. Caroline worked at another home as a housekeeper but continued to live at home. Tony was fourteen years of age, working in his father's fruit shop, ready to seek his fortune, and probably anxious to leave the home environment.

John Nathans, now an old friend of the family, made a propitious visit to the Pastor home. Would Tony like to join the circus just as his younger brothers had done? Frank and William reported favorably on the life of a circus performer. They were well taken care of, well fed, learned a trade, traveled everywhere, and reasonably recognized for their efforts. As Tony recalled, "Mr. Nathans got the consent of my mother and I was apprenticed to him. In reality it was to learn to be an equestrian and acrobat, but as the things were not legally recognized, my apprentice papers read that I was to learn to be a farrier and veterinary man." With good wishes from his parents, Tony left with Nathans to begin his circus career. Now, only Fernando remained at home with Antony and Cornelia.

After twenty years of marriage, and a life style that began well but, unhappily, careened out of control, Antony disappeared. Whether he remained at home, unemployed and destitute, deserted his family or was institutionalized is unknown. No records can be found of Antony's remaining days. Cornelia was now alone with a small child and no income, except a little that might have come from her daughters. Although a respectable and churchgoing woman, Cornelia chose to operate a saloon, thus risking the scorn of the community.[15] She opened at 93 Duane Street. The shop was a few steps off Broadway, a good location since the street had become the primary commercial center of the city.

In 1850, the New York City directory indicated that Cornelia had become a widow, although there is no actual evidence to support that. Women whose husbands had deserted them often claimed, for the sake of propriety, that the husband was deceased. Nevertheless, it was a sorrowful ending for Antony Pastor. That same year, Cornelia was found to be operating a saloon at 424 Broadway, in the midst of concert halls and popular theaters.

2

Circus Days

In April 1844, Welch and Mann's Circus had just returned from Rio de Janeiro. Led by the two- and four-horse rider, John Nathans, they were about to open the summer season in Yonkers, New York. Welch and Mann's Circus had eight riders, one of whom was William Kincade, a six-year-old apprentice to Nathans.[1] It was quite common for traveling circuses to feature children on their roster. Children, some as young as five or six years old, served as apprentices to veteran performers to learn specialties, like high wire, trapeze or equestrian skills. It required many years of training before an apprentice was able to assume a performing role in the circus company. For the apprentice, commitment to the job was essential; for the trainer, it was his responsibility to guide and care for his minion. In effect, the veteran circus man was not only an educator for his ward but he also served as surrogate father. For children who came from dysfunctional families, as many of them did, their lives were transformed.

John Nathans had the reputation for being an excellent teacher and "father" to his apprentices. After his marriage to Amelia Pastor in 1840, he trained his step daughter to become one of the better equestriennes in the business. It would be equally true for William Kincade and Frank and William Pastor.[2]

After playing several weeks in Yonkers, the circus traveled through New York state. They stopped at all towns no more than twenty miles apart to accommodate the horses and wagons, which could not handle more extensive travel.

Wagon circuses traveled on irregular dirt roads, playing one-night stands. The summer of 1844 was so cool that when they appeared in Ithaca, New York, everyone had to wear overcoats.[3] After trudging through western New York, the company moved to Pennsylvania, heading for Harrisburg, Philadelphia, for a two-week engagement, and on to Baltimore. The weather was generally rainy, and everyone was soaked through upon their arrival in Baltimore.

Welch and Mann's Circus opened at the Front Street Theater in Baltimore where, along with the usual business, they staged a sensational piece called "Israel Putnam of '76" which delighted audiences. The skit reprised Putnam's riding feats during the Revolutionary War. Returning to Philadelphia, they played at the National Theater until the spring of 1845. During the winter, circuses often appeared at theaters to continue their season, which improved their receipts and retained their artists. The circus company then traveled to New York and appeared at the old Park Theater, producing a pantomime extravaganza, "Mad Anthony Wayne," another Revolutionary War drama. While in New York, Nathans acquired a new apprentice rider, eight year old Frank Pastor. Amelia, Nathan's wife, was probably responsible for Frank's selection. She was aware of the Pastor family's situation and endeavored to help them.

The company began the summer season of 1845 in Philadelphia with seven riders, two of whom, Kincade and Pastor, were apprenticed to Nathans. Their season featured, for the first time, eight horses driven in a band wagon (later it was increased to ten). It was also the first time that the 5 high act (riders on top of one another) was performed on three horses, led by Nathans. After numerous stops in Pennsylvania, the troupe visited Maryland, New York and the New England states. The company then chose to split its forces, one company to sail to Brazil, the other to continue touring in the U.S. Nathans decided to remain with the U.S. contingent.

Through 1846 and 1847, the circus's travels covered much the same ground as before, although stopping in many villages in between the familiar towns seeking further revenue for their efforts. Frank first appeared in the ring in 1846, in "Introductory Horsemanship"; he rode a horse on a long lead, or safety rein, held by Nathans.[4]

When, in 1846, the company played in New York, Nathans acquired another apprentice, William Pastor, six years old, to be trained as an equestrian. He joined brother Frank, now considered an equestrian performer with a good deal of potential.

In the spring of 1847, twenty circuses emerged from winter quarters, their owners anticipating a successful season. The economic effects of the Panic of 1837 had dissipated, and the country was entering a period of prosperity. Circuses with fifteen to eighteen performers could be organized at a cost of five to seven thousand dollars. A well-run circus could garner profits up to 60 percent of gross receipts. Of course, few circuses enjoyed such success, but owners always began a season with those goals in mind.

The circus had established itself as an important amusement in the U.S. although often criticized from the pulpit and by the press, especially in rural areas and small towns, ironically, the life blood of circus performance and revenue. Still, the circus was a welcome diversion and appealed strongly to rural folks. To assist the circus business at this time, the fledgling railroads were now making their services available for them to travel through the Eastern states.

When the Welch, Mann and Delevan Circus (Delevan was a new investor and part owner) paid New York its annual visit, Nathans again approached the Pastor family to see if he could persuade Tony, now fourteen years old, to join his brothers. The offer was enticing to Tony, who had no employment opportunities in the Bowery. Nathans now had all three brothers under his tutelage.

It did not take Tony long to realize that he did not want to be an equestrian.[5] He did not care for horses and was probably afraid of them. As a circus rider, Tony recalled, "I could ride enough to fall off. I was never a great success as a rider, but I took part in the grand entrees."

Nathans decided that Tony needed some seasoning to learn about the ways of traveling circuses and the various specialties available for an appren-

John Nathans, a veteran equestrian and circus manager, took on Frank, William and Tony Pastor as apprentices when they were children. Nathans was Tony's mentor during his early career and was instrumental in preparing the young man for the challenges of stage performance (Harry Ransom Humanities Research Center, The University of Texas at Austin).

tice performer. For the first part of the season, Tony was sent to Raymond and Waring's Menagerie. The circus performed day shows only, in a tent. Advertising consisted of a Negro with a bell crying out about the show to be performed. While this circus featured wild animals, it also hired equestrians and clowns to supplement the show. Tony had the opportunity to see clowns, tumblers, acrobats, wire artists and other novelties and was given the chance to try each of the skills. Included in the circus was a band, which accompanied singing and dancing and occasional minstrel skits. Tony began his career as a circus performer by singing and playing the tambourine in the band and tumbling.

Tony was particularly attracted to the clowns, who were versatile performers able to present pantomime, songs, cross-talk routines and comic monologues. Their colorful costumes and grotesque makeup always seemed to bring laughs from audiences. Tony embarked on a crash course to learn everything he could from the clowns' performances. Maybe, some day in the future, he would be able to emulate them.

In November 1847, Tony rejoined his brothers in Pittsburgh. In December, he made his debut with the Welch Circus at Welch's National Amphitheater as a tumbler.[6]

In 1848, with the Welch, Delevan and Nathans Circus, Tony got his first experience as a versatile performer, tumbling with the acrobats, dancing "Lucy Long" in the blackface afterpieces, and appearing with the other clowns.[7] After the grand entrée, it was customary to have a comic song, and "I made my first appearance as a comic singer. I wore calico pants, a red vest, a yellow coat, and a vermillion nose." Tony's first song was "Things I Don't Like to See."

For the next three years with Welch and Nathans, Tony perfected his routines and became an accomplished circus entertainer. The circus now traveled by train and was able to cover New England and the Atlantic states, as far west as Ohio and as far south as Richmond, Virginia during the summer season.

Circus routine was almost always the same. After the evening show, the tent was pulled down and stored on the train. While the show had been playing, the sideshow was packed up, the animals put in their cages, and placed in the train's freight cars. While the performers slept, ate and prepared themselves for the next day's shows, the train chugged to the next town. Upon arrival in the new town, the tents were erected and the performers practiced and rested before the afternoon performance. A high-class circus like Welch's played an afternoon and evening show seven days a week, weather permitting. There was little time for anything else in the busy and regimented life of circus personnel.

There were a few occasions when town "toughs" attempted to intimidate the performers. Stories of fights were reported in the press and often magnified in their frequency and intensity. During the 1848 season, the story arose that supposedly initiated the "Hey, Rube" circus call to challenge.[8] Thomas Osbourn, a member of the Welch company, went with some of his friends to attend a dance. He got into an altercation and faced several men who threatened him with wooden clubs. Osbourn shouted out "Hey, Rube" to other members of the company and all of them came to his assistance. From that time on, so the story went, the cry of "Hey, Rube" became known as a rallying signal among circus men in trouble.

During the winter of 1848–49, the Welch, Nathans, Bancker and Christy Circus played at the Federal Street Theater in Boston.[9] Each year, it was common among circus managers to exchange partners and welcome new investors to help continue their operation. James Bancker had already operated circuses, but none as large and as popular as Welch's. George Christy, from the famous Christy Minstrels, wanted to be a circus investor. The circus did well in Boston and moved on to familiar New England cities only to be stopped in July because of a cholera epidemic. Three members of the circus died and the show was closed in Columbus, Ohio. Tony had to travel by stagecoach to Cumberland, Maryland, to ctach a train back to New York.

The circus reunited in September. Ringmaster Neil Jamison had died and Tony was asked to take over his duties. For the first time, Tony sang comic songs, appeared in skits, and tumbled with the acrobats. The salary for ringmasters was six dollars a week. The three Pastor brothers were thriving, each growing in their specialty, Frank and William as riders, Tony as a "grand and lofty tumbler" according to the advertising. Frank was spoken of as the "Pet of the Circle," and William as "elegant in his extraordinary exercises." Nathans pushed Tony to expand his act and to use it in conjunction with other ring activities. For example, Tony was taught to hold objects, a difficult job which required a person of good judgment and quick eye to follow every movement of the rider. Tony passed objects to the rider or retrieved them, while making the entire sequence appear to be funny.

The Welch, Nathans, Bancker, Christy combination played through 1851, culminating their association with a winter engagement in Philadelphia in the fall.[10] The show was so well received that it played until early spring of 1852. These were William's last performances with his brothers. At the age of twelve, now an excellent equestrian, he signed on with Washburn's Circus. His specialty included standing on his head atop a pole thirty feet high.

Tony also found a new set of employers in 1852, John Nathans having brought him along. The Sands, Nathans and Quick Circus traveled New England, as far west as Indiana and as far south as Virginia, like many of the other touring circuses. It was not uncommon to find two circuses entering a town at the same time. Rather than competing with one another, they usually joined to give audiences an enlarged edition, and split the proceeds afterwards. Tony's clown act had gained recognition for its originality. His performing versatility was making him a very noticeable commodity. Another part of his act, that of singing comic songs, gained a strong compliment from John Dingess, a veteran circus agent, said of Tony, "As a comic singer, he was looked upon by the circus-going community to be without a peer."[11] For his efforts, Tony earned six dollars a week.

In the spring of 1853, Tony joined Franconi's Traveling Hippodrome, He performed comic songs and duets with side-show ladies. He was reported to have played banjo solos, but when Tony learned to play the banjo is unknown. In any case, he never played the banjo again.[12]

At the age of seventeen, in 1854, Frank left the Nathans fold to begin his own illustrious career as a star circus equestrian who toured the European continent for many years.[13] He first joined Joe Pentland's Circus. Pentland was a clown who, in 1848, became a well-known circus personality. He opened his own circus in 1852. His troupe went to England in 1856 and performed for the year in the British Isles. The following year, they toured Italy. Back in England in 1858, Frank was the star equestrian playing at the Alhambra Palace in London. For the next nine years, he was a headliner in various circus companies in England, Spain, and Paris—for the 1867 Exposition—with a side trip to Havana, Cuba, in 1866. While performing in Paris, he was feted by Napoleon and the empress for his daring feats. Frank was the first performer to use an American flag in his act, even though the display of any flag except the French was prohibited. He returned from Europe in 1869, to appear with various American circuses. Frank had earned medals and proclamations from royalty across Europe for his equestrian work.

William (nicknamed Billy) Pastor led an equally exciting life in the circus.[14] He joined Mabie's Circus in 1857 as a rider and vaulter; was with Nixon and Kemp in New York the following year; and rejoined Tony with the Sands, Nathans Circus at the Broadway Theater, New York, in the fall of 1858. The next year, Billy went to Spain, as an acrobat, then to Denmark as a trunk clown and with the Chiarin organization to Cuba, clowning in the Spanish language. While in Spain, he was said to have visited his father's birthplace in Seville. On the passage home from Cuba, their ship was wrecked off Barnegat Light; Billy was the only person on board who saved his wardrobe and trunks. Upon his return to America, Billy played a clown, traveling across the country. Billy had always aspired to be a comic singer, possibly because of Tony's influence. He was persuaded by David Bidwell, an agent, to give up the circus business and turn to comic singing on the variety stage.

In 1854, Tony joined the Mabie Circus as a ringmaster and clown performer.[15] The engagement lasted a year, but Tony was dissatisfied with his salary inasmuch as he was doing two jobs. The main reason he stayed with Mabie was the presence of John Nathans and Nathans' stepchildren, Emma and Philo, in the company. Emma was Amelia's child; Philo was another apprentice whom Nathans selected and adopted as his own son. Sol Lipman was the featured clown, but when he became ill, Tony took over his duties.

For the next two years, Tony was headlined as ringmaster and general performer with Levi J. North's Circus. North, a veteran equestrian, had formed his circus in 1843. He was the star of his own show and introduced wrestling bears in American circuses, a unique act at the time. He also introduced the outdoor ascension act where a wire was stretched from the ground to a building on which a wire walker traversed to the top. North established his base of operations in Chicago and became one of the first of western shows, touring through the Midwest. However, North, although an innovative entertainer, had difficulty understanding the financial side of circus operation, and often was on the verge of having to close down.

Tony enjoyed the two years with North because he was given the opportunity to act as ringmaster and versatile actor. When the troupe played in Chicago at North's Amphitheater, during the winter months, Tony established himself as a great

In 1885, at the age of 22, Tony was the lead clown with the Levi J. North Circus (Harry Ransom Humanities Research Center, The University of Texas at Austin).

favorite with the city's audiences. A decade later, audiences welcomed Tony and remembered his pleasing performances.

He left North in 1857 to rejoin Mabie's Circus, where he remained for two years. The Mabie Menagerie and Circus primarily traveled the Midwest, playing one-night stands in small towns with great success. On the program, Tony was listed fourth, as clown, below the manager, the equestrian director and the ringmaster. In the advertisement introducing Tony to a Canton, Ohio, audience, a reviewer said: "Mr. Tony Pastor, the great Yankee clown, who sings new stories which are copied by all the clowns across the country, will open with a new budget of fun. Tony Pastor will also delight the audience by singing his favorite ditty, 'Run High or Die,' as sung by him more than 500 times in all the great circuses of the world, with the most overpowering applause." It was typical circus advertising hyperbole, but it made Tony a headliner.[16] Featured in Mabie's advertising was a long recitation of Tony's skills.

> Mr. Tony Pastor, the great Yankee clown, whose genius for inventing new stories and mirth-provoking hits at the times has been so extensively copied and gagged by all the other clowns in the country, will open an entire new budget of fun, arranged to suit the year 1857. Tony Pastor will also delight the audience by singing his favorite ditty of "Has Anybody Seen My Sister" as sung by him more than 5,000 times in all the great circuses of the world, with the most overpowering applause.[17]

The Panic of 1857 hit circus attendance hard. A sudden collapse in the economy ended a period of prosperity. The immediate event that caused the panic was the failure on August 24 of the New York City branch of the Ohio Life Insurance and Trust Company, up to that moment a major financial force. Massive embezzlement had been discovered. The discovery set off a series of other events that shook public confidence. British investors removed funds from U.S. banks. Grain prices fell. Manufactured goods remained in warehouses, creating massive layoffs. Widespread railroad failures occurred. Land speculation collapsed. Public confidence in banks was further eroded in September when the S.S. *Central America*, on its way to New York from the San Francisco Mint with 30,000 pounds of gold, sank with a loss of 400 lives. A bank holiday — all banks were closed — was declared in New England and New York.

The Mabie Circus was traveling through Ohio when the panic hit. Attendance quickly declined, and the planned route was badly disrupted. Instead of returning to New York for their annual visit, Mabie decided to turn south, to Kentucky, Tennessee, Georgia and South Carolina.[18] Still, many engagements were cancelled: there were sixteen performances in September; only four in October; eight in November; and only Christmas week in December. Mabie ran out of money and performers received very little in wages. Still, they remained with the circus. Where else would they have gone?

Thanks to several investors, Mabie and Crosby's French and American Circus began a new season in January 1858, playing a southern route only. Most of the company, like Tony, were back with renewed enthusiasm. The route was a success and the performers were paid every week.

When the company visited New York in the fall of 1858, they appeared at the recently opened Palace Garden, the first theater located near Union Square.[19] The theater included a two-level octagonal pagoda for the orchestra, a platform for staging fireworks displays, a large fountain and fish pond and a large tent used as a salon. The owners, DeForest and Tinsdale, hoped that the theater would become the "resort of the refined, fashionable and the intellectual." During its first few months, however, it quickly became apparent that the theater would not be attended by the city's elite. The outdoors area became a favorite place for housemaids and the working classes. Theater programs changed to feature variety, minstrel and circus companies. In their first season, the owners offered free gifts to the ladies who patronized the theater, four years before Robert Butler introduced the practice at "444." The one feature that made the theater acceptable to the town fathers was the owners' refusal to serve liquor on the grounds.

Tony appeared as a clown, high on the program's list of headliners. Featured in his specialty act was the singing of comic songs. The most popular were "Wedlock Is a Ticklish Thing," "My Grandfather Was a Most Wonderful Man," and "Has Anybody Seen My Sister." The first and third contained a slight bit of risqué innuendo. "Grandfather" was filled with tear-jerking sentimentality.

At the beginning of the 1859 season, Tony was the top clown and comic singer with Sands, Nathans and Company Circus. Tony was gratified to be with John Nathans again, performing alongside his mentor and to showing off his professional skills. The company traveled in first-class trains now—Tony had his own compartment—and the jumps to each town were quicker, more comfortable and more rewarding. Tony was now earning twenty-five dollars a week, plus the room and board supplied by the circus. A portion of his salary was sent home to his mother. Also in the company for a short while was Billy, who performed equestrian feats. But Billy had other ideas of what he wanted to do, and he left the circus at the end of its run in New York.

Sands, Nathans and Company played at the old Broadway Theater, New York, beginning in late November 1858 until January 1859. A benefit for Tony was given on January 7. The program stated:

> Benefit for Tony Pastor, the Clown
> HA!HA!HA! FUN'S THE WORD
> NOW OR NEVER, BOYS, IS THE TIME TO LEND A HELPING HAND
> FUN, WIT AND FACETIA SHALL BE THE ORDER OF THE NIGHT[20]

Equestrian exercises were performed by Nathans, his stepson Philo, Billy and Frank Rivers. Tony, of course, was the featured clown and was heartily cheered every time he entered the ring. The benefit occurring in New York, it was a gala night for Tony.

In 1859, as clown and comic singer for the Sands, Nathans & Company Circus, Tony was one of the stars of the organization (Harry Ransom Humanities Research Center).

The company played ten shows a week, every evening at 7:30 P.M. (the usual time for all theater performances to begin), and matinees on Tuesday, Thursday and Saturday at 2:00 P.M. Admission was twenty-five cents. Families were particularly welcomed at the matinees.

The company continued their tour of New England, New York, Pennsylvania, and New Jersey, closing finally at Elizabeth, New Jersey, October 10, 1859.[21] Tony returned to New York to find a new engagement, hopefully not with a circus as he was tired of its routinized life. John Nathans helped him once more.

3

"444"

After twelve years, Tony was disenchanted with the circus. He had experienced just about everything: the rigid routines that demanded daily travel and the setting up and tearing down of tents; living for endless months in crowded train cars, where he and his colleagues ate, slept and washed their clothes; the playing of endless games of cards to pass the time; gauging the mysteries of crowd behavior at each performance, with occasional shouts of "Hey, Rube" to enliven a town's visit; the fear of accidents brought on by repetitious performance; the constant appearance of new performers as old ones either retired, were hurt or fired; the battles with egotistical headliners for attention and billing; all of the episodes that made a touring circus company predictable and tedious.

Tony had appeared as a clown and sometimes comic singer for Sands and Nathans Circus in 1859. Nathans continued to watch over and mentor Tony, although he recognized Tony's declining commitment to his job. Their relationship was so good that Nathans was not afraid to ask Tony what he wanted to do apart from circus life. After all, Tony was now twenty-four years old and at a crossroads with regard to his future career. Nathans was aware that Tony had little interest in staying with the circus. Both parties agreed that Tony needed a change. Did Nathans have any suggestions?

Without hesitation, the veteran circus manager recommended that Tony try his act, which had become quite professional, on the variety stage. There were not many variety theaters operating at the time, but there was always at least one in larger cities, enough to keep a good performer employed. Tony immediately accepted the challenge of attempting a career on the theater stage.

As happened often in their long relationship, Nathans assisted Tony in making the transition. With his extensive contacts in the amusement field, Nathans obtained an engagement for Tony at the Varieties Theater in Chicago, Illinois, in January 1860. It would be Tony's first experience on the theater stage. To send Tony away with collegial support, Nathans set up a benefit for Tony at the Chatham Theater in New York to take place on January 12.[1] Tony's benefit garnered many accolades from fellow performers and friends, several speeches of appreciation and a suitcase especially suited for a stage actor, with special sections for costumes and makeup.

Tony opened at the Varieties on January 15, seventh on the bill, a spot usually relegated to newcomers. As was typical of variety houses at the time, the theater was located in a working class neighborhood made up primarily of Irish immigrants. The ticket prices ranged from 10 cents for the gallery to 50 cents for box seats. The bill was long, more than three hours, so that patrons always left the theater feeling they had obtained their money's worth. The ten to fifteen acts included singers, dancers, comedians, contortionists, trapeze and acrobatic artists and animal acts. When Tony first entered the theater's backstage, he was met with a cacophony of noise — singers and musicians practicing, people shouting out instructions, stagehands moving scenery — that seemed to border on the chaotic. Yet, when the show began, everything seemed to follow in order, every performer at their assigned place in time and every act on cue to meet the audience. Tony sang several of the comic songs that he already knew were popular with circus audiences. But he wondered if they would resonate with the more intimate and critical audiences in theaters.

His first song was greeted with seeming indifference. The audience had to get to know the performer. Tony's second song elicited laughs and reasonable applause. At the end of his third song, an Irish ditty, the audience shouted for an encore, the ultimate compliment for an artist. By the end of his first week on the boards, Tony was moved to the fourth position on the bill, one favored because it was considered a headliner's slot. Tony did not disappoint his audiences, and was encored two to three times a night. Because of his immediate success, Tony's engagement lasted six weeks to the end of February. Tony had exhausted his repertoire of comic songs. He quickly realized that he needed fresh material, so he acquired patriotic songs, sentimental ballads, and songs about Irish independence. With the signs of war entering people's minds, the patriotic songs were particularly relevant.

At the conclusion of his Chicago engagement, Tony had no other assignments. A letter to Dan Rice, playing in Philadelphia at the time, got Tony his next job.

Dan Rice, a famous clown, was for many years an even more renowned circus entertainer and manager. He had a prodigious memory, a lightning quick mind and a comic talent. He had gained a reputation as the "great American humorist." Elevating the nature of farce comedy, he almost single-handedly moved it from lowbrow to highbrow entertainment. His opinions on social and political issues were already anticipated by audiences, who responded to them with enthusiasm, whatever side they took. Dan Rice's Great Show was appearing in Philadelphia during March 1860. For a performer to appear with Rice was to share the stage with a master clown. On the other hand, Tony would be back in the circus business.

Tony played the comic singer in a clown's costume with Rice's circus and was quickly reminded of all of the things he wished to escape. At the end of his engagement, he had no choice but to find work with another circus. Rice assisted him in obtaining a spot with the Sands Circus, then on a tour of the New England states. Tony was a clown for five more months, through the summer. In near desperation and afraid that his theater career was quickly disappearing, Tony wrote Nathans to help him get another stage engagement.

John Nathans and Frank Rivers had known one another since the 1840s, and had occasionally worked together. Frank Rivers was born in 1821 in Springfield, Massachusetts. He had entered the circus at the age of ten with Welch's Circus in Boston. He continued in several capacities with Welch until 1851. In a moment of distraction, Rivers traveled to California to prospect for gold. Soon back into the familiarity of circus life, he had to withdraw as a performer due to a leg injury. In 1859, he opened the Melodeon Music Hall in Philadelphia, specializing in variety entertainment, with a strong leaning toward circus performers. The theater afforded many circus performers the opportunity for work during the winter months when circuses were disbanded.

Nathans contacted Rivers, suggesting that Tony was a fine entertainer with audience appeal. When Tony wrote Rivers for work, he was signed for a two-week engagement. Since its opening, the Melodeon had become a popular concert saloon, a large bar featuring various kinds of entertainment. The theater portion of the building displayed a gilded proscenium, a parquet with plush seating and two galleries. Rivers promoted comedy and singing, along with the usual circus acrobats, trapeze artists and animal acts. To this, he added a ballet corps, made up of pretty girls in scanty costumes (for the day) and short skirts, their act positioned as an afterpiece. Tony was paid twenty-five dollars a week—about the same as he was earning in the circus—to perform as a comic singer doing eight performances a week.

Tony's two-week engagement was extended for two months due to his immediate popularity with Philadelphia audiences. Tony also appeared in skits and afterpieces, his first ventures into acting. The time with Rivers convinced Tony even more that the stage was his career path and, as a headliner, a road to financial success.

Rivers changed bills every few weeks. To hold onto Tony for two months was rare. Tony stayed because he was able to introduce new songs each week. But, at the end of that period, Tony had to be replaced with a fresh face, and he found himself temporarily unemployed. Rivers did promise that, in a few months, Tony could return to the Melodeon, if he wished.

Tony went to New York where several circuses were performing. He obtained a job as a comic singer with the Spaulding and Rogers Great New Orleans Circus, appearing at the Old Bowery Theater during the Christmas holidays.[2] It was always a good time to be in New York since shows attracted full houses made up of entire families. Spaulding and Rogers were so successful that they played in New York until early February 1861. During this time, Tony lived at home with his mother and Fernando. They frequently visited the theater to see the young entertainer.

In the middle of February, Tony returned to Rivers' Melodeon, taking up his position as comic singer and headliner. Philadelphia patrons liked the affable performer and treated him to several encores at each performance. Tony acquired comic songs where he could—from the circus, from other performers, from English music halls—and he wrote a few himself. The Melodeon's weekly advertisements mentioned that Tony would introduce new songs in his act, presaging one of his operational themes after assuming theater ownership.

While Tony was appearing in Philadelphia, the country was rapidly moving toward a confrontation about slavery. Philadelphians were particularly sensitive to the disturbing series of events, since Philadelphia had been the nation's capital and was currently an important manufacturing center of military materials, including naval ships. Tony's repertoire of songs now featured patriotic tunes, much to the audience's delight, and they demanded even more from him. When Lincoln won the election the previous November, the undercurrent of revolt became clear as Southern states predicted secession. When he was inaugurated on March 4, the coming dispute seemed inevitable. Tony could sense the edginess of the audience as they were being distracted from theater doings.

Robert Butler, owner of the Continental Theater in Philadelphia and recent purchaser of the American Music Hall in New York, saw Tony perform and offered him a job at 444 to be one of his assortment of headliners. The abbreviated name had been given the American by the press since it was located at that address on Broadway. For thirty-five dollars a week and the opportunity to play in a theater on the city's most popular thoroughfare, Tony could not refuse. He viewed the engagement as the genuine opening he sought to further his career.

Robert Butler began his career in the banking business.[4] In 1857, he was so successful in his financial dealings that he opened a bank that would become one of the leading banking houses on Wall Street. In early 1859, in a move that fellow bankers thought was foolish if not idiotic, Butler decided to enter show business. He bought the Art Union Concert Hall, at 497 Broadway, turned it into a variety house and, after running it for a year, sold it and purchased the theater at 444 Broadway. He wished to feature variety entertainment and make it the most exclusive house in the city. The original theater had been opened in 1847, called Mechanic's Hall, totally devoted to minstrelsy. E.P. Christy and his minstrel company played there for ten years.

Butler opened the American Music Hall (an appropriate name at the time) on August 10, 1860. Known as an upright businessman, well respected by his fellow businessmen, Butler quickly demonstrated his theatrical management abilities, with innovative marketing ideas and an astute eye for talented performers.

Rivers gave Tony a grand testimonial benefit on April 11, 1861, honoring him at the conclusion of his stay at the Melodeon.[5] More than forty-two top performers from variety and minstrelsy performed (at no salary, a common courtesy among performers when participating in a benefit) and a full house gave Tony mementos that he saved for his entire life. The audience called for Tony to sing some of his favorite songs, which he obliged with zest. In Part I of the program, Tony sang three songs, two of which, "The Female M.D." and "Billy Barlow," he had borrowed from the minstrels. In Part II, Tony acted as a clown in the skit "Troobloo, and Infantile Champion, Big Thing on Ice" which elicited much audience applause. In Part III, Tony appeared with the entire company in the skit "The Fairy of the Schuylkill," the performances' afterpiece. At the end of the show, after five recalls, he begged the audience to let him retire since he was tired and his throat was sore. Also appearing in the benefit were three young performers, Kitty Blanchard, William Conrad and Ella Wesner, like himself, early in their careers. All three would later make frequent appearances for Tony at his theater.

The following day, Fort Sumter was attacked. The war produced some odd episodes in New York, some a boon to business and Tony's career and some of cataclysmic proportions, like the 1863 draft riots. Tony closed out his engagement at the Melodeon on April 13. He opened at 444 on April 17.

He stayed with his mother until he could find housing close to the theater. He shortly moved into an apartment at 363 Canal, within three blocks of the theater.[6] Fernando was living at the Pastor home, having spent a short time with Sands and Nathans, like his older brothers. But, unlike them, he cared little for the circus and returned home to seek another occupation. Fernando's temperament did not fit the demands of circus life. He was described as "everybody's friend," a tender and cheerful young man. Contributions from Frank, William and Tony helped to meet Cornelia's needs in a house at 5 Walker Street, just off Broadway, near Canal Street, in a modest and clean neighborhood.

In Butler's advertisement presenting him to New York audiences, Tony was called "the greatest clown and comic singer for the age." While the claim was overstatement, it was a commonly used vehicle designed to get attention and give the artist a colorful image. For newcomers, it was especially helpful as an introduction to audiences. Of course, when audiences witnessed a performer for the first time, they would make their own judgement, vocally and with applause, that either ended or encouraged an actor's career. A new performer had but twelve to fifteen minutes to win over an experienced and critical audience, heightened in anticipation by the amplified advertisements. It was an awesome challenge for any performer.

Tony had several advantages. He was confident in his ability to entertain audiences. He presented a unique act. There were very few comic singers who used topical material and had the knack of creating a camaraderie with patrons. He was good looking, agile on his feet, and exuded a casual and relaxed impression across the footlights. His songs were decidedly funny, a pleasing way to capture an audience seeking humor to escape the trials of the day. He supplemented his initial appearances with patriotic material. As the city streets were seething with war spirit and martial parades, a few selected patriotic songs produced cheering houses.

Tony also had some help from Butler's company. They were already known for purveying fun; they consisted of talented people; and they supplied an assortment of waiter girls to please the needs of primarily male patrons. Waiter girls served drinks, smokes, and offered good fellowship. They were pretty, wore provocative costumes and were available for the patron's desires.

It took Tony but a short time to realize that New York had grown into a metropolis. More than 800,600 people lived in the city, stretching as far north as the country's first urban park, Central Park. All commercial life now centered north of City Hall. Fashionable life was now concentrated in an area bounded by Fourth and Sixth Avenues and from 8th to 40th Streets. Lower Broadway south of Canal Street housed only commercial enterprises, the streets deserted at night. Wood construction was rapidly being replaced by brick and stone and innovative iron and steel construction of tall buildings. In the Bowery, Irish and German neighborhoods had emerged, poor, crowded and unhealthy.

Thanks to a busy harbor, the waterfront grew as commerce flowed into the city. Below 14th Street, there were fifty piers on the Hudson River and more than sixty on the East River. Omnibuses carried 100,000 people a day; taxis wove in and out of seemingly gridlocked streets. Broadway was so clogged with wagons, carts and carriages that crossing the street might take one-half hour. The noise was earsplitting. The city had become the nation's leading manufacturing center and its fastest growing.

Large department stores now dominated Broadway from Canal to Houston Streets. Dozens of hotels had been and were being built, the grandest of them the St. Nicholas Hotel. Others included the elegant Metropolitan Hotel, next to Niblo's Garden, and the Fifth Avenue Hotel, at 23rd Street, featuring private bathrooms. The city had become a tourist attraction, bringing significant dollars to its retail outlets, hotels, restaurants and theaters.

Between 1851 and 1860, 2,640,000 people came to America, mainly to New York and Boston. The immigrants were predominantly Irish and German. Railroads now traveled as far west as Chicago and St. Louis. Five rail lines crisscrossed the Appalachian Mountains and spider-webbed across New England, intersecting most cities and towns. Rail travel to Boston from New York took only ten hours. Ferries crossed the Hudson to Jersey City every fifteen minutes, carrying 2,000 passengers, along with horses and carriages, on every trip.

Inventions like the Otis elevator, the Singer sewing machine, and Steinway pianos set the tone for bigger and better industry. Theaters had become legitimate amusement outlets for all classes of society. Drama still dominated stage presentations, but minstrels and variety appealed to the masses.

Minstrelsy had matured with revised entertainment that helped to humanize Negroes in the eyes of Northerners, as the anti-slavery movement became both social and political. Slavery was no longer a joking matter; plantation life was more idealized. When Harriet Beecher Stowe's book *Uncle Tom's Cabin* was published and became the most widely read book of the century, it was quickly brought to the stage with sympathy for the Negro.

Variety became a distinctly separate amusement from minstrels and circuses, although many of the same people appeared in both. The form, on one bill, featured a series of performers each doing their own specialties. In fact, anyone who claimed to possess a special talent was given the opportunity to perform before a live, and lively, audience. Critical patrons weeded out the good from the bad, the familiar from the novelty. Concert saloons vied with theaters for customers and performers. They were found from lower Broadway to Union Square, bunched up so close it was hard to tell one from another. Cheap concert saloons featured drinking, gambling and available waiter girls and usually some cursory entertainment, designed to keep customers for a longer period of time. Theaters featured performance but, they too, offered drinks, smokes and waiter girls. It cost people only 25 cents to enter; managers believed that the low entrance price attracted a broader base of customers. Managers had quickly learned that by changing the bill each week, patrons would return often. It was especially true when Irish singers and clog dancers performed. Because of the competition for actors and customers, theaters might last only a few months, or hopefully, a full season. Turnover of management, closures and reopenings, and new theater names were common occurrences. For a variety theater to capture audiences and return a profit, it took an astute manager who knew and acted on the tastes of the patrons. Such was Butler's 444. Tony would be a crowd pleaser, in Butler's estimation. Tony opened at the same time that crowds were returning to theaters after several months of war jitters.

Butler filled his program with the best talent he could find and outbid his competitors. He visited other theaters and made a list of possible performers; he selected minstrel and circus actors and persuaded them to appear on the stage; he welcomed new acts. He also installed a ballet troupe made up of women as young as fifteen, and costumed them to please his male audiences. The *New York Clipper* in May 1861 summarized Butler's philosophy of operation.

> R.W. Butler makes every effort to keep up with the demands of the times. The variety in the entertainment, supported by a good company, makes it just the place for an evening's amusement, a state of things that the public are not slow to appreciate. To witness the evolution of the sylphs of the ballet troupe is alone worth the price of admission.[7]

Tony was an immediate hit. The joy of performing, a trait he would never lose, crossed the footlights to capture and entrance his audiences. He was a small man; pictures of him and his colleagues showed him mostly shorter. However, he was strong and wiry, due to his circus clown days. Tony was also a handsome man, with a full moustache, bright, friendly eyes and an equally affable smile. When he entered the stage, there was a strut in his step. He displayed agility and was light on his feet, with expressive body movements. When he talked to the audience from the front of the stage — reaching out, he could almost touch them — Tony greeted them with a genial, casual, direct voice that seemed to convey a passion for what he was about to do. His effect on audiences was magnetic.

Although of small stature, Tony was big on stage. Behind the casual and genial demeanor was a determined, motivated person, under control, with a keen desire to succeed. He would do what he could to win over audiences. It is very likely that this drive to succeed had been influenced by his early life of poverty and the devastating events that affected family relationships. He was energetic, handled himself with confidence, and was obsessed with preparation — planning, practicing and delivering — so that every performance would come as close to perfection as he could make it. While he was by no means a finished professional when he opened at 444, the talent and artistry was already in place. He played for keeps.

Tony possessed a phenomenal memory. He mastered song lyrics quickly, several in a matter of days. At any one time, he was able to recall three hundred songs to sing. This attribute contributed greatly to his future success as a manager, since he recalled performers' routines and audience reactions.

Tony had a constant desire to improve and to innovate. He came to understand that audiences demanded fresh material and he worked hard to meet their needs. The new songs he introduced each week were both comic and sentimental, touching the audience's psyche. Later, as a manager, he directed each performer to offer new material each week. Those that were unable to meet his demands were quickly replaced. Those who were versatile and flexible enough to play many roles became stock company performers for several seasons. Their loyalty to Tony and his to them made for a happy troupe. He gave his colleagues the opportunity for adulation; they could get as many encores as the audience meted out and they could try new ideas without Tony's supervision. But while Tony was sympathetic to an actor's problems and responsibilities off stage, outside the theater, inside it must be all business and commitment. Still, as hard a person he was with respect to performance, he was always genial to others and enjoyed many friendships that lasted for years. If Tony had a fault, it was his desire to help others in need, from destitute actors to newcomers who needed stage polish. He made time for all of them. He gave out a great deal of money during his prime to anyone in financial need.

Tony was also a passionate competitor, at first among other actors and later with other managers. He aspired to be the best performer on the bill. As a manager, he led by doing, setting goals for himself and his colleagues and never hesitating to put them into practice.

While performing with the circus, and during his brief stint at the Melodeon, Tony learned to read audiences. His songs and lyrics were topical, often taken from current events or neighborhood experiences. He would modify the lyrics of songs to make them topical. Audiences were familiar with the subject matter; they could identify and they cheered for more of the same. During the early days of Tony's theater ownership, on the bill there were always Irish vocalists, clog dancers and skits related to the Bowery environment.

Tony also had an excellent sense for the business part of entertainment and, as his career blossomed, thoughts of management were being formed. He had a good mentor in John Nathans and found one equally good in Robert Butler. Tony watched Butler run his business, carefully selecting out those attributes he believed would make a variety theater successful. He saw how Butler handled his finances, selected performers, advertised and promoted, and strove to meet the public's approval. Tony was also learning to become a clever evaluator of talent by observing an act, the audience response, and the performer's desire for challenge. He made a mental note of the kind of people he wanted on his bill; later, many of the same people appeared at Pastor's theater. Butler, in turn, was aware of Tony's interest and assisted in his learning.

Tony's joy for performing grew each year. Audiences sensed it, as only audiences could pick up the "vibrations" of commitment to them. It was contagious. The pleasure derived from his performance and patrons' reactions to it bred confidence and success.

In May 1861, Butler took over the lease of Wallack's Theater at 483–485 Broadway and converted it to a variety house, calling it the Broadway Music Hall. Although it was only a short distance from 444, Butler believed that a second high-class theater would attract new customers.

When Tony began his career in variety, he still used costumes to illustrate his comic songs (Harry Ransom Humanities Research Center).

There were economies as well: performers could be signed for longer engagements that included appearances at both theaters; advertising could include both theaters; and the same management team could handle both. In June, Butler moved Tony to the Broadway to head the bill. For the first several months, Butler's decision looked promising.

Along with singing comic songs, Tony had his first variety experience appearing in farcical skits. They were quickly made up, rehearsed and presented within a week of their inception with the intent of varying an actor's role and introducing new material on a bill. More often than not, the skits fell flat due to poor scripts and inadequate rehearsals. Still, Tony saw the value of a well written and rehearsed skit. He filed it away for future use.

Tony was also responsible for introducing the "Star-Spangled Banner" to theater audiences.[8] Noticing its use in military parades and rallies, he copied the words, purchased the music, and sang it to the audience. He asked them to join him in the chorus. The result was a spontaneous outpouring of cheers and shouts of approval. From that moment, Tony sang it every night and the results were always the same. Within a week, the song was being sung at 444 as well.

His comic songs, however, were the items that got critics' notice. "Tony Pastor's 'Lord Lovell' is not only a most damnable taking off," said the *Clipper* reviewer, "but, in reality, a first-rate character song, wherein he eschews some of the great Lovell's peculiarities and adds improvements of his own."[9] Songs like "Female at Ease," "That's What's the Matter," "Ragged Coat," and the patriotic "Union Forever," enthused audiences which demanded they be sung again.

Tony published *Tony Pastor's Union Songster* in 1862, a 5 by 7 inch booklet with thirty-nine songs dealing with the war. Tony wrote the music and lyrics for eight of them. In the rest of the songs, Tony reworked the lyrics to reflect the conflict between the North and South. The songs reflected a variety of topics. The booklet included "The March of the Union," "The Monitor and the Merrimack" (formerly "The Landlady of France"), "The Union Train" (formerly "Old Dan Tucker"), and "A Yankee Boy Is Trim and Tall" (formerly "Yankee Doodle"). Lyrics were handed out to audiences, and Tony encouraged them to sing along with him. Patrons responded enthusiastically and applauded for encores. It was common for Tony to sing four or five encores at each evening's performance.

Butler hired several veteran minstrel personalities to bolster the bill at the Broadway. Old-timers like Ben Cotton and Billy Birch seemed to blend well with Tony. He saw how audiences took to "Ethiopian eccentricities," as Negro acts were called at the time. On the other hand, when Butler hired Charley White to replace Tony at 444, he did not care for the intrusion, as he interpreted it. There seemed to be a little static between them at first, but the more Tony watched White perform, the more he respected him. Rather than a competitor, White was a compatriot. They quickly became fast friends and enjoyed sharing the stage.

In August, an old circus manager, Sam Sharpley, was appearing at 585 Broadway with his troupe. They had modified their circus acts to conform to the theater venue and attracted large audiences, due primarily to Sharpley's colorful and exaggerated advertising. Tony visited 585 to see the company perform and was quite impressed by its professionalism. He met Sharpley, who was already familiar with Tony, and they discussed teaming up some day. They would meet and discuss the possibility several more times over the next few years.

The Broadway Music Hall prospered during the summer with its variety programs which featured top talent, although its success was mitigated by the fact it was the only variety theater open during this time. Surprisingly, business improved even more in September and October as the opening for the new season of other theaters attracted more patrons to theaters. It appeared that the public's interest in attending theater, whatever the offering, had sizably increased. An observer would not guess a war was in progress by the enthusiasm for theater amusement. A newspaper reviewer commented on the phenomenon.

> A stranger coming to New York would not believe that the nation is engaged in a great civil strife and that one section of the country is engaged in open warfare against the other. On the contrary, everything wears quite a lively aspect, and the city presents a greater variety of amusements than we ever remember to have seen presented for public patronage before.[10]

However, the Broadway Music Hall began showing the first signs of decline. Competition had become fierce. At the end of October, offers were being made to Butler to sell out since his theater was not performing up to expectation. The theater community was well aware of what the receipts were for each theater because the *New York Clipper* printed them each month. Tony noticed it too, from across the footlights; many empty seats and less involved patrons. But Butler refused.

At the same time, performers' salaries declined because there were more actors available than there were spaces for them to perform. Actors earning $100 a week, like Tony, were reduced to $75; those earning $50 were getting $25 or $35; women in the chorus or ballet who had been earning $15 a week were dropped to $8 or $5. Some performers returned to the circus or minstrels. Some went to England. The situation continued for more than a year.[11]

To make up for the decline in business, Butler introduced Saturday matinees expressly for women and children. These were immediately popular and he offered them at 444 as well. To performers, however, it meant an additional appearance at no additional salary. The Broadway Music Hall, its life renewed, flourished to the end of the year. Tony took careful note of Butler's successful business decision. To date, no other theater, dramatic or popular, had catered to women and children.

Tony's extended engagement at the Broadway established him as a variety headliner. In fact, advertisements for the theater usually

The Irish song and dance routine was variety's most popular act. Tony, dressed for the part, captured audiences with his comic renditions (Harry Ransom Humanities Research Center).

placed his name at the top of the program and mentioned him with superlatives like "the greatest comic singer in America." His comic songs "gratified the patrons of the house" and "could not serve them better." When Tony appeared in skits, such as "Virginy Mummy," he was labeled "a military spark." Every few weeks, the stock company put on a burlesque or farce, and Tony usually played an important role. The attempt was always to be funny. Satires on current events were heartily welcomed by audiences. With Billy Birch and Ben Cotton, minstrel sketches sometimes included Tony, in blackface, in minor roles. The company also performed pantomimes, in which Tony appeared, like "The Red Gnome," "The Ape of Borneo," and "Friend of the Lake of Fire." Pantomimes were particularly pleasing to an immigrant audience because of the colorful props and scenery and exaggerated grotesque humor. In "Fortune's Frolics," a Christmas show, Tony played the lead role and won favorable approval from reviewers for his "dramatic" acting. The following week, the entire company played "Broadway Minstrels" in blackface, demonstrating their artistic versatility.

But the Broadway Music Hall again lost business—no one seemed to know why—and, at the beginning of 1862, Butler realized he could not run two theaters at once. He put up the Broadway for sale and moved his headliners back to 444. In contrast, 444 was reaping the benefits of a surge in popular theater patronage.

At this time, several local groups of evangelist ministers and town fathers attempted to close down variety houses because of their "sinfulness" and "undue influence." The effort caused public attention to the theaters and, instead of diminishing attendance, increased it. Hundreds of people complained that the closing of these theaters would deprive them of the entertainment they enjoyed. Those involved in theater knew that such an act would put them out of business. The movement quickly disappeared because of the protests.

In its place, however, this same group of "do-gooders" attacked theaters for "giving comfort to those in the South by hiring actors who had come from Southern states seeking employment in New York. Theater managers responded by giving benefits for military groups and expounding on their patriotism. That argument, too, died quickly.

One issue not only caught the attention of the public and politicians, but also forced them into action in a short time. The Concert Saloon Law was passed because the social elite of the city, in conjunction with influential religious figures, pressed local politicians to get rid of the vice running rampant in concert saloons and theaters, primarily those concentrated along lower Broadway.[12]

The effect was disastrous, and unsettled theater patronage for some time as well as putting hundreds of proprietors out of business.

4

"Greatest Comic Singer of the Age"

In December 1861, a New York grand jury submitted a report to the superintendent of police. The report recommended that "attention be paid by the Police to the current concert saloons in the city since they harbored a significant source of crime," that they were especially concerned about its effect on the young, and that such nuisances should be abolished. The grand jury demanded that lists be compiled which included the owners of buildings who ran concert saloons along with lessees and sub-lessees. Thirty-nine names were listed, twenty-three of them located on Broadway, between 401 and 679, and eight on Bowery. The 444 was one of the buildings on the list. However, the superintendent stated that, at present, there was no law to remove these "nuisances" and only an act of the state legislature would enable the authorities to shut down the concert saloons.

Reaction to the issue quickly became heated. Owners disputed the report, claiming such a law would put them out of business. Employees, especially the waiter girls, complained about the potential loss of jobs. Liberal advocates for the concert saloon owners suggested that the waiter girls were at least working in legitimate jobs instead of having to work on the streets. However, the legislature, under pressure from religious organizations and some influential town fathers, put the issue on a fast track, putting together a law by the end of January and starting debate about it in February. Robert Butler was convinced that the law would ultimately be passed and that owners like himself would be put out of business, or would have their revenue considerably reduced.

In early March, the Senate bill to suppress concert saloons was reported favorably and moved forward into committee. In the Assembly, however, local politicians representing the Bowery district fought against the passage, causing many demonstrations. Also against the law was the *Staats Zeitung,* a German language newspaper that was very popular and influential in the Bowery neighborhoods. The newspaper claimed that the proposed law would "outrage all Christian citizens" with the establishment of a rigid system governing businesses.

Nevertheless, the law passed both houses in early April and was signed by the governor. An editorial in the *New York Times* suggested the end of concert saloons.

> Should the legislature fail of its duty in regard to the physical health of the city, what it has done for its moral hygiene may be received as atonement. The Concert saloon Bill is a law, and Concert saloons, with their mirth and meretriciousness, lubricity, drunkenness and multiform indecency, are things of the unsavory past. And the age of pretty "waiter girls" being over, we hope the police may be trusted with seeing that the law is thoroughly executed, and the nuisance finally quelled.[1]

Three days later, the superintendent of police let all establishments know that strict compliance would be required. Most of the small places, housed in basements, closed up immediately. The larger halls stayed open with business as usual, except for the disappearance of waiter girls. Some theaters closed down their bars but retained the entertainment. Butler followed the law but decided to test its constitutionality. The girls were omitted. A bar was installed adjacent to the theater. There were some ladies that roamed in the audience. Performances went on as scheduled.

A number of businesses got together and went to court to test the law's constitutionality. Concert saloons still open awaited the results. "Why," they asked, "can we get a license and the city taxes us for the performances and liquor-selling, that some happen to employ waiter girls; since we combine all three in our business, why should we be punished for a misdemeanor?"

Even as everyone waited for the court decision, the police maintained rigorous compliance with the statute and did not permit theatrical entertainment, liquor and waiter girls to be enjoyed together. Attendance at saloons and theaters dropped off. Those people who had the misfortune of being arrested were fined $500 or jail. One theater ad boasted that they "were still alive," but when one looked in there were few patrons. The 444 was identified by the *Times* as a "good house." They had the bar next door, with no inside communication between it and the theater. Without the part normally played by the waiter girls, performances continued.

The owner of Volk's Garden, the German theater, was arrested for selling lager, which he claimed was not beer. He lost the case and his theater was temporarily shut down. In May, the Supreme Court decision upheld the law, which put all but the largest theaters out of business. It appeared that Broadway had finally been "cleaned up." Within a few years, however, saloons were reopening and waiter girls returned. The police did little about it, likely due to the Tweed faction in the city council, strong supporters of businesses in the Bowery.

Butler had handled his situation well, with no diminishment of business. In fact, his theater was more crowded than usual due to the demise of the concert saloons in his vicinity. Even the *New York Clipper,* which had come out against concert saloons, praised 444's operation.

> The American Music Hall continues to develop itself as an attractive place of amusement. The funny fellows, beautiful women and clever artists, there engaged, are so numerous that we cannot begin to mention their names. But we know a man who never has a good laugh without thinking directly of Tony Pastor, Charley White, Johnny Wild and some such rib-ticklers at the American.[2]

Charley White, a minstrel veteran and well-known Ethiopian delineator, had recently joined the company. In ads for 444, Tony was called "the greatest comic singer in America." While the Supreme Court was deciding the fate of the new law, Butler promised his patrons that he would "run his establishment as long as the people demand it, law or no law." It was an astute public relations ploy; he had little fear of being closed down, having complied with the provisions of the law. After the court decision, Butler's business continued better than anyone expected. Butler survived because he was a good businessman who offered top entertainment with low admission prices. He also had the only first-class variety theater in town.

Tony learned a good deal from Butler during his first year at 444. He auditioned actors and saw what "top talent" really meant. He realized the importance of putting good people on longer contracts. He saw the benefit of keeping admission prices low. (Prices ranged from ten cents in the gallery to orchestra chairs for fifty cents.) He heartily embraced Butler's decision to present new programs each week. He saw the advantage of hiring performers who were versatile, who could formulate their own material and, in addition, appear in other roles to support the company. He appreciated Butler's use of the ballet; "women for women," Butler said, but they appealed to all patrons and were always warmly received.

The 444 closed the end of June for the summer. Butler had made it through a turbulent period and prospered. The potential for the coming season which was to open August 11—earlier than any other theater, another Butler strategy—appeared even better, since the cast was made up of already familiar and favored performers. And, 444 continued to be the only first-class variety theater in operation.

Tony could not rest during the summer nor could he afford to be unemployed. During July and August, he appeared at the Continental Theater, Philadelphia, along with Charley White. Apart and together, they gave a good show, much to the delight of audiences, who were getting quite attached to the two men. Tony and Charley experimented with some sketches in which Charley appeared in blackface and played against Tony's New York style. Audiences were convulsed with their absurdities. They planned to bring the idea back to 444 for the new season.

The 444's season opening week played to full houses and excellent box office receipts. Pastor, White, Simmons and Hart were singled out as audience pleasers. Butler offered another innovation by getting Miss Agnes Sutherland, called the Scottish Nightingale, to head the bill. Bringing in a performer from England was a rare occurrence, usually found only in the dramatic side of the theater business. Sutherland had audiences cheering for her and obliged them with several encores. The success of her appearance persuaded Butler to look to Europe for future performers. Tony's act consisted of singing three comic songs, with two more as encores, and he was favorably received. The more he sang his comic songs, the more audiences seemed to like him.

During 1862, Tony published nine songsters, sold at ten cents each.[3] Together, they included more than 500 songs, mostly comic, a few sentimental. The titles of the songsters reflect their content: *Tony Pastor's Bowery Songster, Waterfall Songster, 444 Combination Songster, Open House Songster, Carte de Visite Songster, Great Sensation Songster, Own Comic Songster, Comic Irish Songster*, and *Comic Songster*. The vast majority of songs were taken from music and lyrics written by other authors; Tony adapted his own lyrics. Tony had a prodigious talent for preparing rhyming lyrics that audiences easily understood. He produced at least one new song each week. Tony usually signed a contract with the song's authors, giving them a fee for use ranging from one dollar to fifteen dollars for the rights to sing the song several times over an agreed-upon period. Tony employed this pattern for three decades.

Many of Tony's songs became audience favorites, frequently requested as encores. "The Bill-Poster's Dream" (written by E. T. Johnston, music from "The Captain with his Whiskers") began:

> If you walk through the streets of New York City,
> You can daily see the subject I have chosen for my ditty;
> Upon almost every fence and wall that you may espy,
> Posted bills, of every size and shape, are sure to meet your eye.[4]

One of the audience's most popular requests was "The Upper and Lower Ten Thousand," a travesty about the differences in life between the city's elite and its poor.

> And now, when rebellion o'ershadows the land,
> And the nation sends forth each brave volunteer band,
> Who is it in battle the valientest proves–
> Isn't it the Upper Ten Thousand that wears its kid gloves?
> Or isn't it the Lower Ten Thousand, that's found
> (Whose hands by labor been hardened and browned)
> With his steel in his hand and afire in his eye,
> Rushing into battle to conquer or die?[5]

Audience response to the song was electric. Tony had revealed his philosophy of the war and where he stood with regard to his neighbors, and the theater rocked with appreciative cheers and applause, asking for more of the same.

Tony's songs about family relations, especially between husbands and wives, always aroused

At the height of his appeal at 444 Broadway, Tony published songbooks containing the lyrics of his most popular songs.

the audiences. While these songs were all farcical, they offered a sensitivity to familiar relationships. "The Wife that Wears the Breeches" was a song Tony sang particularly at matinees when the theater was filled with women. Others included "All Men Are Liars (Especially to Their Wives)," "The Seven Ages of Women," and "He's a Grand Old Has-Been."

Included at almost every performance were songs and skits about the Irish and their foibles. "Miles O'Reilly's Love-Letter" (music from "Dennis McCastor") was one of the patrons' sentimental favorites.

> Dear Molly, me darlin,' me thrush and me starlin,'
> I'm bitin' and snarlin' at this fate of mine!
> Of joy you bereft me, of happiness cleft me,
> And so coldly left me to sorrow and pine:
> It's bad that I'm lookin,' with grief I am chokin,'
> And sorely is breakin' this poor heart of mine–
> To keep it from sinkin' right off, I'm thinkin'
> I must take to drinkin' old whiskey and wine.[6]

Tony sung his songs of the Irish about lost loves, working conditions, the Bowery atmosphere, and marriage with a dialect that was as real as the subject matter.

Over the years, people talked approvingly of Tony's management style. But even more pronounced was his talent for humor and poetry. Tony's comic songs were not only unique, but they also captured audiences with their topical lyrics and Tony's inimitable presentation. No one else wrote telling verse like Tony until, much later, Tin Pan Alley dominated the music business. Tony was able to successfully entertain in this manner for forty years; it was only after he died that nostalgic admirers and theater historians recognized his special abilities.

Even with the opening of other theaters in September, attendance at 444 continued to be high. The New York theatrical season held the potential of bringing in significant box office profits, as the public seemed intent on making this amusement its most important escape from the war. The city was enjoying a war-related prosperity with industry in full swing, most people employed and money available to spend. To an outsider, it may have seemed incredible to see so much joy and merriment on the streets of New York at the same time that a bloody war was in progress. Of course, the war was far away and no one believed it would last very long. Theaters were filled the entire 1862-63 season.

On October 1862, a benefit was held for Charley White at 444. He was to be drafted into the army. "The benefit was headed by the ever fresh Tony Pastor, high cockalorum of comic singers," the *Clipper* reported.[7] His colleagues gave White a steel portrait engraving and a great sendoff. Behind the scenes, Butler and local political officials were seeing about a deferment. Two weeks later, White was back at 444, assuming his usual place on the bill. Somehow, he had found someone else to take his place. The same was true for Tony, a prime specimen for the army. He, too, was able to avoid military service throughout the Civil War. In fact, examining the list of performers in variety theaters, minstrels and circuses, very few of them ever served in the armed forces. Information suggests that the passing of money to avoid conscription was a critical element, one that helped to incite the draft riots a year later.

The American Music Hall continued to prosper throughout the winter of 1862-63. Butler advertised his theater as "the music hall of the masses," with no cessation of novelties—any act that contained a unique feature was labeled a novelty—the "most popular place of amusement in the world."[8] With Butler's Melodeon business in Philadelphia floundering, he sent Tony to play there through the Christmas holidays. Business increased and Tony's reputation as a crowd pleaser was further enhanced. Tony also received a salary increase for his work in Philadelphia. He was back at 444 in January 1863, singing his comic songs.

To begin the year, Butler made another strategic business move by raising admission prices and restructuring seating arrangements in the theater; "suits all classes," he declared. The gallery remained at ten cents, but a new section, "the colored gallery," was fifteen cents, and "colored boxes" were twenty-five cents. It was the first recognition in any popular theater of a Negro audience. The war against slavery broke many previous perceptions of Negroes. They were allowed freedoms heretofore unthought of by the general public, for example, attending white theaters. Unfortunately, after the war, all of this would revert to previously held beliefs.

The parquet was raised to twenty-five cents, orchestra chairs to thirty-seven cents and seats in private boxes to fifty cents. Butler added two more sections: upper private boxes at two dollars and lower private boxes at three dollars. Attendance never faltered.

The ballet company, now directed and choreographed by a Frenchman, M. Le Thorne, put on new dances weekly and quickly became an important element on the bill. It especially appealed to the men in the audience, since "the girls were pretty, had pretty understandings (legs) and prettily used them." Tony was featured again, this time with T.G. Riggs and J.C. Wallace, Ethiopian comedians. A new item was added to the bill. Besides performing their specialties, the actors put on a sketch in which they played various roles. It was all farce and burlesque comedy, meant to create laughter.

At the beginning of 1863, there were fifteen theaters operating in New York City. Only two of them served up variety: 444 and Barnum's Museum, which featured more oddities than professional artists. Two offered minstrel companies; Wood's Minstrel Hall, which featured the Christy company, and Bryant's Opera House, led by the famous Dan Bryant. One theater, the Broadway Menagerie (formerly Broadway Amphitheater) featured circuses and wild animals. An arena in Brooklyn gave shows of horsemanship. The remaining seven played legitimate drama, starring performers that included Edwin Booth, Miss Bateman, Laura Keene, Mrs. Sarah Siddons and John E. Owens. The 444 remained the only high-class variety house in the city.

Tony was able to take advantage of his comic song popularity by publishing another songster made up of twenty-five of his favorites. The songbook sold for twenty-five cents. It was publicly advertised but its success was questionable because of its high price.

Even the advent of Lent, a normally slow time for theater attendance, did not diminish audiences at 444 as Tony continued as a headliner among a talented group of performers. Butler was now reaching out to include circus performers to enliven the bill — trapeze artists, contortionists, jugglers, magicians and high wire acts. Because they performed the same routine at every performance, they had to be changed each week. Circus performers were more available because the war had all but eliminated their ability to tour.

In March, Tony reappeared at the Continental Music Hall, Philadelphia, for a special four-week engagement where he headed the bill. He added to his routine by dressing in costume (sometimes a tuxedo) and including a few dance steps. Philadelphia audiences had come to love Tony and he was

Charley White, an exponent of "Ethiopian eccentricities," co-starred with Tony at 444 Broadway. He later managed his own company and owned a theater.

amply feted for his performances with several encores each night. The Continental Music Hall seated 2,500 people and claimed to be the largest theater in the country. Filling the hall was a managerial challenge. Even half full, one could hear his voice echo. Tony did not care to play there because of its size and his inability to connect familiarly with audiences. He preferred smaller theaters, because his act was more intimate and he needed closeness with audiences to put it over in the manner he desired. At one memorable performance at the Continental, Tony sang selections from Dutch opera, as he styled it. For those patrons close to the stage, it was a hilarious act; those further back were unable to clearly hear the lyrics. He withdrew the routine and reserved it for a better occasion.

In April, Tony returned to 444 and appeared in a minstrel company act. His acting ability was deemed good and was getting better. Given the opportunity by Butler, Tony was acting in roles beyond his usual specialty and audiences liked it as well. Butler was now advertising Tony as "the greatest comic singer, clown, jester and burlesque orator of the age."[9] Sketches by the stock company, those who continued in the cast for a long period of time, were becoming a familiar part of the 444 bill. Their versatility gave a fresh look every week. No other theater could claim to have a group of actors playing together every week. The actors themselves found the arrangement enjoyable and exhilarating. Audiences loved the change of roles, the humor and the sheer delight the performers had in rendering the skits. As new people were added to the program, they were incorporated into the fun. If they fit in, they were retained for several weeks or months; if not, others replaced them.

During the middle of May, Tony again appeared at the Continental, in Philadelphia. There was an incentive: he was paid a higher salary to play there and Butler was paid a fee to release him to appear there. When Tony came on stage, he was met with a large reception. "Welcome back Tony," they shouted, which continued throughout his five-week engagement. Philadelphia newspapers called him "the prince of all comic singers and jesters."

Theaters were closing the middle of June for the summer months, as was usual in New York. However, Butler had another idea to prolong the season and acquire additional profit. For a short season of six weeks, Butler booked the company into the Boston Museum. The company included his top headliners and a ballet troupe of twenty-six young women. In the meantime, 444 was to be refurbished for the coming season.

After the outbreak of war, the New York was filled with political zeal. But, as the war dragged on, ideas of a quick victory were denied and opposition by the Democratic Party increased. During the summer of 1862, the Democrats convened a large meeting, which included delegates from the state's districts. The Democratic contingent from the Bowery, led by the Tweed organization, was especially vocal and demonstrative. Resolutions coming out of the meeting condemned President Lincoln and demanded peace with the South. Tony was a Democrat and against the war but did not let his political leanings affect his performance; he sang patriotic songs and promoted use of the American flag in the theater.

By February 1863, the city had become a center for anti-war activity. The new mayor, a Republican, had no control over the city council, that role being taken by "Boss" William Macy Tweed. Tweed was also against the war and his minions in the Bowery, primarily Irish, were his strongest supporters. In March 1863, Congress passed the Enrollment and Conscription Act; the Tweed organization fought it bitterly. A convenient loophole in the act allowed a drafted man to avoid army service by paying $300 to obtain a substitute. The act clearly favored the wealthy; it was the poor who suffered most from its consequences.

Also against the act and quotas given to New York was Governor Seymour, who threatened the Republicans with turbulence in the streets. "Boss" Tweed believed that the act discriminated most in his territory with its 200,000 poor Irish. The draft began on July 11 at Third

Avenue and 46th Street. There were crowds milling around the building but all remained quiet. On July 13, drafting was to continue. Based on a prearranged plan, a group of men and women assembled and then moved north, picking up supporters from surrounding factories to a place near Central Park. They were armed with clubs and other weapons. The riots were about to commence.

The city was put into a stage of siege. No stores opened. No transportation operated. Buildings were set afire. Thousands of panicky people attempted to leave the city, mainly on the ferries. Police and called-in federal troops fought running battles with the rioters. What had begun as a dispute against the Conscription Act turned into violence by mostly Irish against Negroes living in the area. In effect, Negroes were held responsible for the war and, thus, the draft.

After four days of rioting, thirteen regiments of soldiers finally quieted the crowds and put the city under military control. More than a thousand people were killed and millions of dollars of property destroyed. Streets in the Bowery were littered with debris for weeks. A month later, the draft was resumed with no problem.

Surprisingly overlooked, none of the city's theaters were harmed. Most had already closed for the summer and those few that were open put up their shutters quickly. The 444 sustained no damage, and the artists were not in jeopardy because Butler's entire company was performing in Boston. Their departure from the city was fortuitous. Still, everyone worried about their loved ones and the theater while they played at the Boston Museum. Butler was receiving daily messages from his agent in New York, which reassured the company.

The Butler Combination made a big hit in Boston, filling the theater nightly. Tony's first appearance as a headliner quickly made him a city favorite, one whom audiences never forgot. Newspapers suggested that the public see "the great company from famous 444." Tony was singled out for singing about topics of the day and was "vociferously applauded." By the fourth week of their engagement, the *Clipper's* stringer reported on the troupe's triumphs.

> The great secret of their success is in the excellence and variety of the entertainment offered. The acts are short and each is diversified from its predecessor. Singing, dancing, gymnastics, pantomime, Ethiopian minstrelsy follow each other in rapid succession, the whole constituting a delightful melange.[10]

Butler discovered that six weeks of box office receipts on the road equaled three months receipts at home. Touring was found to be very profitable and should be employed whenever possible, Butler concluded. Other variety theater managers had not yet discovered this because they had no resident companies to put on tour and no star power to make it work.

The company returned to New York on August 1, readying their acts to reopen 444 on the tenth. In spite of the insurgency, the entire interior of the theater had been refurbished. In a newspaper ad alerting the public to 444's season's opening (again, almost a month before any of the other theaters), the theater was labeled "the great institution of the age, the only place of amusement in America nightly presenting a stock company composed exclusively of star artists."[11] No one could argue against them. In the ad, each headliner was afforded a few words of hyperbole and identification. Butler may have omitted his name in the ad to feature his performers but everyone knew who was behind this theater's success. He was being called a business genius and, considering the high risk and singular peculiarities of theater operation, he earned the title.

During September and October, however, box office receipts suffered badly when General Lee and his troops invaded Pennsylvania. The Democrats again spoke out in favor of peace but were ignored by a majority of people who believed the North's army had to prevent Lee from threatening any Northern cities. Attendance at theaters remained low until Lee retreated. Then, euphoria seemed to return and the theaters were again well attended.

In the August and September issues of the *New York Clipper,* both Frank and William Pastor had engraved portraits on the front page and brief bios of their successful circus exploits. This recognition in the *Clipper* was public affirmation of their ascendance to stardom in the circus world. The accolades they received were comparable to those of Tony. For that brief moment, the three Pastor brothers were the pride of New York.

Patrons returned to 444 to standing room only signs hung out an hour before the performance began. Standing room was allowed in theaters as long as the patrons did not block aisles. However, enforcement was lax and bribes frequent, allowing the theater to jam as many people into the auditorium as they could fit. Although the situation was dangerous and the press made complaints, it was several years before real enforcement was enacted. Still, standing room was not outlawed. Some theaters worked on short margins because they charged low admission, and standing room patrons meant the difference between profit and loss.

With the full season came an influx of tourists. It had been an increasing phenomenon the past few years and had become an excellent source of revenue for retail outlets, hotels, restaurants and theaters. The 444 benefited because newspapers suggested to tourists that if they wished to experience "good variety," the American Music Hall was the place to visit. Said the *Clipper,* "444 seems to be the center of attraction with out-of-town seekers of pleasure." Regarding Tony: "Tony Pastor continues an immense card to the manager, for he is nightly the recipient of three or four encores for each song."[12]

One of the newer features at 444 was the inclusion of farce and burlesque skits put on by the whole company. The first of them had melodramatic-style plots, like "The Ghost," "The Haunted Cave," and "The Secret Conclave." Stock company members usually formulated the skits and prepared the script which, when actually presented, was freely ad-libbed with humorous material. The skits were changed each week, so preparing and rehearsing them had to take up some time prior to their presentation. Only very talented and skillful performers could take various roles in the skits while still performing, and keeping fresh, their own specialties. Audiences became enamored with them and came to expect new skits each week. While it gave them an additional reason to visit the theater frequently, it was a very demanding task for performers. Yet, everyone recognized how popular such skits were and other theaters began incorporating sketches of their own.

The skits themselves became more sophisticated, emphasizing humor over all other considerations, much to everyone's delight. Performers now were able to include their specialty into the skit plot and the ridiculousness on stage provided even more audience laughter. The flexi-

Top: After beginning his career as a circus equestrian, William (Billy) Pastor switched to variety and joined Tony in various stage ventures. *Bottom:* Frank Pastor spent most of his life as a circus equestrian. He became world famous for his breathtaking performances. During the last years of his life, he assisted Tony.

bility of the material, costuming, scenery, and music offered the opportunity for burlesquing anything from current dramas to current events. In November, 444 put on a skit called "Lonergan's Ball" in which Tony "sang with much gusto." The skit was so well received that it was played for three weeks in a row. The performers were as pleased as the audience. Each night, one performer ad-libbed business that broke up his colleagues so that they had a hard time playing their roles. Audiences loved the spontaneity of the experience.

Sam Sharpley and his circus company visited New York during the Christmas holidays. Sharpley attempted to persuade Tony to leave 444 and be his partner in a new troupe. Tony refused because he was doing so well as a local performer. Actually, Tony had a more grandiose idea for his future. He revealed to Sharpley that he wished to own and run a variety theater. Sharpley was not yet prepared to deal with that suggestion; his own troupe was still on tour. They promised to discuss the issue again when Sharpley returned to town.

January 1864 brought several changes to 444. Butler formally introduced programs especially for women and children and advertised that his theater was a "clean place." Matinees three times a week were promoted and the bill was modified to include shorter routines with an emphasis on humor. The theater's success was immediate, an event Tony filed away for future consideration.

The other change occurred when Tony was booked, for a fee, to appear at the Varieties Theater, Chicago, for three weeks. He was so well received that he stayed for six weeks. An ad in the *Chicago Tribune* called Tony "the celebrated jester and champion comic vocalist of the world."[13]

The Varieties Theater was Chicago's best variety house, in many ways comparable to 444. Admission prices ran from fifteen cents to fifty cents. Each bill featured fifteen to sixteen acts, the show running beyond three hours. Tony was paid fifty dollars a week for nine appearances. On February 15, the Varieties announced Tony's last week with the report that "this place of amusement is nightly filled with its patrons, and are highly delighted with its reigning star, Tony Pastor."[14] Chicago audiences would not forget Tony.

Tony returned triumphantly to 444 in March; he generated full houses and shouts for encores after every song. Butler continued to reap the benefits of large crowds and excellent public recognition for his high-class shows. He delayed the theater's summer closing until early July to take advantage of the tourist trade and reopened the new season on August 15. Tony was listed at the top of the bill, which included Charley White; Nelse Seymour, an Ethiopian comedian; James Wambold, one of the best of minstrel end men; Ed Murray, song and dance man; orchestra leader David Braham (his first major assignment); and a ballet which included fifteen pretty young women.

In September 1864, Tony's portrait appeared on the front page of the *Clipper*. At the same time, fellow performers gave Tony a benefit at the New Bowery Theater on September 9; 4,000 people were present. The event revealed to the press how well known and popular he had become.

> The Pastor of the diocese (444), the refulgent Tony, had a full house for his benefit at the New Bowery Theater on Friday evening. It was a pretty sight to Tony, and made his heart rejoice with thankful emotions. We guess he made money enough out of the benefit to enable him to put in a reasonable bid for a new loan.[15]

Were they aware of what Tony was planning?

Butler had raised admission prices again to begin the 1864-65 season but it made no difference; audiences continued to fill the hall. Doors opened at 6:00 P.M. and patrons streamed in; the show commenced at 7:30 P.M. and ran for four hours. In October, the *Clipper* reported:

> There can be no question as to the success of manager Butler's 444 Broadway, for people of all political stripes and platform make the three 4s their place of amusement.[16]

Few knew of Tony's marriage until the announcement of Anna Pastor's death in 1866. Tony retained artifacts of this relationship, which were ultimately dispensed in his will (Harry Ransom Humanities Research Center).

No other theater in the city received such outstanding recognition from the press.

But Tony was getting restless. He had been fully recognized for his performances by New York audiences. He was getting offers from theater managers to appear at their houses. His salary had increased so much that he moved into better lodgings, with a maid and a dresser. Butler was unable to offer him more money than he was already getting. In late November, Butler reluctantly announced that Tony was going on tour to appear in the month of December in Washington, D.C., as a variety headliner. Butler could not promise that Tony would return in January or, if he did, for how long.

On December 5, Tony began his engagement at the Canterbury Theater, Washington, D.C. He brought with him Charley Fox, from Wood's Minstrels, and, to Butler's consternation, Charley White, James Wambold and Johnny Wild from the 444 company. It appeared to observers that Tony was managing this engagement and the people playing with him.

At the same time, a new variety theater, aptly called Varieties, opened at 37–39 Bowery early in December and was attracting customers away from 444. George Lea, who owned the Canterbury, also owned the Varieties, and it was no secret that he was attempting to compete with Butler head on.

On January 7, 1865, the *Washington Post* declared that Tony had a successful engagement. He was given a benefit at his last appearance and was proclaimed by the *Post* "a great favorite in Washington."[17] Tony returned to 444 a few days later and people had to be turned away. Sam Sharpley returned to New York at the conclusion of his company's tour. He and Tony met to discuss merging their talent. It seemed that the timing of their possible association was precipitous.

Sam Sharpley was born in Philadelphia on June 13, 1831, and entered the burnt cork business when only sixteen years of age. His success was rapid and in a few years was acknowledged as one of the best performers in the business. He had made himself a popular favorite with Philadelphia audiences. In November 1860, he opened Jayne's Hall with a first-class minstrel band. The following year, Sharpley led his company on tour. In the fall of 1862, he returned to appear at the Melodeon; his banjo playing and songs got him a salary of one hundred dollars a week. He decided to form his own troupe and toured the New England states with success. He then took the company, called Sharpley's "Iron Clads," west on another successful tour.

Sharpley gained the reputation as an astute businessman, honorable in all his dealings, and an excellent manager of performers. His business acumen led him to talk to Tony about the opportunities that would be theirs if they merged their skills. This time, Tony agreed.

Through January and February 1865, Tony continued to star at 444. He introduced new comic songs and "the people never seemed to tire of him." In the meantime, Sharpley sold one-half interest in his company to S.S. Sanford for $3,000. It was reported that, at the time of their announced partnership, Tony had saved $2,000 of his own. In February, Sharpley reported that he had begun the farewell tour of his "Iron Clads" to Philadelphia, Baltimore and Washington, D.C. They would close in early March.

On March 11, 1865, the *Clipper* announced that:

> A new variety troupe is at present organizing in this city, under the direction of Tony Pastor and a well-known popular minstrel manager, and is to be called "Tony Pastor's Variety Show." Gymnastic exercises, pantomime, ballet, comic and sentimental singing will be the order of the program. They give their first show at Patterson, New Jersey, on the 22nd, and continue two days. They go thence to Newark for two days, New Brunswick, 27th and 28th, Trenton, 29th, 30th, Elizabeth, Orange, etc.[18]

At the age of thirty-two, Tony had realized his ambition. After eighteen years in the amusement business and six years in variety, he now had his own company to manage. He was determined not to fail.

5

Tony Pastor's Opera House

The New York public had exploded into a seven-mile procession of cheering men and women celebrating Lincoln's second term and recent Union victories. Five days later, city newspapers and theatrical journals announced that Tony Pastor was forming his own variety troupe. It was a bold move for a young performer with no managerial experience and no theater in which to perform. But, according to critics, if anyone had a chance to succeed, it was the genial Tony Pastor.

Tony had spent the last several years studying the variety business, with mentoring from Robert Butler. He was aware of the changes taking place in local amusements and sensitive enough to anticipate their influence on his managerial plans.

Lower Manhattan at this time included factories, commercial enterprises like the Ladies Mile on Broadway, pockets of abject poverty and crowded tenements. There was a significant Irish population made up of recent immigrants, and the area was a bastion for the Democratic Party. After the Civil War, New York began to improve its city services: changing from a volunteer fire department to a professional one; forming a health department to track down pockets of disease, with doctors to assist the ill and equipment to clean the streets; reclaiming old buildings, renewing neighborhoods and making them affordable; and building new department stores, hotels and restaurants.

Theaters were being built near Union Square. Older ones were being refurbished to attract a better clientele. The more established and recognized theaters adjusted their bills to reflect the neighborhoods in which they were located. Theater owners and managers created stock companies to perform over an entire season, and when summer closed them, they sent companies on tour, thanks to an improving railroad system that made every city and town easily accessible. As the theater business expanded, an entire support system came into being. A flourishing poster and playbill industry supplied every theater and every flat surface in the neighborhood with advertisements of coming attractions.

At the time, obtaining acts and actors, except for the Laura Keenes and Edwin Booths, meant making deals on Union Square's benches (called the slave market) or in surrounding restaurants. The emergent brokers allowed actors to be represented and theaters to find performers. Within a few years, most local performers could obtain bookings through brokers. Actors lived in boarding houses situated near their brokers and theaters.

A growing printing industry prospered with the manufacture of advertising material, trade newspapers, sheet music for the middle-class families with pianos in their parlors, and even programs and tickets. Support services, consisting of costumers, scenery painters, prop builders, and theater furniture makers, became important elements in a theater's operation.

The theatrical business had matured considerably from its concert hall days. Opportunities for success or failure were more clearly delineated: they involved risk, daring, venturesome experimentation and money. The survivors were the ones who grasped the intricacies of the theater business. But there was no single model for success. Each manager and performer developed a unique system. What mattered most, what determined success or failure were the audiences, how they responded to what was presented to them in the name of entertainment.

Tony learned from Butler the importance of advertising and promotion. The scope of news coverage had dramatically expanded in recent years; sixteen newspapers were published in New York, most of them dailies. New readers were attracted by specific feature material, like theater programming, music venues and circus locations. With the addition of features devoted to fashions, homemaking and other women's interests, an active female constituency arose, one that was not deterred from attending the theater.

The *New York Herald* offered the most coverage of theater doings in the city. Its publisher, James Gordon Bennett, cared nothing for public policy, only money. The *New York Ledger,* a weekly, offered the most space for theater activities. The *New York Clipper,* another weekly, specialized in sports and public amusements. By 1865, nearly half of the city's papers devoted space to entertainment — drama, minstrelsy, circuses and variety halls— and included detailed reportage of the events at each of the New York theaters. They also offered plenty of room for theaters to place ads, allowing them freedom to say what they wished in the ad. Exaggeration and hyperbole were rampant.

No sooner did Tony put together his company than he began advertising in the *Herald* and *Clipper.* Ads featuring statements like "incomparable troupe," "newest and best combinations," and "the original and only Tony Pastor" signaled the direction in which Tony wished to formulate his management philosophy. The effect was almost immediate success, crowding theaters with audiences anticipating the amusement they were about to witness.

In March 1865, when Tony and Sam Sharpley formed their company, they had no theater in New York in which to perform. Instead, they decided to tour New England for several months while a local theater could be found. The tour afforded the opportunity for the troupe to gain the reputation as a first-class variety organization. It was an excellent device for promotional purposes once they returned to New York. The feature of the tour was a week's engagement at Morris Bros. Opera House in Boston, opening in the middle of June. Their appearance was so successful that they played there for four weeks to full houses each evening and every matinee. Local advertising and extensive billboarding surely helped to attract audiences.

About the time the company was to leave Boston, Pastor and Sharpley announced they had leased the theater at 201 Bowery. They planned to begin their New York residence on July 31. The theater had previously been a minstrel hall. It would need only minimal refurbishing to prepare for the new variety company.

After stops in Massachusetts and Connecticut towns, the troupe entered New York on a triumphal note. Newspapers hailed the combination as "the greatest concentration of artistic talent" and "Tony Pastor, the unequalled clown, comedian and comic vocalist."[1]

The Tony Pastor Company, his first as theater owner and manager, consisted of the following performers: Ernestine de Faiber, a dancer and already a local favorite; Mlle. Bertha, ballet; Amelia Wells, a repertoire of Irish songs; Ellen Collene, vocalist; Carrie Austin, Zouave drill; Walter Caldwell, comedian; James Gaynor, banjo solos; Johnny Wild, Ethiopian delineator; Robert Butler, Willis Armstrong, and Doty Duly, skit comedians and pantomimists; and Sheridan and Mack, clog dancers. Each week, Tony introduced two or three new people: Sam Ryan, Irish comedian; El Nino Eddie, a daring gymnast; Tim O'Brien in "The Irish Emigrant," a farce-comedy; Laura Taylor, vocalist, advertised as having come directly from England; Bob

Hart, with a stump speech; Master Barry, a teenage fast song and dance artist. Of course, at every performance was the redoubtable Tony Pastor.

The show lasted from three to three and a half hours, depending on the number of encores each performer received. Evening performances began at 7:30 P.M.; Saturday matinees began at 2:30 P.M. Tickets ranged in price from fifteen cents in the gallery to one dollar in the box seats. A good attendance for the week would generate about $2,000 in receipts. Out-of-pocket expenses, like salaries and other operational expenses, would come to about $1,200. The highest salaried performer would receive thirty dollars a week. The profit margin was good as long as the theater was at least three-quarters full. For the first several months, Tony had no problem making a profit. By the end of September, Pastor and Sharpley purchased the building and now were performing in their own hall.

Tony quickly learned several operational procedures and put them to good use. Performers who initially pleased audiences—applause and recalls were excellent evaluators—were called back to the Opera House to appear again. Some were signed to return numerous times during the season. The emphasis on

In 1865, Tony's picture appeared on the front cover of the *New York Clipper* when he opened his own theater. Theatrical people doubted the success of his venture, but agreed that if anyone could do it, it would be Tony.

fresh material was critical with audiences. Even a favorite who appeared several weeks in a row had to have new business to present each week. That requirement culled the versatile artists from the limited act performers. Tony, too, had to introduce new comic songs each week, although he could sing familiar favorites for encores. As a compliment to his recent comic song successes, Tony published a complete set of comic songs, edited by John F. Poole, taken from the previous songsters published in the early 1860s.[2] The lyrics were all Tony's but some of the music was quite familiar to people, like "Jim Crack-Corn," "O Susanna," "Derry Down," "Auld Lang Syne," "Columbia, the Gem of the Ocean," and "Yankee Doodle."

Tony continued to collect his comic songs from various sources. He had kept dozens of them from his circus days. In his files were songs with lyrics written out on small pieces of paper accompanied by one sheet with the music theme to be expanded by the orchestra. He bought songs from local composers who were happy to supply him as long as they got credit for the composition. He was sent songs from English music hall performers for a small fee. With a few words changed, they were ready to present to local audiences. He also composed a few himself.

Tony's primary topics were local social and political subjects, with which audiences could readily identify. Not all songs were comic; some were sentimental ballads, as long as they were related to subject matter the audience understood. The overall impression as seen by reviewers and audiences was that Tony's routines were fresh, unique, humorous and warm-hearted. Tony's voice was only average, maybe somewhat gravelly, but he handled it in such a way as to make it pleasing. Audiences felt that they could sing "like Tony." But it was his delivery that was so outstanding. To the patrons, he was a genial friend, a next-door neighbor, using an almost shy sort of humor, with a twinkle of the eye and a strut of the step.

This year's favorite song was "The Streets of New York," an original song composed by Tony. The song had a catchy musical cadence, and the lyrics told of the relationship between one's occupation and local street names, i.e., butchers on Market Street, jewelers on Gold Street, and virgins on Maiden Lane.

> All you who've been around the town,
> Or travelled through the city,
> Just list to what I've noted down,
> And strung into my ditty.
> Perhaps you never thought of what
> I've got in my narration—
> How every street is fitted for
> A certain occupation.
> Chorus: Oh, yes we know—
> For, as you travel through the town,
> You'll find it so.[3]

The original song had four verses. By the second week it was featured, Tony had added two more verses, thanks to contributions made by audiences. The song became so popular that Tony reprised it for several years.

At the beginning of the 1865-66 season, there were twenty-one theaters open in New York. Most featured drama, three played minstrels. Four were considered variety houses: the Varieties Theater (old Stadt Theater) with 1,600 seats; Butler's American Theater (444) with 1,100 seats; Barnum's Museum with 1,700 seats; and Tony Pastor's Opera House with 1,055 seats, one of the smallest theaters in the city. By the end of 1865, only sixteen theaters were in operation, which included two new entries. Changes in management, closures and changes of name were common, demonstrating the volatility of the business. Few believed Pastor and Sharpley would last six months. Yet, at the beginning of 1866, the *New York Clipper* reported the Opera House's 1865 receipts since its opening July 31 as close to $31,000, with a profit of $7,000.[4] Tony put the money back into the business.

During November and December, Tony initiated holiday programs, the first to do so among variety houses. He featured skits and pantomimes with Christmas themes. At the same time he was mounting these bills, orchestra members and ballet performers began a strike for higher wages. Orchestra members were earning from five to fifteen dollars a week; ballet performers earned seven to eight dollars a week. Several managers closed their theaters rather than pay an increased salary. Some attempted to replace their employees but found few to take their place. Tony raised the salaries so his personnel never went on strike. After a few weeks without box office receipts, all theater owners recognized the wisdom of increasing salaries, the orchestra from ten to twenty dollars a week, the ballet to ten dollars a week.

With the addition of John F. Poole, a prodigious skit writer, Tony was able to incorporate into his weekly program humorous burlesque and farcical short plays to conclude the evening. Such skits were called "afterpieces" and were commonly used in variety and minstrels. Most were loosely plotted and actors usually improvised their roles. Audiences were quite demonstrative when an afterpiece did not meet their expectations. An evening that ended with a sour note greatly affected future attendance and diminished the creditability of the theater. With a written script, definite subject matter and rehearsal time, the presentation had a finished look, better character development, and pleased audiences.

John F. Poole was born in Dublin, Ireland, in 1833.[5] His family came to the United States when he was twelve years old. Poole graduated from St. John's College and obtained work as a clerk. At the age of thirty, he embarked on a theatrical career, writing songs and one-act plays. Tony hired him to prepare sketches on various topics to be introduced and performed each week as part of the program. "Old Dame Grimes or the Good Fairy of the Harvest Home" was Poole's first production for Tony. It was well received, and played for two weeks. "Fenian's Dream or

Ireland Free At Last" followed, with even greater success. The sketch ran for a month. Poole's holiday contribution was "The Demon's Revel," a Christmas pantomime. Poole worked almost exclusively for Tony for more than three years.

Poole retired to his rooms each Sunday evening, equipped with a clay pipe, a pencil and pads of paper. He would not get up until he had written a sketch and copied all the parts, sometimes drawing a humorous cover. On Monday morning, he would deliver the sketch to Tony. The stock company would rehearse it, adding or subtracting jokes or farce elements, and prepare it for presentation the next week.

The weekly skits placed additional demands on members of the company, particularly those with continuing contracts. Not only did they perform their specialty during the program, which had to be freshened each week, but they also had to perform in the afterpiece, which was changed each week. Stock players worked all day to prepare their roles for both their specialty and the skits to be performed that evening. For this additional effort, Tony gave them better salaries.

The combination of versatility and commitment from Tony's actors was significant; they played their parts with professionalism and verve. Each year, the skits became more complex and the demands on the artists greater, but none flinched from the challenge. Performers were so anxious to appear in these afterpieces that they would bet with one another for the parts. None was ever repeated unless requested by the audience. Many were no longer afterpieces; they appeared in the middle of the program. Some involved the entire company, including Tony. Topics dealing with the Irish and local current events were especially enjoyed.

Tony's Bowery audiences wanted something hearty, genial, racy and varied in character. They looked for something familiar to their own nature, who loved mirth in its broadest phases, delineated by strong dramatic actions. They expressed little time for sentiment, but sufficient time for fun and a relief from the obligations of everyday life. Variety was a necessity; music and acting had to be laden with histrionics. Each week, Poole tailored his presentations to satisfy the audience.

The comic Christmas pantomime, "The Demon's Revel," was advertised as "written expressly for this establishment and produced at immense expense, with new scenery, new dresses, new properties, new tricks, transformations, etc."[6] The plot and characters were copied from the Commedia dell'Arte, with the featured players resembling Pantaloon, Harlequin and Columbine in their traditional roles. Slapstick was prevalent throughout, to the delight of the audience.

During the fall of 1865, Tony and Sam Sharpley put together another traveling company to appear in New England towns for a period of months. Due to their summer success, they believed the company could generate additional revenue and, at the same time, give needed experience to new performers who could later play at the Opera House. Billy Pastor was made manager of the touring group.

While Billy had spent most of his career in the circus, one of his ambitions was to become a comic singer like his brother Tony. In the summer of 1865, Billy left the circus and made his singing debut at the Academy of Music in New Orleans. The engagement was a success, and Billy returned to New York to further his new career. Tony hired him to both manage and perform in the new touring company. It began the tour in November and initial reports suggested a reasonable success. The touring company played through May 1866, and returned a good profit. Billy was proud of his accomplishment, but was not entirely satisfied working under the aegis of his brother and the ever-present Sharpley.

The year 1866 began with a flourish of business at the Opera House. Reviewers suggested that visitors to the city not to miss Tony Pastor's. Copies of the program were posted at all the hotels located on lower Broadway.

An 1865 engraving of Tony Pastor's Opera House at 201 Bowery. It was opening week, listing the names of the entire company who initiated Tony's long career as a theater manager (Harry Ransom Humanities Research Center).

During the early part of the year, performers included contortionists, trapeze artists and minstrel artists along with the stock company's specialties. Also in prominence were Poole's skits. "The Female Clerks of Washington" featured men in female attire in a satire on how the government operated in the nation's capital. Bumbling and fumbling highlighted the farce. "Mountain Devil" had the principals in broadsword combat full of pratfalls and stilted English dialogue. "The Bells of Central Park" was a play on words that featured young women dressed as bells singing different sounds in unison. "Stephen's Escape or English Rule in Ireland" attracted a good deal of audience participation with boos and cheers in appropriate places for the Irish heroes and English villains. Poole was quickly building a reputation as a prolific writer, producing a new skit for each week's bill.

Tony remained the star of the show singing his comic songs. The *Clipper* called him "a whole show within himself."[7] To add to Tony's appeal, Poole wrote him into some of his skits, which engendered even greater enthusiasm from audiences.

Although the traveling company was reported to have returned a profit of over $20,000 on its tour, Billy Pastor was unhappy with his job. It was decided that Sharpley would resurrect his Iron Clad minstrel group, unite with Billy's company and continue to tour. But neither Sharpley nor Billy was comfortable with the new arrangement. The only thing that kept them together was the company's profitability and, of course, Tony's influence. That did not prevent Billy from placing an ad in the *Clipper* seeking other engagements.

Although four variety theaters began the season in September 1865, only Tony's Opera House remained in operation in the spring of 1866. Two had closed and Butler's 444 burned down. Butler attempted to move his company to the New Bowery Theater, but lease disagreements delayed him. Tony used this situation in all of his newspaper advertising. The result was continuously full houses at the Opera House. In fact, Tony would have no competition until late in the year.

The spring programs continued with emphasis on Poole's skits and the ballet troupe. "Ireland in 1866" had Tony playing Jedediah Bestroot, a Yankee, who gave a stump speech full of malapropisms. So well was he received in his dramatic role that Poole followed with "The Yankee Inventor" that had Tony inventing everything from shoes to vegetables. The ballet put on a different routine each week. It consisted of ten young women, led by Mlle. Bertha, who performed a variety of ethnic dances. They had become a feature of the program, particularly among the male audience members.

Several of the artists who signed to appear for a week's engagement were carried over for an extended time. A few were added to the stock company. William Carleton, a recent visitor from Ireland, sang Irish songs that delighted audiences. The Gorenflo Sisters put on a successful song and dance; but their versatility so impressed Tony that he signed them for the season. They stayed with Tony for five years. T.G. Riggs, a minstrel comedian, was so well received that Tony had him appear in skits as well. Riggs was an excellent character actor and he, too, became an important part of the stock company. Riggs remained with Tony for seven years and later became a well-known dramatic actor. Jennie Engel, a pretty vocalist, received an invitation to appear at the Opera House whenever she had an opening. During some periods, she stayed for months. As late as 1880, she was still honoring Tony with her presence.

A typical Opera House program consisted of the following: El Nino Eddie, a teenage rope walker; Jennie Engel, vocalist; Johnny Mack in skits on Negro life; William Carleton, Irish songs; the corps de ballet; Tony singing several comic songs, which always received encores; Lew Brimmer, in banjo solos in blackface; Billy Emmet, pathetic ballads with humor; and a Poole skit which featured Riggs, Willis Armstrong, G.F. McDonald and the La Point Sisters, all stock company players.

By April, reviewers were calling the Pastor Opera House one of the institutions of the city.

> An excellent company of performers is engaged there who appear in as varied a bill as can be found in any similar establishment in the country.[8]

Although Lent was traditionally a time when theater attendance declined, this did not occur at the Opera House. Tony brought back performers who had previously pleased audiences, and they appreciated his decisions.

Tony announced that the current season at the Opera House would conclude June 9. His summer traveling company would open in Boston June 11 at Morris Bros. Opera House for a short season and then tour the Eastern states. At the same time, he stated that the Opera House would remain open during the summer, featuring various companies and performers who rented the hall. It was another revenue source for the proprietor. The first company to play there was Sharpley's Iron Clad minstrel company with Billy Pastor as comic singer. Although Billy had been advertising his availability for some months, no other engagements had come his way.

On June 9, Tony was given a benefit. The company gave him a diamond-studded watch and several testimonials were presented. Performers who had appeared at the Opera House during the season came back to honor Tony. Such benefit performances were always given voluntarily. Tony sang some new songs and appeared in a skit called "The City Messenger" in which messages between various political figures got mixed up and were delivered to the wrong people, with comic reactions. As soon as the show closed, Tony and the company boarded a train for Boston.

The traveling company was made up of familiar names and established performers: besides Tony, there were William Carleton, Billy Emmet, Johnny Wild, Lew Brimmer, Jennie Engel, McDonald, Riggs and Armstrong, and Johnny Mack. The ballet was led by M. Szollosay, a new member of the company, a choreographer from Europe. Tony filled out the company with eight other performers who had done well on the Sam Sharpley & Billy Pastor tour.

Once on tour, the need for new material each week was greatly diminished. Artists could do their favorite specialties; skits could be repeated; Tony's comic songs would be new to each audience. Except for travel and living on a train, performance life was much less demanding. Expenses were less, ticket prices higher, and profit more easily achieved, even with less than crowded houses. Nearly every stop on the tour of twenty-one towns had full houses. The company returned to New York on July 30.

Tony's earnings for his first full year at the Opera House netted him a profit of over $21,000. With a large portion of the money, he bought a brownstone home on 40th Street for his mother.

The Sharpley & Billy Pastor company left the Opera House and continued their tour of Eastern states. They were said to be "meeting with splendid success." A new member of the cast was Fernando "Dody" Pastor. He performed various acrobatic tricks which, it was reported, he had learned while appearing in the circus. In the census, Tony, Billy, and Fernando gave the same New York address, a home on 17th Street.

On July 31, almost one full month before the opening of any other theater in New York, the Opera House began its season. The press announced that Tony had bought out Sam Sharpley's share of the theater and the traveling company for $3,000. Sharpley planned to operate a minstrel group. Billy went out on his own, seeking engagements in Eastern theaters. Fernando was brought in by Tony to serve as his treasurer. Observers saw Billy living in his brother's shadow because he did not possess the talent that made Tony a headliner. On numerous occasions, Tony helped Billy, particularly obtaining stage engagements for him. This pattern would continue for as long as Billy lived.

The press made a big issue about Tony becoming the sole proprietor of his "expanding dynasty." He now owned a prosperous theater in New York; he headed a profitable traveling company; he rented out his theater during the summer. He had put together a coterie of artists who either stayed with him or returned often to appear at his theater. He paid them well and gave them latitude to innovate their own specialties. And he did all of this by example, working as hard as his performers, if not harder, to satisfy his clientele.

There was no question that Tony possessed a passion for what he did. People around him and the audience could feel that passion. He was happiest when at the theater conducting all aspects of his business. He loved it. He lived it. This message was conveyed to all who interacted with him. This passion made him genuine, approachable, cheerful and honest, and generated loyalty and respect from his fellow artists.

For those who were learning the art of performing, Tony was a mentor and guide. For those who suffered from hard times, Tony was kind and generous. An examination of Tony's expense sheet revealed loans and outright gifts to needy performers. It was apparent that Tony never forgot where he had come from or the trials he had experienced as a young man.

Although he had little formal education, Tony had an intelligence acquired from personal experience and life on the streets. By the time he became a theater owner, Tony demonstrated a talent for selecting artists and understanding the desires of his audiences. He also had the ability to keep a perspective on his own business and maintain a detachment from it that contributed to its stability. If Tony had lived today, people would have declared that he had charisma.

The opening of the Opera House created a "densely packed house, many being unable to obtain standing room."[9] As each old favorite appeared, he was warmly welcomed and encored. Tony's entrance signaled cheering from the gallery and stomping of feet and applause from the lower part of the theater. He was encored five times. Although it was early in the season, the Opera House was full almost every performance.

Even when the other theaters opened in September, business at the Opera House remained good. Apart from Barnum's menagerie and oddity show, there was only one other variety theater open, run by Tony's old friend, Charley White. They often shared performers on successive weeks.

In September, Tony decided to launch another traveling company to tour the East, hopefully to continue until the holidays. The new company's manager was Billy Pastor. He had been unable to find other engagements for the new season. Similar to last year, the company attracted "splendid business." Tony planned to evaluate their profitability at holiday time.

Tony obtained performers from a number of sources. Some he had observed appearing at other theaters. Some were recommended. Some wrote to him directly asking to play at his theater. The majority of acts had to audition for Tony before being accepted to appear at the Opera House. Only if the act seemed unique enough to excite audiences would Tony agree to sign them without an audition. All acts were signed for one week. If they pleased the audience, they would be signed for another week. Their ability to successfully build their audience appeal and create a demand for encores enhanced their chances for additional stage time. In coming years, the broker business would change the way performers were selected and booked. Even then, Tony required the performer to audition for him.

The list of new faces to appear at the Opera House was extensive. M. La Thorne, called "The Man of Iron," juggled 60 pound cannon balls; James Gaynor was an Ethiopian comedian; Billy Emerson, soon to become a minstrel headliner and manager of his own company, pleased the crowd with his "Negroisms"; and Celia Brown did clog dances with speed, precision and clarity. The skits were handled by the team of Riggs, Armstrong, McDonald and others in a variety of roles in pieces like "The Mysteries of Gotham," "The Yankee Sailor," "Young America in Ireland," and "Life Among the Mormons," all farce-comedies written by Poole, which the audience came to expect each week and enthusiastically endorsed.

Just prior to the holidays, the New Bowery Theater was destroyed by fire, creating even more business for the Opera House. Once again, Pastor's was the only first-class variety theater in the city. A Christmas pantomime was performed by the entire cast along with two new sketches with Christmas themes, "The Heart of Erin" and "Americans in Turkey." The *Times* reported, "Great times at Tony's the current week."[10] In the Christmas pantomime, Poole again used the Commedia dell'Arte characters as the featured players, complete with their traditional slapstick routines.

The traveling company, under Billy Pastor's management, disbanded in Buffalo on December 17, with most of the performers returning to New York. Apparently, the tour had begun well but suffered a continuous decline in attendance when they played the smaller towns in New England. Billy was again unemployed.

January 1867 led off with a now familiar Pastor program: Tony sang a new song, "The Famous East Side of Town"; the ballet performed "Les Sabotieres"; a burlesque featuring the entire company was presented, called "A Night in New York"; and a farce-drama, "Little Tom Tucker," concluded the show. To begin, a group of acrobats, claimed to be Bedouin Arabs, excited the audience with their daring feats of leaping. Whether they were really Arabs was open to speculation.

Tony followed the first week's bill with a grand skit that occupied almost the entire show. Called "Tour Around the World," the company performed in "a dramatic illustration of life in many lands, with a new grand panorama, abounding in songs, choruses, dances, etc., grand mechanical effects" and ended with the "birth of the stars and stripes, the most startling novelty of the age." Tony had enlisted John W. Collier, a well-known local painter, to paint each scene's background and a team of engineers to develop the mechanical displays. It was the first time a variety theater had put on such an elaborate show of the kind more likely to be found in dramatic presentations. The show was so successful that Tony later used portions of it in small skits.

In late January, theater receipts for 1866 were released. Pastor's Opera House was reported to have made over $67,000 in eleven months of operation, the highest amount for all of the variety houses in town.[11] Tony admitted to a profit of $17,000. It had been a good year for Tony, made even better because he was the theater's sole proprietor. He expressed a determination to do even better in the coming years.

Tony was now the recipient of accolades from local newspapers regarding his entertaining shows. The *Herald* was most complimentary.

> If you want to pass two hours pleasantly, drop into Tony Pastor's Opera house and you will be sure of getting your money's worth and come away delighted. Tony manages to give one of the best variety shows in the city and all who go once are sure of doing so some more.[12]

It is possible such comments were influenced by his purchase of a considerable amount of space from the *Herald*. The quote closely resembled what an ad for the Opera House had claimed in a previous issue. All theater managers were known to give gratuities to the press, but Tony easily outspent the competition.

In the spring, Tony signed new novelty acts that had heretofore not been presented at variety houses. Sports figures were featured. Boxer Sam Collyer and his two sons, Dan and Eddie, appeared several times. He also included a runner who claimed to sprint a mile on stage in less than five minutes; a skater who performed acrobatic tricks; and a scullist who demonstrated his technique. Tony also persuaded his new performers to take part in the stock company's skits, for many, quite a departure from their specialties. It worked out well; performers obtained new stage experience and Tony got additional stage time from them.

John F. Poole was Tony's in-house writer of skits, satires and travesties, performed by members of the company. Poole was a prolific author who set the example for future writers of variety and vaudeville sketches and burlesques.

Often, Tony opened up his theater to benefits on behalf of charities and destitute actors' families. He handed over the receipts from the show to the subject—a widow, a sick actor, a children's orphanage—for whom the benefit was given. In a few years, Tony became known for making his theater available for benefits and many needy people and organizations were beneficiaries of thousands of dollars. For benefits that honored a current performer, the company worked voluntarily. Often, performers from other theaters would appear at Pastor's voluntarily to enhance the program.

John Poole was turning out new skits every week: "The New York Volunteers," "The Working Girls of New York," "The Scottish Hero," "The River Rats of New York." All were topical stories, laced with Irishisms, which made them very appealing to the patrons. Stock company members were the primary performers in these skits with others playing cameo roles. New skits demanded a great deal of time and effort from the company, what with preparation of the skit, suggestions for dialogue changes and comic bits, costuming, scenery and continuous rehearsals. The collaborative effort was hard work, but it paid off by entertaining the audience. When Tony appeared in a skit, the sight of him in an acting role delighted patrons.

In May, another of Tony's innovations was to offer free ice water to patrons. Time was allowed between the acts for people to go to the lobby to obtain the drinks. He also brought in large fans to cool off the auditorium. In his ads, Tony claimed he had "the coolest house in the city, windows on every side, fans and ice water in abundance."[13]

The spring season closed June 29 with a grand finale benefit for Tony, an occasion for a full house of cheering patrons. Tony entertained them by singing many of their favorite comic songs. After several encores, shouts for a speech brought Tony to the front of the stage to thank the audience for visiting his theater. In a final gesture, he called out the entire company to take their bows. The noise was deafening.

At the same time, Tony announced that his traveling company would begin their tour in Boston for four weeks and then hit the road with one-night stands in New England cities and towns. Heading up the combination were Tony and Billy Pastor. Fernando was also included in the cast. A mixture of Irish actors, acrobats, song and dance people, female vocalists and comedians filled out the company. Billy acted as stage manager; Fernando performed some acrobatic feats. In the meantime, the Opera House was to be completely refurbished during the summer.

It was strange, then, to see an ad in the *New York Clipper* placed by Billy seeking to be engaged by "responsible managers only." The ad ran for several weeks.

During the summer of 1867, there were very few variety-style touring companies in operation. Tony's only real competition came from traveling circuses and minstrel shows. A first-class variety company was a decided treat for small town audiences and they crowded theaters to see the Pastor combination perform. The tour proved quite profitable, with lower expenses and salaries and excellent box office receipts. However, it would be the last summer that Tony faced no competition. Other managers were already planning to send out companies in 1868 on the same routes.

It was likely a shock to the public that Tony had been married. It was also a sad revelation, since the information was publicized at the time of his wife's death. Anna Pastor, age twenty-eight, was suffering from consumption. She had gone to Saratoga Springs to recover. On July 18, she died there. Tony was appearing in Boston when he was informed. He returned to New York at the same time Anna's body reached the city. After a brief funeral and burial, Tony returned to Boston to continue the tour, but his heart was not in it. The only recognition of the relationship was the erection of a large monument in her honor in the newly purchased Pastor plot in Evergreens Cemetery. No other information about Anna exists.

Anna's death did shorten the tour. Tony decided to bring the company back to New York and open the new season on July 29, rather early, even for Tony. Most theaters opened in late August and early September. Attendance at theaters during the "hot months" was light and it was no different for the Opera House. It is likely that Tony was grieving at this time and chose to bury his feelings in his work. The theater's refurbishing was not yet complete and Tony had not begun to sign up performers for fall dates.

The New York entertainment scene at the beginning of the 1867-68 season consisted of seventeen theaters: eight dramatic houses that featured such stars as Lotta, F.S. Chanfrau, John Brougham and the very successful "The Black Crook"; the New York circus; three minstrel shows; Barnum's Museum; and, for the first time, four variety theaters. Number 472 Broadway, owned by Robert Butler, and Griffin and Christy New Opera House were newcomers; Banvard's Museum was run by Charley White. Tony's competition suffered from a lack of awareness and an inability to sign first-class artists. They also did not open until September, by which time Tony's theater was already in full swing. He opened with the "Tour Around the World" extravaganza and followed with a Poole skit, "William Du Tell," in which Tony took the lead role. Sam Collyer, Jennie Engel, and Billy Emmet were back again, and the ballet performed at its beautiful best. By the end of August, the Opera House was enjoying full houses again.

New features introduced this season included trained canary birds and white mice, a female club wielder, gymnasts and trapeze artists, magicians, ventriloquists and contortionists. They typically played only one week because their act was so specialized. Song and dance people, vocalists and comedians could remain longer because they were able to vary their routines and also appear in the weekly skit. Tony continued to introduce at least one new song each week. An interesting guest performer in October was a young clogger and song and dance man named Jerry Cohan. Another was Charles Vivian, in his first appearance in America, a pleasing singer having matriculated from the English music halls. Vivian was an immediate hit on stage. Off stage, his engaging personality and amiability gathered many friends, several of them from Tony's cast, and included Fernando and Tony himself.

Poole's take-off on "The Black Crook," entitled "The White Crook," was one of his best works. His full length play, one of the first done at 201 Bowery, was a burlesque on "The Black Crook," which had premiered at Niblo's Garden in 1866. The original production was immediately popular and played for an unprecedented fifteen months to full houses. Poole wrote the play in rhyme, adding to the humor of the dialogue. Tony played Ran-dolf (Rodolphe in the original), singing a popular song, "I am a Bowery Boy." The principal male stock company members dressed as blushing danseuses in white skirts and "cut up queer capers." Riggs, in particular, as a sylph with two left feet, was especially funny. Audiences demanded specific numbers to be encored. The play was repeated for three weeks. The success of the show prompted the *New York Clipper,* not one to trumpet a specific theater or act, to report:

> Tony Pastor flourishes at his Opera House in the Bowery, and deservedly so, for he has got one of the best variety companies seen in this city. Each and every department is represented by first-class performers. They all arrive to please their patrons, and the crowded houses that are seen every night is a sure proof that they succeed in pleasing.[14]

By November, one variety house closed and the other two were struggling for attendance. Two new ones were about to open. When Tony claimed in his ads that he gave the best variety show in town, no one could dispute his statement.

The holiday program featured two skits: "The Female Forty Thieves," a burlesque on "Arabian Nights" in which the men played female roles in grotesque Oriental costumes, and a Commedia dell'Arte pantomime called "There Was an Old Woman Who Lived in a Shoe." In both plays, the entire company participated except Tony. He sang several London music hall songs and was nightly encored. The plays were advertised to appeal to "young and old," with scenery said to cost over $3,000.

Tony and the company were quite pleased that the holiday shows had attracted so many women and children. After the New Year's Eve show, Tony and several of the stock company members retired to a "free and easy" to celebrate.

6

The Elks, John Poole and Touring Success

They called themselves The Jolly Corks.

Charles Vivian had proven himself a popular singer at the Opera House. After a performance one evening, Vivian and his accompanist visited a "free and easy," a place that served steaks and offered tobies of ale in private rooms. Someone suggested they roll dice to see who would pay for the next round of drinks. Vivian volunteered to introduce a new game. He got three corks from the bartender. The object was to drop the corks on the floor and pick them up as quickly as possible. The last one to retrieve his cork would be the loser and pay for the drinks. The cork trick became a routine for a group of friends, including several performers from Pastor's stock company, George McDonald, T.G. Riggs and Billy Sheppard. McDonald labeled the group Jolly Corks.

At this time in New York City, excise laws prevented the sale and consumption of alcohol on Sundays. The group collected a stock of beer during the week, and on Sunday they would meet in the attic of a boarding house to hold a "convention." The group now numbered fifteen members, including William Carleton, G.W. Thompson, Fernando, Billy and Tony Pastor. Vivian was elected imperial cork.

McDonald recommended that the group of entertainers become a fraternal and benevolent society. Vivian agreed and called a meeting of the group on February 2, 1868, to discuss organizing the Corks as a lodge, then formed a committee to draw up a charter and by-laws and select a name. While debating the charter, the committee visited the Cooper Institute Library, where they discovered an elk head and a description of the animal as fast and protective. The idea appealed to the members, and the Elk was recommended to the entire group.

Charles A. Vivian, a popular performer with both audiences and colleagues, was the founder of "The Jolly Corks," which later became the Benevolent and Protective Order of Elks.

The committee gave its report February 16, 1868, on the stage of Pastor's Opera House. They recommended that the Jolly Corks be renamed the Benevolent and Protective Order of Elks (B.P.O.E.). After much debate, the vote in favor was 8 to 7. The new fraternal order was born.[1]

A montage of the original members of Elks Lodge No. 1 at its inception in 1868. Included are Tony and Fernando Pastor, Charley White and Gus Williams (Museum of the City of New York).

Within a few months, the lodge grew to fifty-eight members, including businessmen as well as entertainers. Membership doubled in 1869 and doubled again in 1870. New lodges were being formed in other cities. Tony petitioned the New York legislature for an official charter. A grand lodge charter was issued on March 10, 1871, with the first local charter designated as New York Lodge No. 1.

During the lodge's early years, Tony produced annual balls and benefits to collect money for destitute actors. As the organization grew, it assisted many needy institutions. Every year, Tony participated in the lodge's events, meetings, benefit performances and funerals.

Total receipts for all theaters in New York in 1867 amounted to more than $2.8 million. Theater had become a popular and commercial business enterprise that now attracted banks, businessmen and investors beyond the former theater owners and managers. As the theater business grew larger each year, it attracted real estate people, builders and an entire ancillary support business — printing, costuming, theater supplies, booking agencies and newspaper coverage for every amusement in town. The Opera House receipts for 1867 amounted to over $84,000, not including receipts for the traveling company.[2] It appears that Tony had signed some long-term contracts with artists and rented them out for a fee to appear at other variety houses. At the beginning of 1868, Tony was advertising "fun for the ladies, fun for the children, fun for the big folks."

After a series of near-disaster events (several theater fires), theaters were found to be overlooking the laws regarding easy egress from halls. The city invoked new laws about how standing room patrons must be handled. At first, they proposed the elimination of all standing room in theaters. Theater managers quickly responded, showing that such a law would be the difference between profit and loss for them. The city then came up with more modest rules: no seats placed in any aisles or passageways; no standing room in any places that obstructed passage; violators subject to arrest and closure of the theater. Within months, however, the law was not being enforced and patrons packed the auditoriums as before.

Like other theaters, Tony's enjoyed a considerable standing room business. He quickly moved to clear the aisles of his theater in order to satisfy the new fire department rules. He, too, tended to ignore the rules when they were not enforced.

In late February, the Opera House introduced the can-can to New York. This so-called erotic dance was currently sweeping Europe. The dance was not presented as duplicating the original, which was considered too risque for American audiences. In one sequence, a man and woman danced together, the laughs coming when the woman kicked the hat off the man's head, a high-kicking and revealing act. At the Opera House, a short man danced with a tall woman and the act of kicking was conducted in a modest manner. Still, audiences were enthusiastic about the new dance.

With box office receipts topping $7,000 a month for the first three months of 1868, Tony appeared to be heading for a banner year. During the final months of the season, however, the Opera House did not do as well, some weeks barely breaking even. Tony made plans to change his offerings. It was obvious that audiences were becoming tired of the same format. He decided to experiment with some new ideas when the traveling company launched their summer tour. This past season had amounted to forty-seven weeks and 336 performances; maybe the season had been too long. Even though the press complimented Tony on his ability to manage a variety theater, he was not satisfied with the results.

On the last day of the season, June 27, the company gave Tony a benefit. The theater was filled and a large number of people were turned away, unable to obtain even standing room. Tony sang a few familiar songs and was encored until he consented to give a speech. He thanked the audience for their loyalty and sincerely promised to do better next season.

On June 29, Tony's third annual summer tour began at Morris Bros. Opera House, Boston. Unlike the previous year, business was only moderate, probably due to the hot weather the city was experiencing. Before embarking on one-night stands, Tony added Jennie Engel and Johnny Thompson to the cast, familiar performers whom he knew would create more audience excitement. The tour took the company through New England, New York and Pennsylvania to most of the cities they had visited before. This time, however, receipts were only fair and there were several weeks when the company played at a deficit.

Tony decided to shorten the tour and return to New York to reopen at the Opera House on August 3. The tour had netted slightly more than $1,000, far short of estimates. Again, Tony took the risk of opening earlier than other theaters and fighting to attract audiences through the hot months. Advertising about fans and ice water did little to get patrons in the door. Tony was anxious to try some new ideas.

During the summer, the number of seats had been increased by 139, to 1,194, still less than other variety houses. The additional seating, however, had the potential to generate up to more than $9,000 in receipts during the season. Tony reformulated his advertising, expressed in even greater hyperbole than before. "Star artists," "mammoth troupe"; the entertainment is "strictly recherché, select, chaste and fashionable"; the company is "the best in the world."

Tony also changed his program's format. Instead of presenting a skit only as an afterpiece, the bill would open with a skit, a comedy featuring the stock company, to get people in the mood. Tony planned to sing duets with the leading female vocalist of the week. More child performers and Ethiopian comedians would be booked. Minstrelsy was having a resurgence at the time. He would include more gymnasts and circus oddities. The more gasps from the audience, the better the act. Poole continued to write skits, but Tony had him concentrate on local topics. Poole, however, was already unhappy with the demands on his productivity. Now he chafed at being told what to write. He would soon revolt.

For the 1868-69 season, the company included many continuing favorites: Johnny Thompson, Jennie Engel, Frank Kerns, Billy Sheppard, T.G. Riggs, Billy Emmet, Addie le Brun, and the Gorenflo Sisters. They could perform their own specialties and also play diverse roles. Tony planned to introduce three or four new acts each week.

There were eighteen theaters that opened the new season, four of them variety houses: Pastor's, the Olympic, Pike's Opera House, and the Theater Comique, the latter two new entries. Wood's Museum, with its Barnum-like exhibitions, was held over from last year. The scent of a profitable business, as demonstrated by Tony, had attracted several entrepreneurs into variety. The ever-increasing number of Irish and German immigrants in the Bowery provided an attractive audience, as long as the ticket prices were kept low. But it was the caliber of talent and the composition of bills that made for success or failure. Tony had supplied the model; the others attempted to emulate his ideas, but they had no Tony Pastor to implement them. They quickly found that individual personalities, the kind of performers that could, by themselves, attract crowds and fill theaters, still drove the business.

Tony's changes in the Opera House's program helped increase business. Attendance went from moderate, to pretty good, to excellent by mid–September. The *Clipper* reported that "the Opera House had one of the best variety entertainments yet offered at any house in the city."[3] The other variety houses were already suffering sporadic attendance.

With the inclusion of new acts, some without prior auditions, Tony found himself dealing with problems, not enough to affect attendance, but sufficient to cost him time and money. Little Nell, a young "California wonder" who sang ballads, was prevented from performing because she was underage. Although Tony attempted to persuade city officials that she was old enough to appear in New York, he failed. Several of his newer performers were considered mediocre by audiences and reviewers, causing some remarks about Tony's ill-fated choices. Speculators were a continuing problem for theater owners; it was reported that the Opera House was attracting bums who hung around the entrance of the theater looking for handouts. Tony contacted the police to disperse them, but when policemen began patrolling in front of the theater, he called them off. In the fall, illness struck hard at cast members, and several were out each week, forcing Tony to juggle performers and skits, seeking substitutes to fill in. Fall receipts showed little profit.

The annual holiday program turned it all around. "Hickety Pickety My Black Hen" was the Christmas pantomime, again structured on the Commedia dell'Arte format. The theater was full with ladies and children that made business "first-rate," according to the *Times*.[4]

The year 1869 opened with only two variety theaters in operation and a new one at Tammany Hall to be opened soon. The New York Circus was in town, and minstrel and dramatic houses were said to be doing good business. Theaters continued changing management, names and programs. Pike's Opera House became the Grand Opera House, playing variety. Number 718 Broadway, a dramatic house, became the Waverly Theater, advertised to feature a variety bill. The Fifth Avenue Opera House was changed to John Brougham's Theater, for dramatic productions. When the receipts for 1868 were reported, the Pastor Opera House had made over $84,000.[5] Tony bought another brownstone uptown as an investment.

During the latter part of January, Tony and several of his top artists took a two-week engagement in Boston, at the Howard Athenaeum. It surprised everyone that he would leave his theater during the season, even for a short time. Reviewers suggested he did it for the money. They appeared to be correct when a rumor was passed that Tony was looking for a new theater. The rumor quickly disappeared when he returned to the Opera House and talked about refurbishing it during the summer.

The new theater at Tammany Hall and the reopening of the Theater Comique after a fire offered patrons new entries into the variety business. Tammany reported "immense business, crowded every evening." The top trends for the spring were matinees, burlesques and performers coming from England. Every variety house had two matinees a week, on Wednesday and Saturday. Tony had his on Tuesday and Friday, and used every holiday as a special time to offer another matinee. Regarding the burlesque craze, Tony had his performers incorporate their specialties into parody skits so he could claim to offer more burlesques than any other theater. Tony also took the lead in importing performers from Europe, primarily acrobats, trapeze artists and contortionists, less risky acts than vocalists and dancers. The experience of booking people from another country captured Tony's interest because it gave him another opportunity for promotion.

The situation with John Poole had become contentious. He balked at preparing skits every week; he demanded a higher salary, and he began negotiating with other theater managers for his services. Tony was unsure when a Poole skit would be available; he began to lean on Riggs and Kerns to supply him with material. After one confrontation, Poole was released. Three weeks later, he was back with a new skit. After a month, he walked out of the Opera House. He returned a few weeks later with a new skit.

While Poole presented a problem, his skits were well received. "New York Now-a-Days" and "Irish Hearts and Irish Homes" were big hits with the audience, while those prepared by other company artists did not fare well. Finally, when "High Life and Low Life or Scenes in New York" was produced and did well, Tony persuaded Poole to remain for the rest of the season. It was a tenuous arrangement. Poole did not show up for rehearsals but he wrote one of the biggest hits of the season.

"Broadway and the Bowery" began as a short afterpiece, but it was so well received by audiences that Poole was requested to expand it into a full skit. In a departure from the usual program listing, Tony included a complete outline of the new skit so audiences knew what the story was about, what the scenes depicted and what the action was about. This practice was well suited to the audiences attending 201 Bowery. Tony decided to include this information in subsequent programs, and other theater managers soon copied the idea.

Any patron, regardless of his level of education or command of the English language, could easily understand and follow "Broadway and the Bowery."[6]

> Scene I—carpenters workshop—mechanics at work. A visit from an old friend. Orville Short on a collecting tour. A dead beat. How to settle a dispute. A row—police! Bustle and striking tableau. Scene II—New York street—A working girl. An insult. George Henley's ruse. Abijad Brown, the hard up gentleman. Mrs. Brown's experience. A dollar on hand. Struggles of the dissapated. Saved! Saved! Scene III—interior of tenement—house, showing two apartments. Home of the mechanic and of the working girl. Orville Short and the mutilated mudturtles. Attempted outrage. The alarm. Jackson Callendar on hand at the right time. Exciting tableau. Scene IV—the Bowery—The seedy gentleman's tour around New York. How to astonish the browns. City charity and Albany commissions. Scene V—plain apartment—The two friends. Mutual congratulations. Love making. Jackson Callendar caught. The fly in the spider's web. Scene VI—Union Square—The missionary from Timbuckto. George Henley's lost plan. Brown accepts employment. The watch and chain. Arrest of Harrison Hall, the charge robbery. A slight change. Caught in his own trap. Cleared from a foul charge. Innocence vindicated. Guilt foiled. Union of Broadway and Bowery. Joyous denouement.

The skit ran for a month. New jokes were inserted each week to keep the dialogue fresh.

In the process of signing up new people to appear during the spring, Tony selected several stellar entertainers. Jenny Benson, a jig and clog dancer, became an immediate audience favorite. Delehanty and Hengler, song and dance artists, were versatile actors who appeared in skits as well. Maggie Fielding, a vocalist, received four encores each evening. All returned often to the Opera House and later became part of the traveling company.

Poole's final skit for the season was "Othello and His Man Friday" in which Tony appeared as Othello in blackface. It had been more than a decade since Tony had used the burned cork, in a circus clown routine. The skit was a decided hit. Poole followed the original closely, giving the principal situations. Soliloquies and speeches were given in songs using the popular tunes of the day, all very laughable. Tony was said to have acted his part well, in true burlesque style. The skit ran for three weeks.

The final week of the season was filled with benefits. In succession each night, benefits were given for Frank Kerns, T.G. Riggs, John Mulligan (a backstage man), Fernando, and, on the last day, Tony himself. The theater was crowded each evening, because audiences did not know who would be appearing as special guests for each honoree. Games were played with the audience in which winners received gifts, songs were sung in unison and, on Tony's night, speeches given. The season had been good and Tony expressed his appreciation to the audience. Everyone left the theater having been happily entertained.

On June 21, Pastor's traveling company opened at the Howard Athenaeum, Boston, beginning a six-week tour. The company consisted of an entirely new cast, none of them ever having appeared at the Opera House. It was a calculated risk by Tony to include relative unknowns to knowledgeable audiences. It also meant lower salaries. They attracted patrons so well that the company remained in Boston the entire time.

Tony also launched another touring company made up of more familiar performers, under Billy's management. They planned to travel as far west as Michigan and stay on the road for as long as they obtained engagements. It was another opportunity for Billy to prove his managerial style and make money for the Pastor organization. Billy actually did quite well, bringing home more than $20,000 in receipts. The tour did not close until September 1870.

On August 2, the Opera House was opened for the 1869–70 season. The theater had been repainted, the seats and chairs recovered, a new drop curtain installed, the dome painted gold, the rugs replaced, and the lobby freshened up. Variety theater competition came from Tammany Hall, which remained in business the entire season, Varieties Theater (formerly Union Hall, 53 Bowery), and the Waverly Theater, managed by Robert Butler. Tony's new company was filled with familiar faces: Kerns, Riggs, Thompson, Collier, Graver, Clifford, Addie le Brun, the Gorenflo Sisters and Jenny Benson. New advertising for the Opera House was filled with overstatement: "the best company in America," "composed of the best star artists in the profession," "no comparison can be instituted between it and any other."

In a rare interview, Tony revealed the kinds of expenses he managed. Actors made anywhere from ten dollars to $100; ballet girls from eight to fifteen dollars; supers, fifty cents a night; a carpenter, fifty dollars; a property man, thirty dollars; scene painters, thirty to fifty dollars; the orchestra leader, $100 and the players, eighteen to thirty dollars. Fernando, the treasurer, received thirty dollars a week; doorkeepers twelve dollars; and billposters fifteen dollars. Advertising amounted to $450 a month, outside of salaries, Tony's most expensive item. Tony added that he paid these people more than at any other variety house, which was likely true.

Variety was growing, not only in stature but also in the number of theaters being built across the country. Fifteen new theaters had opened in September alone, in places like Johnstown and Reading, Pennsylvania; Champaign, Illinois; Indianapolis and Ft. Wayne, Indiana;

Houston, Texas; Rutland, Vermont; Akron, Ohio; Council Bluffs, Iowa; and even Cheyenne, Wyoming. Chicago, Louisville, Cincinnati and Pittsburgh were adding new theaters to those already operating there. The variety business was thriving, and developing performers of all descriptions and specialties.

Tony introduced to New York audiences three performers who quickly became headliners: Gus Williams, Nels Seymour and Ella Wesner. Williams was one of the first variety performers to present a Dutch act, in dialect and in costume, with songs and monologues. He wrote all his own material. Other actors copied his routine, but none could give as hilarious a presentation as Williams could. He frequented Pastor's often for the next four decades. Nels Seymour had been a minstrel performer and a song and dance man. Tony found that he was an excellent comedian and enlisted him in the stock company to play various roles each week. Seymour was also an accomplished eccentric dancer. He played at Pastor's periodically for a decade, until his premature death. Ella Wesner began her career at the Opera House as a jig and clog dancer. She added character songs and rapid changes to her routine and scored a decided hit with audiences. She played in four of Tony's traveling companies and returned to the Opera House frequently. Of all the female stars Tony nurtured, Ella was his favorite.

Fall highlights included gymnasts, clog dancers, banjoists, Irish song and dance artists, a drum soloist, impersonators, stump orators, sports specialists and magicians. Several came from circus backgrounds, like the "man-fly," who crawled up a wall to the ceiling and then over the heads of the audience; a giant and dwarf who performed a comical song and dance; Australian grotesque clowns; the "flying man," a high wire performer; and a set of comic skaters. Another act that Tony introduced was a female appearing in male attire in song and dance. Reviewers seemed uncomfortable with her act, suggesting she would be better received "in her own habiments." This was the first time a female impersonated a male on the variety stage.

Tony continued to present new songs and published a new songster. The ballet performed exotic dances. And the stock company appeared in new sketches, led by Kerns, Riggs, Armstrong, McDonald, Seymour and Jenny Benson.

By the holidays, the Theater Comique and Waverly were closed. Tammany staggered along, and the Varieties Theater continued, using performers who had previously appeared at the Opera House. The press acknowledged that Tony still served up the best variety show in the city.

While the farce-drama of "Santa Claus" was a highlight of the holiday program, Harry Gur, the "man-fish." stole the show. His performance of eating, drinking and smoking while under water elicited cheers from the audience and several curtain calls. One evening, he stayed under water for two and a half minutes, said to be the longest anyone had accomplished the feat. The audience called out the seconds excitedly as he remained under water and burst into applause when Gur surfaced.

Tony's 1869 receipts amounted to $86,000 for eleven months, slightly more than the previous year.[8] The figures steadily rose as other variety houses closed their doors. For the remainder of the season, little competition helped to insure another fine return for the Opera House.

The new year brought an influx of plays and perform-

Gus Williams began his long career as a Dutch comedian at Tony's theater. He was one of the first to introduce ethnic humor into the variety program.

ers from Europe, primarily for drama but also for variety, and Tony was first to have these people open in America at the Opera House. The English horizontal bar champion appeared in January. Catherine Lucette, an actress and vocalist (obtained at "enormous expense" said the ad) played in February. Her act, "Statuesque Vocal Visions," was not considered fitting at a Bowery theater, according to reviewers. Audiences did not take kindly to her drinking songs. Another English import was advertised as "the world's greatest female gymnast." An act featuring performing dogs was said to have been imported from France. The introduction of foreign performers helped to build audience anticipation, but the actual performances were not very exciting. Tony planned to continue using foreigners but would select out those who presented routines more familiar to his audiences, particularly vocalists and song and dance artists. In the near future, foreign performers would become an important part of the variety program and no one used them more judiciously than Tony.

During the spring, Tony was featured in several burlesques. He began with "Richard III," then "Hamlet II," and finally "Macbeth." In all three skits, the scenery and costumes represented the period and the dialogue was a polyglot of Old English, Irish and German dialects. In "Richard II," Tony limped around the stage shouting for a horse, which dutifully appeared. He was unable to mount it because the center, between the two players in horse costume, continually collapsed. For "Hamlet II," Tony appeared in a suspiciously familiar New York public court pleading his case. Those who disagreed with him were stabbed to death. The ghost wore a high silk hat. The grave digger turned up hoop skirts and tin cans. Ophelia entered the stage to the tune of "Walking Down Broadway" and soliloquies contained local allusions. In "Macbeth," Tony and Jenny Benson sang the dialogue and participated in the witch's clog dances. Tony was continually cheered and encored scenes from the skits.

A fourth Shakespearean piece was later offered, "Romeo and Juliet; or, the beautiful Blonde who Dyed for Love."[9] Tony played Romeo; T.G. Riggs was Juliet; Addie Le Brun and Maggie Fielding were Mercutio and Paris. The cross-dressing was a key element of the humor. Poole closely followed the original script, although he condensed it. Poole did not have Juliet stab herself; rather, she appeared in the closing scene, a minstrel walkabout (the usual ending for a minstrel show) with the entire cast. Most important, Poole wrote the dialogue in rhyme, with a good deal of humor coming from mispronunciations to make the rhymes work. There was also stage combat, complete with pratfalls. This was Tony's first full length burlesque.

In March, Frank Pastor returned home after performing in circuses in Europe for some years. He was immediately signed to appear in the European Circus currently playing at the Empire Rink in New York. From there, he went on a tour of the United States. Billy was still on tour in the Midwest and heading back East, reported by reviewers to be enjoying a successful route. When Frank arrived in New York, Tony and Fernando and their mother met him at the dock. It was reported to be a joyful reunion.

The 1869–70 season at the Opera House closed on June 18. During the final week, there was a succession of benefits, for Kerns, Seymour, Riggs, Fernando and, on the final night, for Tony. For the summer, the theater was rented to John Poole, who planned to produce a number of plays he had written. Instead of going on tour this summer, Tony and a select number of artists—Frank Kerns, Nels Seymour, T.G. Riggs and Helene Smith—had an engagement at Fox's American Theater in Philadelphia. Originally booked for two weeks, beginning June 20, they played through July 23. The group returned to the Opera House on July 25 to open the new season.

The company for the 1870–71 season again included many familiar performers: Kerns, Riggs, Graver, Smith, the Gorenflo Sisters, Alice Somers and Ella Wesner. New people added to the stock company included Kitty O'Neil and Billy Carter. To fill the first week's bill, Tony featured a pantomime troupe, gymnasts and clog dancers. Joseph Braham remained orchestra conductor; Fernando was treasurer; Riggs, stage manager; and, to everyone's surprise, John Poole as acting manager.

The fall season was filled with favorite specialties, minstrel acts and a few oddities. The favorites, those who had appeared at the Opera House before and were well received by audiences, were Billy Sheppard, Harry Gur, Johnny Wild, Jennie Engel and Polly Daly. Minstrel routines and skits were put on by Kerns, Seymour, Riggs and Carter. The oddities included Mlle. Irma, the Statue Queen, offering a series of living pictures; Charles F. Seabert, a character actor; Prof. O'Reardon, inventor of the tumbleronium (playing on glass goblets); the Romelli family of female gymnasts; a child gymnast and juvenile dancers (both of whom were unhampered by city authorities for being underage); Prof. Mawley, the man with a talking hand (ventriloquist); and a can-can group.

Poole wrote the first two skits, "The Magic Flute" and "Jack Tait and His Monkey." But three weeks into the new season, Poole withdrew from the Opera House, reportedly due to an argument with Tony regarding Poole's compensation for the scripts. Not sure where the next skit would come from, Tony enlisted Charles Seabert to prepare one. "The Black Detective" was well received and Seabert became the stock company's new creative force.

In September, there were sixteen theaters in operation, only two of which were variety houses, the Theater Comique and Pastor's. Two others featured minstrel companies, and Wood's Museum had taken over from Barnum's presenting curiosities and tableaux. In October, the old New York Theater changed its name to the Globe and promised to offer variety. Still, Pastor's Opera House remained the only first-class variety theater, as reported by the press. Reviewers spoke of the "large numbers of talented and versatile artists" who "assemble large audiences each week." "Business continues to be excellent," reported the *Herald*.[10]

Fernando's brief appearances in the circus and on the variety stage were unsatisfactory. He was treasurer of Tony's theater until his early death at the age of thirty-three (Harry Ransom Humanities Research Center).

When Tony raised admission prices from twenty-five cents to thirty-five cents, reviewers and theater owners were surprised and believed it was Tony's first bad business decision. However, audiences either did not seem to notice the change or did not care, because the Opera House continued to be crowded every evening. A month later, Tony told the press that he had raised ticket prices to accommodate increased salaries for his performers.

Seabert proved to be an adequate replacement for Poole. A succession of skits; a musical burlesque, "Robinson Crusoe"; a farce-drama, "The New York Bank Clerk"; and an Irish sketch, "1, 2, 3," all were applauded by audiences. The annual Thanksgiving matinee was designed to simulate a Christmas program and was "jammed with people and little urchins." Ella Wesner, now featuring a singing and quick-change costume act, was encored several times at each performance and had become a particular favorite with the patrons. Included in her act was the adoption of male attire but, unlike previous performers who had tried the routine and failed, Ella received a warm reception. A new Dutch comedian, D.L. Morris, performed in a skit, "Intelligent Dutchman," and later in the program did a Teutonic specialty. It had become common at the Opera House for performers to appear twice on the program, demonstrating their acting versatility.

The annual Christmas pantomime was "Ba Ba Black Sheep," in which the stock company players switched gender roles. Kerns was Columbine; Helene Smith, Harlequin; and Annie Wood, a burlesque actress, Pantaloon. Also on the family program were a strong man, and a pair of female aerial gymnasts who worked over the audience's heads. Hanging from the dome of the theater, with her head downwards, one held a leather thong in her teeth from which her partner hung. They then reversed positions. Along with the gasps of astonishment, they received strong applause.

At the beginning of 1871, a recurring rumor passed through the press suggested that Tony was seeking another theater. It intimated that Tony was seeking a broader audience by moving up Broadway. There was no question that the neighborhood was changing, with the influx of a new wave of German and Italian immigrants, the building of tenements of questionable construction, heating and health considerations identified as problems, and the loss of commercial business uptown. The opening of the Globe Theater and Robert Butler's announcement that he was going to build the most modern variety theater in New York contributed to the rumor. Under scrutiny by the press, Tony announced that he had no inclination to leave his friends and neighbors at 201 Bowery.

The press printed a series of articles about variety's increasing popularity, particularly as it attracted the working classes.

> That theatrical entertainments are growing in favor more and more every year is evident to all who take an interest in amusements. Nearly every city and town of any importance has its theater adapted to variety or other performances. Every few weeks, we place upon our record the opening of some new theater, music hall, or concert saloon; these new structures are a vast benefit to traveling companies of various kinds, enabling them to give performances with every convenience at hand, the same as are found in the large cities. Companies laying out routes may now do so without losing much time between stands, so general has been the erection of halls in towns and villages during the past year.[11]

Several New York entrepreneurs and investors spoke of building variety houses or reconfiguring dramatic theaters to variety. There was talk of opening them around Union Square, almost a mile north of the current theater district. The area had high traffic commercial business and better neighborhoods, very attractive for new theaters. But it would be a few more years before the movement uptown really took hold.

Another business enterprise that hastened the move toward variety entertainment was the formation of theatrical booking agencies in the heart of the theater district. The Eureka Dramatic Agency was located at 636 Broadway; Riggs and Fitzgerald (T.G. Riggs, one of Tony's star stock company performers had decided to take on another business) was located at 681 Broadway. The biggest and most aggressive, Colonel T. Allston Brown, Dramatic Agent, was found at 718 Broadway. Brown backed his business with heavy advertising and a concerted effort to sign as many performers as he could, as long as they had already shown their value. He announced each artist he signed, and featured them and their accomplishments in his ads, some of them covering a full half-page of the *Clipper*. Theater managers were now relieved of the effort to hire their own acts. They could more readily negotiate salaries and engagements. Even Tony decided to work with a booking agency, in May agreeing to work with Allston Brown. But this did not deter him from auditioning people on his own. Everyone seemed to acknowledge that popular theater was about to enter a new era of development and big business.

The spring of 1871 was highlighted with a series of special programs at the Opera House. Tony again brought over some performers from Europe. He engaged more circus acts. He emphasized Irish artists and skits. He opened a refreshment saloon adjacent to the theater's entrance where alcohol was served, but not brought into the theater. And he led off each week's bill with a burlesque skit.

The female minstrels were introduced in the middle of February. They became so popular that the act appeared for eight weeks. Bones was played by Larry Tooley, a veteran minstrel performer; Frank Girard was the Interlocutor; and newcomer Billy Barry played Tambo. Stock company players shared the skit with weekly newcomers. Men played women's roles, and comedic situations were freshened; songs were replaced; and dance routines varied by the ballet. During the final week, Tony joined the group singing old minstrel ditties. The female minstrels had been an unqualified success. For several weeks after the act had been withdrawn, audiences were shouting to have it replayed. Several of the skit's songs, like "Don't Be Angry with Me, Darling," "Sailing in the Moonlight," and "Tis But a Little Faded Flower" were reprised frequently by female vocalists since they had become so popular with audiences.

Seymour and Seabert had taken over writing the weekly skits, dealing with topical subjects. Comedy had now become the primary force of these performances, interspersed with song and dance. "The Working Girl's Holiday," "Life in a Tenement House," "The Lady's Picnic," and "The Dressmakers of the Bowery" were all subjects that the audience could readily identify with, laughing at the comic exaggerations of their own life styles.

The new weekly features included clog dancing (a perennial favorite), magicians, impersonators, trapeze and acrobats, along with the familiar specialties performed by stock company members. Playing of "The Star-Spangled Banner" was shifted to the end of the program.

In the middle of April, Tony announced that a traveling company would perform during the summer, beginning June 12, visiting "the interior cities" for the first time in six years. The company consisted of Ella Wesner, Kitty O'Neil, Ada Wray (banjo and vocal soloist), William Carleton and the local favorites, Kerns, Riggs, Seymour, Carter, Smith, Wild, and a new entry, Frank Girard, a talented and versatile character actor. Girard would become a permanent member of the Pastor organization. In a significant departure from previous seasons, Tony said that his Opera House would not open until the middle of September, well after the other variety houses began operations. By extending his tour and delaying his return to New York, Tony was counting on a profitable summer that would more than compensate for a later opening. And with the reputation he had built for variety entertainment in the city, he was confident of immediately attracting crowded houses to the Opera House when he opened, no matter what the competition. He was also acknowledging that a tour company had the potential to make more money than one in the city.

Billy Pastor worked various jobs for Tony, from managing a touring company to running the Opera House during the summer. Each time Billy attempted to go out on his own, he failed and returned to Tony's employ (Harry Ransom Humanities Research Center).

The *Clipper* reported that Tony's past season had been "a complete triumph." Claiming he had the "leading variety talent of the city," Tony acknowledged that his season had been a profitable one.[12]

Unannounced but noticed by everyone was that nine theaters were attempting to remain open for as long as they could for the summer months. None were variety houses, but their managers were watching the situation closely. They were all closed by the middle of July, but the experiment was not a failure. Managers planned to try again next year, adjusting their programs to suit "hot months" audiences.

7

Variety's Triumph

New variety theaters were opening across the country. Traveling companies reported profitable engagements. Theatrical newspapers ran ads seeking performers no matter the specialty, and 1871 appeared to be a banner year for theater managers.

When the Tony Pastor Combination began its summer tour in Bridgeport, Connecticut, on June 19, Tony confidently predicted that he would enjoy a profitable trip. The route took the company through the New England states, New York, Pennsylvania, Ohio and to the new territory of Terre Haute and Indianapolis, Indiana. Weeklong engagements were booked for Cincinnati and Pittsburgh.

The company visited fifty-four towns and cities in twelve weeks, concluding the tour in Newark, New Jersey, on September 8. Newspaper reports from various stops told of full houses and enthusiastic audiences. Tony's appearances in new locations—they amounted to twenty out of the fifty-four—helped to reinforce his reputation as a genial performer and manager of one of the best variety companies in the country. When the company appeared before audiences in the "provinces," the results were all the more impressive.

Besides the summer tour, Tony kept the Opera House open for rental to dramatic and variety troupes. During this period, Billy managed the theater and Fernando looked after the finances.

The Tony Pastor Opera House opened its 1871-72 season on September 11. The auditorium had been freshly painted and decorated. Matinees were to be given twice a week, on Tuesday (in a break from the traditional Wednesday), and Saturday. The new season's company consisted of Frank Kerns, Sam Devere, Johnny Queen, H.W. Ragen, Charles Walters, J.W. Collier, all part of the stock company, as well as specialty performers Kitty O'Neil, Jennie Gilmer, Josie Farran, William Carleton, Turner and Lester, Frank Girard, Charles F. Seabert, J. A. Graver, orchestra conductor Joseph Braham, Jennie Eagan and the Gorenflo Sisters. Most were familiar faces.

Sixteen New York theaters were open in September, three featuring minstrels and four variety houses, including Pastor's Opera House. Richard Butler had opened a new variety theater, the Union Square. Tony's decision to have Tuesday matinees was derided by theater managers and the local press. However, by October reviewers reported good attendance at the Tuesday matinees. By November, they said, "The Tuesday matinees have become quite popular and are well-attended."[1]

The fall season was filled with novelty acts such as acrobats, magicians, ventriloquists and contortionists; the usual Irish routines of clog and jig dancers and vocalists; comedy sketches;

Tony donned a tuxedo to reinforce his claim for running a "fashionable house" with "clean" entertainment. He also was demonstrating the theater's prosperity due to his management (Harvard Theater Collection).

minstrel performers in stump speeches, comic songs and plantation skits; a few visitors from the English music halls; and burlesques and farces by the stock company, usually written by Seabert and Hen Mason.

Audience pleasers included Mason's quick changes from black to white with appropriate character songs; Sam Devere's banjo playing and comic dialogue; a concertina soloist; a Dutch comedian; Sam Sanford, the venerable Ethiopian artist; Lilliputian comedians and, of course, Tony's comic songs. The burlesques performed by the stock company ranged from "The Streets of New York" and "Drink, or the Perils of City Life," to the holiday pantomime, "The Clown's Misfortunes."

In October, reports of the devastating Chicago fire led to benefits at most theaters, to collect money and clothing for the survivors. Tony ran benefits for an entire week, and collected several thousand dollars.

The fourth annual meeting of the Elks was highlighted by voluntary performances from actors across the city. Tony and his company were among the participants. The Elks collected money for destitute actors.

A new variety house, the Theater Comique, opened in October and quickly attracted large audiences. This was Tony's first real competition. Two dramatic theaters closed and a new one, the St. James Theater, opened. In late September, Billy put an ad in the *New York Clipper* saying he was open for engagements. The ad ran through December; Billy received no offers.

In late November, Tony announced plans for his annual summer tour, which was to begin May 6, 1872, and asked performers desiring engagements to contact him. His announcement was designed to sign up a high-class company before any of his competitors and serve notice of his dominant position as a touring company. Within a few weeks, Tony had the company he desired, made up of Pastor veterans and new acts offering potential, like Harrigan & Hart.

Tony began 1872 by offering ladies, accompanied by a male escort, free admission on Friday evenings. This was a first among New York theaters and was quickly copied by other variety and minstrel houses. The offer was another effort by Tony to attract women to the Opera House. Not so obvious was the effect the Theater Comique was having on the Opera House's attendance. Josh Hart, the Theater Comique manager, had patterned his operation after Tony's, and, in a matter of a few months had become a healthy competitor. After performers appeared at the Opera House, Hart engaged them, advertised their recent success, and gave them a higher salary. A battle for audiences had begun and would continue for several years.

Eighteen seventy-two was also a year in which Fernando experienced the joys and sorrows of life. In March, he married Dora Wehmann, a twenty-one year old who was working in her father's grocery store. She became pregnant in July. In late fall, Fernando became ill, with a dry cough that persisted. A visit to a doctor suggested that Fernando was in the early stages of consumption.

Consumption and phthisis were nineteenth century names for tuberculosis.[2] During the middle and late nineteenth century, the major killers of Americans were tuberculosis and childhood diseases. In large cities like New York, tuberculosis was the leading cause of death. At the time, doctors had freedom to use a wide variety of treatments to combat disease. Most were of no value.

The microscope was invented in Europe in the late 1850s, stimulating the development of bacteriology, but it took almost two decades for it to influence American doctors. In 1870, Pasteur warned physicians to sterilize their hands and clean their instruments with boiling water. The thermometer came into use as a better means to diagnose diseases. But no laboratories existed to analyze body fluids. During the 1870s, physicians began to believe that consumption was contagious. None of these discoveries helped Fernando. As far as physicians were concerned, anyone contracting consumption would suffer a slow and painful death.

Symptoms included loss of appetite (treated by stimulants and nutritional supplements), a dry cough that progressed into the expectoration of pus-like sputum (sometimes with blood), and fever, bringing on periods of profuse sweating. Physicians had no means to really combat these symptoms except to quiet the patient down with narcotics.

Tony relieved Fernando of his treasurer's responsibilities. He assigned Fernando to manage the saloon. In reality, it was nothing more than a gesture to keep his brother on the payroll, which he continued until Fernando's death. Fernando lingered for three years; in his final months, his mother cared for him. He died in April 1876.

The winter and spring of 1872 saw Tony featuring the same lineup of performers supplemented with three or four new people each week. If they did well during their introduction to Bowery audiences, Tony signed them to return a second week. He used more children's acts, since the group crusading to rid children under sixteen from the stage was in disarray. To embellish his own act, Tony urged the audience to sing along with him. The boys in the gallery were a particularly vocal group and participated often, complete with whistling and foot stomping. It all added to the camaraderie of the show.

One particular song was a departure from Tony's usual fare. Briefly apologizing to the audience for the selection he was about to introduce, he launched into a sentimental ballad about a small child about to die who was attempting to dispose of his toys, annoying the entire neighborhood for several weeks. Tony convulsed the audience with laughter due to the lyrics and his unique interpretation and delivery.

While "ladies free Friday" and the presentation of local favorites helped to maintain business, competition from the Theater Comique was affecting attendance at the Opera House. For that reason and because summer tours offered the attractive potential for large profits, Tony decided to begin the tour in early May. Billy would manage a variety group at the Opera House to keep it open during the "hot months" for as long as patrons would attend.

Special features of the spring included Sam Sanford, the veteran minstrel entertainer, playing an old plantation darky in "The Old Kentucky Home" with apologies to Stephen Foster; the French Twin Sisters, two pretty girls of seven and eight who danced an Irish jig; the introduction of John T. Kelly, a comedian on the threshold of a long and outstanding career as one of the popular stage's most beloved actors; ballad duets by Tony and Jennie Engel that brought diversity to his usual comic songs; a ventriloquist, Prof. Hilton, who presented three talking heads, representing Ireland, Scotland and England; Sam Devere with his banjo and musical witticisms; and skits like "An Irishman in Greece," "The Mysteries of Gotham," "Mazeppa, the Wild Mule of Turkey" and an Ethiopian opera, "Oh, Hush," featuring Girard, Kerns, Devere, Mason, Graver and other stock company regulars. When the season closed May 4 at the Opera House, Tony declared that the past season had been profitable. Reviewers questioned him just how profitable it had been when Tony was fined $500 for using the song "When the Band Begins to Play" without authorization.

The summer company consisted of Ella Wesner; Emma Alford; Jennie Engel; Kitty O'Neil; Sydney Franks, a Dutch comedian; Frank Kerns; Sam Devere; Frank Girard and a new comedy team, Harrigan & Hart.

Edward Harrigan was born in New York in 1844.[3] As a teenager, he apprenticed in the shipbuilding trade. He ran away from home to San Francisco where he entered the stage. He appeared briefly with Campbell's Minstrels and moved on to become a favorite comedian in West Coast variety. Harrigan teamed with Alex O'Brien and then Sam Rickey in an Irish two-act. While in Chicago, seeking a new partner, he found Tony Hart.

Tony Hart (Anthony J. Cannon) was born into a poor family in Worcester, Massachusetts, in 1855.[4] He left home for New York and appeared in concert saloons singing and dancing. He then played in various circus and minstrel companies. After Harrigan saw him, they formed a team. Hart was sixteen at the time, small, handsome, with a fine tenor voice. In contrast, Harrigan was taller, more mature looking and a baritone. They recognized their talents to be complementary.

Their rendering of "The Little Fraud," a skit performed in Dutch dialect, with Hart playing a feminine role, was an immediate hit with New York audiences. Several successful months in New York and New England brought them to Tony's attention. He hired them for his 1872 summer tour.

The annual summer tour began May 6 in Providence, Rhode Island, to an SRO audience. The company traveled through New England for the next two weeks, appearing before familiar audiences anticipating a fun evening with their old friend, Tony. The high-class performers did not disappoint. Stops in New Jersey and Pennsylvania were equally successful. A report from Wilkes-Barre said that "the master troupe of the world, now being greeted with overflowing houses, was pronounced the strongest array of talent ever seen."[5] Tony took the statement and quoted it in his weekly newspaper ads.

The tour visited cities in Ohio, Kentucky, Indiana, went as far west as St. Louis, and played in Chicago, at Nixon's Amphitheater, for one week. They were so successful that the company stayed for three weeks. Nixon's had a seating capacity of over 2,000 and was filled at nearly every performance. The *Clipper* reported that "every seat was occupied, no less than 500 people were standing throughout the entire performance, the average receipts reaching within a trifle of $1,400 a night." At each performance, Tony was recalled no less than four times; Jennie Engel and Ella Wesner were given tremendous applause; Kitty O'Neil's jig dancing delighted the crowds; and Harrigan & Hart were "stupendous." Attendance at Nixon's had never been larger.

The *New York Times* reported an episode at Nixon's about two drunken men who came to see the show and began disrupting it with shouts and bad language. Ushers attempted to stop them but they ran on the stage and claimed they would fight any two men in the house. Several members of the company carried them off. The police later found them in an alley, unconscious with their heads cut. No one seemed to know what had happened to them.[6]

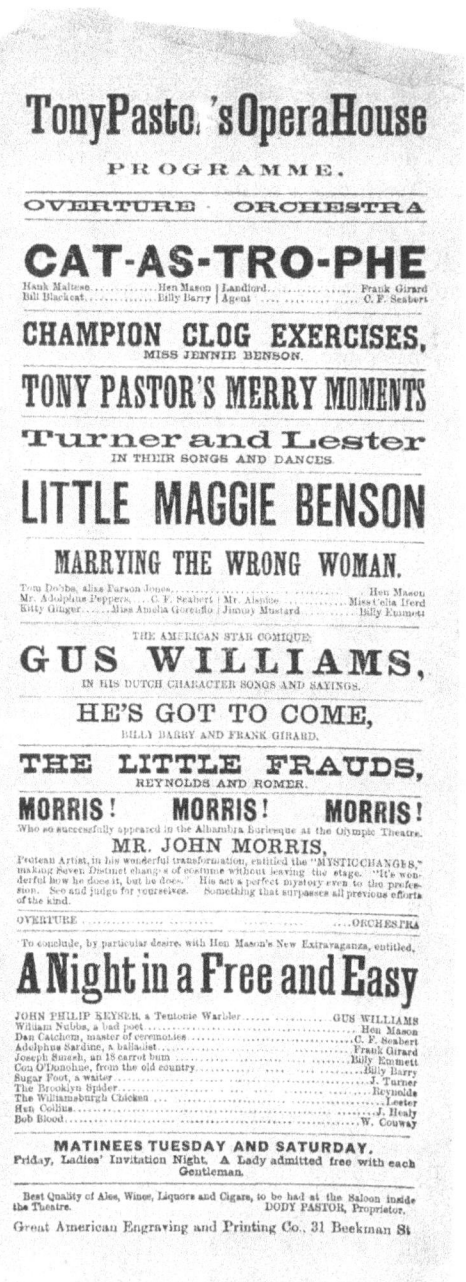

A typical playbill from the early 1870s shows the versatile program Tony presented. Performers not only played their specialty but also appeared in skits.

Fresh from their triumph in Chicago, the company played three days in Milwaukee, two in Detroit, and three in Cleveland as they worked their way back East. A three-day engagement in Buffalo won accolades from the *Clipper*.

> St. James Hall had overflowing houses, standing room only being at a premium. The performances were first-class throughout, fully sustaining the excellent reputation of the troupe.[7]

Again, Harrigan & Hart were singled out for their zany comedy.

The remainder of the tour returned the company to cities in New England, and then closed in Trenton, New Jersey, on September 9. The tour was the most successful Tony had ever had. His company was considered the best in terms of artistic merit. Tony arrived home with a profit of more than $30,000.

The Opera House had stayed open during the summer to mixed results. "Hot days" diminished attendance but "normal days" helped Billy return a slight profit. Many of the performers had played there earlier in the year. They were happy to be performing during the summer, otherwise a time of unemployment.

The Opera House opened the 1872-73 season on September 16. The theater had been refitted and decorated. Harry Sanderson was engaged as Tony's business manager. Joseph Braham remained as orchestra conductor. Matinees were on Tuesday and Friday. Ladies were admitted free on Friday evenings; it had become a permanent feature of the Opera House, not yet copied by other variety theaters. In addition, the front seats of the gallery were fitted up for the ladies.

Henry (Harry) S. Sanderson was born in Baltimore, Maryland, in November 1842, the son of Col. Harry S. Sanderson, well known in amusement circles and the father of Thomas Sanderson, a popular Ethiopian comedian known professionally as Nelse Seymour.[8] Harry began as a telegraph operator and railroad purchasing agent. He then tried the real estate business, was a jeweler and manufactured rubber goods. In 1868, he was engaged in Tammany Hall when Jarrett & Palmer ran a minstrel group. Tony hired him to take over Fernando's duties in 1872. In his first stint with Pastor, he stayed until 1875. Sanderson then managed a concert company, a pantomime company and, in 1876–77, he became treasurer and business manager of the Olympic Theater, New York. San-

Tony introduced Harrigan & Hart to New York audiences. The duo later became famous at their own theater while appearing in a succession of ethnic comedies (Harry Ransom Humanities Research Center).

derson returned to Tony in 1878 and remained continuously until 1908. Sanderson not only ran the business side of Tony's enterprises but also became his confidante and liaison between booking agents, advertisers and performers. His loyalty to Tony was unbounded and his relations with the performers at Tony's theaters were warm and respectful. Sanderson kept books of each day's expenses and receipts, both at home and on tour, for every year he worked for Pastor. These records are available to researchers.[9]

Opening night at the Opera House saw a cheerful crowd eager to welcome their favorites back home. The fall company included Jennie Engel, Kitty Leroy (jig danseuse), Clara Brooks (character vocalist), Celia Iferd, Gus Williams, Harrigan & Hart, Billy Carter, Hen Mason, Harry Kernell, Johnny Manning, Frank Girard, Charles Seabert and the Gorenflo Sisters. Most of the performers appeared twice during the evening, once in their specialty and once in a skit. Mason and Seabert were the designated skit writers. Breaking with the traditional variety format, the program opened with a skit, "The Artful Dodger," which featured Mason, Girard, Seabert and Iferd. Johnny Manning gave a song and dance entitled "A Dollar a Dozen for Shirts." Jennie Engel, richly costumed, sang several songs that were encored. Harrigan & Hart followed with a double song and dance, "The Big and the Little of It," and later appeared in a skit, "The German Immigrant." Hart appeared in female dress. Tony then skipped on stage, was vigorously applauded and satisfied the audience with a dozen encores. Harry Kernell, as an Ethiopian comedian, played "Old John Hutchinson." Billy Carter entertained with his banjo and funny witticisms. Tony and Jennie Engel performed a comic duet called "Courtship" that had to be repeated three times. Gus Williams sang Dutch character songs and starred in the skit "The Dutch Justice," which closed the program. There was no intermission. The show ran for more than three hours. It was a typical Pastor bill.

In September 1872, sixteen theaters were operating in New York. There were four variety theaters besides the Opera House: the Theater Comique; (Charley) White's Athenaeum, the Bowery Theater, and a new entry, Charley Shea's Opera House on 34th Street. Another variety theater, Hooley's Opera House, opened in Brooklyn.

The fall season at the Opera House included novelty acts: magicians, infant gymnasts, a fire king who ate burning coals and drank boiling liquids, a child singer and Zouave drill team; the usual Irish dancers and vocalists; skits on topical issues; and the promotion of several recent newcomers to high-class variety, Harry Kernell, Gus Williams and John T. Kelly.[10] Tony retained these performers through December and garnered generous receipts from their efforts. Of course, Tony introduced new songs each week, as audiences had come to expect and enjoy.

Other highlights of the fall were the appearances of Annie Hindle, a quick-change vocalist, and the blackface team of Delehanty and Hengler. Hindle excited audiences with her Irish patter songs, stayed on the bill for several weeks, and returned often to the Opera House. Delehanty and Hengler's skit, "Africa's Hottentots," was performed entirely in song and dance. Instead of the usual blackface act, the team brought new ideas and characterizations to audiences, portraying Negroes in a much more positive and dynamic way. The team remained with Tony for a month and reappeared often later. Their versatility also made them prime performers in skits (sans blackface).

Other firsts at the Opera House included a ten-year-old Herbert Cawthorne, singing in a musical sketch, "The Old Man's Drunk Again." Cawthorne matured into one of vaudeville's most colorful comedians. A mother-daughter team of Jenny Benson and Baby Benson performed songs and dances. When Baby Benson grew up, she became Marguerite Fish, a renowned comic opera and musical performer. Fanny Herring, a dramatic actress, was persuaded to appear with Tony for one week, reprising her comic role in the drama "The French Spy." Audiences were undecided whether they liked her or not.

The end of 1872 brought additional sad news to the Pastor family. Fernando, Jr., Fernando and Dora's seven-month-old child, died of pneumonia on November 20. There were rumors about how much longer the marriage would last.

Charley Shea's Opera House was forced to close due to financial losses. Charley White left 585 Broadway and the theater switched to offering minstrels. However, the Theater Comique continued to attract large audiences and put pressure on Tony to retain his once-loyal patronage. Josh Hart attempted to copy every move that Tony made and proved to be quite successful at it. His biggest coup was the signing of Harrigan & Hart for the winter and spring season.

Frank Kerns became ill and was forced to retire from the stock company. Fire inspectors made one of their periodic crusades checking theaters to see that they complied with the access laws. For the interim, Tony had to eliminate SRO patrons, which reduced his receipts. He was also forced to replace a furnace because it was too close to a retaining wall in the basement. To improve his matinee audience during the holiday season, Tony gave away six sewing machines to the ladies.

Although all New York's theaters made claims of prosperity at the box office, Tony saw his receipts diminish because of the increasing competition, particularly from the Theater Comique, but more generally from other theaters who changed their policies to cater more directly to neighborhood audiences. He was forced to recognize the new challenges to his position as supreme purveyor of high-class variety in the city.

At the beginning of 1873, Tony made several business decisions designed to protect and improve receipts. He increased advertising expenditures, enlarged his ads and placed them in more newspapers. In the ads, he extolled the virtues of his performers even more, to the point where some claims seemed beyond reason. He continued the practice for the remainder of the season and it seemed to have stimulated attendance. The boost of performers' specialties was needed because Tony chose to engage lesser-known acts more frequently in order to reduce his salary obligations. Only when it looked like a bill might be weak in local favorites did Tony call on Gus Williams, Jennie Engel and Sam Sanford to highlight the company.

When Tony announced that his annual summer tour would begin on April 7, everyone was surprised to see Tony give up spring and early summer business at the Opera House, usually a good period for theater attendance. However, Tony chose the early date because of the profit potential of playing longer on the road. In fact, his previous summer tour had earned larger profits than his entire season at home. Beginning in April and playing to September, a total of twenty-three weeks, could deliver sizable profits.

The winter and spring season saw a succession of novelty acts and Irish vocalists, with an added emphasis on Ethiopian comedians. The novelty acts changed every week and included a steel wire walker, Chinese juggler, rope skipper, plate spinner, and the usual acrobats, gymnasts and contortionists, many of them appearing for the first time in New York. Irish skits, written by Mason and Seabert, played on local politics and current events and always elicited laughter.

New performers to the Opera House, Billy Barry and Billy Emmet, the former an Ethiopian comedian, the latter a song and dance artist, made a great hit with audiences and were retained for the season. They also were enlisted to play in skits and their acting versatility served them well. Their addition to the stock company became more important when Hen Mason died suddenly, leaving the company with only one writer. Tony approached John Poole to help out, but Poole was currently in negotiation to be manager of a rival variety house.

With his comic song repertoire, Tony remained the star of the program. His call for new material was so universal that songs were reaching him by the dozens each week, some from as far away as England. Composers offered cheap fees to Tony since a selected song would give them good exposure. As usual, Tony wrote most of the lyrics to fit audience interests. At every performance, Tony was encored repeatedly and presented old favorites to crowds. Many of the familiar songs were copied and passed out to patrons, encouraging them to sing along with Tony.

High esteem from the audience and community were seen at Tony's annual benefit on March 14. The festivities began with his company serenading Tony and Frank Girard making a presentation speech. Tony was given an inscribed gold watch. A well-known local lawyer, Charles W. Brooke, talked about Tony's contributions to local charities and the church. The Navy Yard Band furnished music. More than one hundred performers from other theaters paid their respects to the man who they said "started their careers." Actors and audience members then escorted Tony to his home where a group of prominent businessmen awaited him. The party lasted until morning, the wine flowing freely.

In March, Tony reported and reviewers verified good business at the Opera House, but sellouts and SRO were rare. The Theater Comique and the growing reputation of its stars, Harrigan & Hart, continued to attract full houses. Tony seemed almost glad his season was nearly over. When he published his traveling company, there were few surprises. Tony had again engaged a high-class troupe already familiar with his management. They included Ella Wesner, Jennie Engel, the Freeman Sisters, Gus Williams, Delehanty & Hengler, Billy Carter, Kitty Henderson, George F. Moore and Frank Girard. Tony had contracted with a printer in Philadelphia to produce his billboarding in color and in various sizes to fit different locations. They would appear in every city, plastered on every high traffic surface a week ahead of the company's arrival. This represented a first for traveling variety companies and became a model for touring advertising. Billy would again manage the Opera House and rent the facilities out to variety and dramatic companies. No one paid attention to the news that a number of banks had failed, several of them having had good reputations.

The Tony Pastor Combination 1873 summer tour was highly successful, the best ever. The company opened in Poughkeepsie, New York on April 7 and proceeded to New Jersey, Connecticut and Massachusetts. It was a familiar route and attracted Tony's admirers at each stop. Various correspondents reported "immense business." In May, they played in New York cities to "very large business." The company then traveled through Ohio, Indiana, and Michigan with a stay of two weeks in St. Louis. They were said to have the "best entertainment of the kind ever presented to our community." Engagements in Cleveland and Pittsburgh played to "packed audiences." Tony added several acts to the company: the Fieldings, a husband and wife song and dance team; Baby Benson; and the St. Felix Infant Ballet Troupe with success.

The news that Tony purchased a house at 118 East 78th Street went unnoticed. He paid $21,000 for the building. This was his third purchase of property in the last few years.

The middle of July brought the company to Cincinnati for two weeks of "big houses" and a return to Nixon's Amphitheater in Chicago for another two weeks. Like the previous visit, the summer of '72, response to the Pastor Combination was overwhelming. On opening night, 500 people were turned away, unable to get even standing room. "The building has an enormous seating capacity," said the *Tribune* reporter, "but there are not seats sufficient to accommodate the would be attendants."[11] Tony's ads in the newspapers proclaimed "the most successful Western tour on record!" and his claim was very likely true.

August found the company returning to New York and New England for a series of one-night stands, The company's final engagement was at the Howard Athenaeum, Boston, for four weeks. The *Clipper* reported that the theater had "larger nightly receipts than ever taken on any previous occasion."[12]

The tour concluded September 13. A *Clipper* correspondent claimed that it was "one of the most successful tours, in a pecuniary as well as an artistic sense, ever made in this country and, it is said with a profit exceeding $50,000."¹³ Tony would need to use every dollar of it in the coming months.

The Opera House's new season opened on September 15. Ads for theater said it was "newly refitted, chaste and elegant." Matinees were to be given on Tuesday and Saturdays, the Tuesday matinee having proven to be successful with the ladies. And, on Friday evenings, ladies would be admitted free.

The lineup of performers was the same as the traveling company, which had been such a success. Newcomers included a fine character comedian, George S. Knight, and Fanny Fordham, an Irish vocalist making her first appearance in America. In a surprise announcement, John F. Poole was engaged as business manager. Part of the arrangement with Poole included the preparation of skits.

The Opera House was crowded "to the rafters" with enthusiastic admirers who cheered every performer before they began their routine, cheered them while they performed, and cheered them afterwards. Tony was given a long ovation, responded with a short speech of thanks and was then encored six times before he was able to leave the stage. It appeared that an auspicious season had begun.

Four days later, one of the worst economic disasters ever to affect the country burst on the scene. The Panic of 1873 was so calamitous its effects lasted for five years.[14]

America had experienced an economic boom following the end of the Civil War. Banks played an integral part in financing a large industrial expansion and the fast-growing railroad system. There was no unemployment, salaries were good, and spending expressed the public's optimism of the future. Theaters were among the recipients of this largesse.

In April, a number of banks failed. On September 18, Jay Cooke & Co., one of the largest and most respected of financial institutions, failed. The bank had been one of the major investors in the transcontinental railroad but had overextended itself by issuing millions of dollars of worthless stock. Other banks tied to it also failed. The New York Stock Exchange closed its doors.

The effect on New York City was devastating. In the matter of weeks, construction was cut in half. One hundred thousand people, one-quarter of the entire labor force, were thrown out of work. Not surprisingly, Bowery families were the hardest hit. Ten thousand homeless roamed the streets. Those who were lucky enough to be working saw a severe drop in their wages.

In January 1874, with the loss of jobs and the government's suppression of labor unions, unemployed mobs marched to demand that the city find them work. Unfortunately, the event ended in a police attack on the marchers in Tompkins Square, with the result that scores were killed. For several years, little was done to assist the unemployed.

During the second week of the new season, the Opera House experienced a significant drop in attendance and the matinees attracted few patrons. The same was true for all variety and minstrel houses. Dramatic theaters fared slightly better because their clientele was more upscale. Almost half of Tony's usual customers were either out of work or had their salaries slashed.

As a consequence, Tony published a "preliminary announcement: Tony Pastor, with his traveling company for 1874 will start Monday April 6, visiting all the principal cities of the East, West, North and South. Season, thirty weeks. Specialty artists (first class only) desiring engagements with this mammoth combination will apply early, stating terms, etc." Tony wished to corner the best performers he could obtain before anyone else. He also wanted the world to know that he would continue to operate no matter the financial risks. It was a bold and brave move, considering the current economically unstable situation.

Tony already had many of his regulars on long-term contracts. He was able to engage new people at lower salaries. No one complained since they were happy just to be employed. Tony also introduced a benefit for Saturday evenings, two people admitted free for the price of one.

And ladies would be admitted free for Saturday matinees. The decline in attendance was temporarily halted.

Tony discovered that it had become difficult to sign new people for each week's program. Some performers had left New York, hoping to find jobs in other cities. Some decided to stay where they were, even at reduced salaries, avoiding the need to seek employment on the open market. Some just quit the profession, reducing the number of performers available in variety houses. Circus people and child performers were sought out. Tony had to reduce the number of skits he normally put on. John Poole was not being cooperative and good talent to supplement the stock company was hard to find. Instead, Tony promoted his regulars to fashion their specialties into short skits with titles to suggest they were presenting actual playlets.

Poole did write a skit called "Wall Street or the Curse of Gold" but audience reaction was mixed. The plot seemed to be more reality than farce. "A Trip to Paris" and "The Match Girl of New York" were better received. The number of available novelty acts had declined, so Tony had to fill the spots with more dancers and vocalists. The quality of some of them was not up to Pastor standards, as audiences quickly pointed out. Tony's comic songs remained popular, but he had to be more selective of his lyrics not to touch on issues too sensitive to patrons. He repeated many of the favorites and brought back some old patriotic numbers.

In mid–November, the *New York Times* summed up the conditions for entertainment in the city.

> The amusements of this city remain in about the same condition as per last quotations; that is to say, theatricals are weak, and money scarce.[15]

With audience size ranging from "good average" to "fair," Tony barely broke even in weekly receipts, and some weeks lost money. With unemployment and homelessness a familiar sight around the theater, Tony had to acknowledge that his neighborhood could no longer support his Opera House. The area was in transition, with an influx of Irish and German immigrants, mostly unskilled and poor. The regular residents had been frequent patrons of his theater and were loyal customers but they, too, found it difficult to afford the price of tickets.

In a further attempt to improve attendance, Tony reduced admission prices. The orchestra was reduced from a dollar to fifty cents; the parquet from fifty cents to thirty-five cents; and the family circle from thirty-five cents to twenty-five cents. The response to his decision was almost instantaneous. Attendance improved and the other variety theaters lowered their prices as well.

Benefits for the poor became a weekly happening, each theater designating one performance to collect money. To collect food, clothing and money for his own neighborhood, Tony gave a benefit on November 20, at a rare Thursday matinee. He was also giving money to the local church to help its members.

For the holiday season, Tony planned the usual pantomime based on a children's fairy tale, this year "Goosey, Goosey, Gander," with clown Harry Thorne. He also booked a children's act — two sisters, aged three and five, who performed hat spinning and acrobatic feats. He engaged Prof. Richards, who, while submerged in a tank of water, ate, drank and smoked. When he simulated sleep while on the bottom of the tank for more than two minutes, the large audience broke out in cheers and applause of approval. The program did such a good job of attracting audiences that Tony held them over to the middle of January.

Tony had three more months of programs to consider before the beginning of the summer tour. What could he do to sustain and attract patrons to the Opera House during the normally slow season, now made bleak by the economic conditions? Newspapers no longer described theater attendance in superlatives; words like "average," "satisfactory," and "fair" were the most frequently used. The reviews identified the problems Tony was having getting a large enough box office to avoid losses. All of the profits he had collected from the previous summer's tour had been exhausted. Yet Tony refused to cheapen his show as other variety managers were doing to stay in business.

He engaged new people, like Pat Rooney, an Irish song and dance man, and Patti Rosa, a clog and jig dancer. He brought in novelty acts not yet seen in New York: a pedestal dancer; a Chinese man-serpent; trained dogs and monkeys; skaters and child acrobats. He changed the bill each week and retained low prices. He prevailed upon John Poole to write skits that would appeal to local audiences, like "The Masked Robbers" (funny), "The Last of the Mohicans" (humorous farce), "The Effects of the Panic" (flop), and "Life in Ireland" (a hit). But Poole was again looking to better himself in the variety business by seeking ownership of a theater.

Tony searched for new songs and props to improve his own act. One in particular captured audience interest. He employed a Stereopticon to illustrate his lyrics and picture famous people mentioned in the songs, patriotic figures like Washington, Grant, and Lincoln. The presentation was repeated for a month.

He also renewed advertising for the 1874 summer tour, ads that would continue weekly until April. The company featured the familiar faces of Ella Wesner, Billy Barry, the Fieldings, Freeman Sisters, Larry Tooley and Frank Girard. Newcomers were Kitty Brooke, an Irish vocalist; the Garnella Brothers, acrobats; and Billy Ashcroft, an Ethiopian comedian. The summer tour was scheduled to open April 6, in Trenton, New Jersey.

At about the same time, the *Clipper* revealed that Tony would manage the Olympic Theater during the 1874-75 season, running it as a variety house. Tony had been looking at the Olympic as a possible upgrade but no deal was made. He assured his patrons that he was not abandoning them, but there was no question Tony was looking to move to a better neighborhood.

It was during this period that forty-one-year-old Tony met Josephine Foley, a pretty twenty-year-old woman from Bridgeport, Connecticut, visiting New York relatives. The attraction was mutual. However, Tony could not court Josephine in the traditional way because he was on tour. When he was in the city, late hours and busy days prevented them from meeting often. Josephine would be often seen at morning rehearsals and meals between matinees and evening performances. When Tony returned from the summer tour, they announced their forthcoming marriage, to be held in December.

The Tony Pastor Combination for the summer of 1874 was not the only variety company on tour. Six others advertised their schedules and routes but none of them began until June. Their routes were not as ambitious as Tony's. Managers were concerned about the success of their tours due to the current economic situation. Would patrons come to the theater? Would they accept the advanced prices (higher admissions) demanded by touring companies? Tony wondered whether his admirers would come out to see their favorite performers. Critics wondered why any variety manager would choose to go on the road at all in such uncertain times.

The company opened to an average audience in Trenton. Other stops in New Jersey were equally uninspiring. But when they reached Connecticut, the theaters were full and audiences were excited that they were able to see the company. Tony took this display of appreciation and placed ads in the *Clipper* and *Dramatic Mirror:*

> Success unparalleled. Standing room only. Hundreds turned away
> nightly, unable to gain admission to see Tony Pastor and his
> traveling company.[16]

Whether the claims were true or not, they did have the effect of attracting patrons in cities to be visited. The ads also signaled to the industry that Tony was bringing in audiences at his usual first-class level.

Tony and Josephine were quietly married in December 1874 in Bridgeport, Connecticut. Mrs. Pastor became active in organizations devoted to the recovery of destitute and crippled children (Harvard Theater Collection).

In Hartford, "large and enthusiastic audiences" greeted the company. They played to the "largest audience of the season" in New Haven. Anticipating good receipts, Tony added bookings in New York and the Midwest. Results had been so positive it seemed that these places had been little affected by the current economic situation.

Actually, business conditions helped Tony. Theaters in the cities he visited had been closed because of poor attendance. Performers had curtailed traveling to conserve expenses. Audiences were hungry for amusement. When Tony arrived in town, an outpouring of people seeking entertainment greeted him. The fact that he brought high-class performers excited audiences even more. In contrast, the six other touring companies had been reduced to three and, by July, all were finished for the summer, leaving Tony the only company on tour.

Tony added Sam Collyer, a boxer, to the program in a skit called "The Champion of the Ring," in which he emulated Joe Kidd. Sam also included his two young sons, who sparred two rounds and made a hit. E.D. Davies, a ventriloquist, was also added and became an immediate attraction. The program began with a skit, "The Actor's Studio," performed by Barry, Girard and Tooley that set the mood for comedy.

In July, a review of the summer season by the *Clipper* attempted to offer a clearer picture of the variety business and specifically referred to Tony's company as an example of perseverance "in trying times."

> Tony Pastor's Combination, which is still traveling, now has a clear field. John Stetson's Company and Josh Hart's Combination having closed their season. When Tony first started he did an excellent business in New England cities, but when he arrived in the West, owing to the depressed state of trade and being compelled to compete with the two companies above referred to, who were playing just before him, his business dropped off somewhat. We are informed, however, upon good authority, that up to the present time he has lost no money on the season. He had determined to travel during the entire summer term, whatever may be the result. Although his profits will, by no means compare with those of last season, which was an unprecedentally successful one, still we think he may meet with a reasonable reward for his labors. His company is a strong one, and Tony is an energetic manager, and all of his assistants are both capable and infatigable.[17]

Two weeks in Chicago proved to be most profitable. The *Tribune* cautioned readers to make "an early visit to the box office." Hooley's Theater was filled at every performance with cheering audiences. Tony's ad campaign followed him out of Chicago in blazing rhetoric.

> Hail! Hail!! All Hail!!!
> Returning East. The best and only successful
> Traveling Company on the Road!
> The People's Favorite and ever popular Tony Pastor
> And his entire Star Troupe.[18]

The company enjoyed a two-week engagement in Boston, at the Howard Athenaeum. They were reported to have had "a smashing business." One-night stands in Massachusetts and Connecticut attracted crowded houses. And, in a new twist for closing a summer season, they played in Brooklyn for a week, at the Academy of Music, to full houses. From the *Clipper*:

> They have stayed out the length of time he originally proposed; and notwithstanding he had much opposition in the early part of the season, he has weathered the storm and his treasurer's account shows a handsome balance on the right side of the ledger.[19]

Tony had taken a decided risk with the summer tour. In the process, he demonstrated his management ability and personal reputation. He continued as the top variety manager in the country.

On September 14, the Opera House opened the 1874-75 season. Traveling company members were the featured attraction, with the addition of Gus Williams. The *New York Times* reviewer observed how compatible both performers and audiences were at Pastor's, a unique feature of the house.

> It may be said with candor that Mr. Tony Pastor, thoroughly understanding the peculiarities of his patrons, succeeds admirably, and always has full houses. The actors and actresses are always in complete accord with their hearers, who never fail to evince their delight at the triumph of long-suffering virtue over vice. An innocent stranger will never forget a visit to this place, and he will undoubtedly be delighted as much with the people in the auditorium as well as those on the stage. There is novelty on both sides of the footlights.[20]

A new rumor circulated that Tony was planning to build a new theater on Broadway. What was actually taking place was a discussion between Tony and M. B. Leavitt, one of the city's first theater impresarios. Leavitt had met Tony in Boston during the Civil War and struck up a friendship that lasted until Tony's death. They had many business dealings throughout the years.

Leavitt owned the lease of the Metropolitan Theater at 585 Broadway, opposite the Metropolitan Hotel. He was seeking someone to take over the lease. Tony believed that moving to a Broadway address would improve his business, and negotiations became serious in early 1875.

The theatrical business in New York was still depressed. Audiences were slim; just breaking even generated exclamations of triumph from theater managers. Tony's neighborhood, in particular, was steeped in poverty and unemployment. To attract patrons, he sought out additional incentives to enhance receipts.

In November, Tony announced that ladies would be admitted free on both Tuesday and Friday. Reactions to the offer were positive but actual attendance increased minimally. At the opening of a new week's program on Monday, Tony declared he would give away sixty hams and on Thursday evenings, he would give away sixty turkeys, all by lottery. Attendance picked up. Food giveaways proved to be just what patrons wanted.

The holiday program featured the performers of Tony's 1875 summer traveling company in a preview of their routines. They included Gus Williams, Venus and Adonis (infant velocipedists), the Foy Sisters (character duetists), the Fieldings, Jennie Morgan (serio-comic songs), the Garnella Brothers, Harry Kernell, Sanford and Wilson (funny song and dance team), and Girard, Barry and Tooley. At the same time, Tony announced that the summer tour would begin March 29, even earlier than the previous year, with "the most perfect combination ever submitted to the approval of the American public."

Also on the holiday program was a skit, "The Flats and Sharps of New York," a farce on Christmas carols in which the audience participated. In addition, a thousand toys were distributed to children at both the Christmas matinee and evening performances. The theater was filled with happy families.

On December 23, Tony and Josephine Foley were married. The marriage took place in Hartford where her family was currently living. After the ceremony and reception, the couple returned to New York where Tony prepared for his theater's holiday festivities. There was no mention of the marriage in the local press or theatrical newspapers.

At the beginning of 1875, the theater situation showed little improvement. Several dramatic theaters had closed. Others reduced prices, making them comparable to variety houses. The police were enforcing the access law. They began fining managers who hired young children to perform. And they put an end to can-can performances, which had gotten quite "blue." Tony continued to look for strategies to improve attendance.

Changing the usual bill, the performance began with a minstrel act, "The Female Minstrels," given by eight "ladies" of dubious age, actually the stock company men in costume, all dressed as women. The entire act was performed with an Irish brogue although everyone was in blackface. The skit was so well received that Tony decided to continue the act on the following week's program. The "Female Minstrels" ran for eight weeks. Each week, the routine was changed, as were the performers, adding to the hilarity. New performers, no matter their specialty, like trained dogs, contortionists or acrobats, were included in the minstrel skit. Blanche Selwyn, a male impersonator, impersonated a woman. The act's incongruities only served to make it funnier.

January 30, 1875, at the Opera House was the season's outstanding event. Ten tons of coal were given away. And Tony's conversation with the "boys" in the gallery, who now only paid fifteen cents for a ticket, brought down the house.

The auspicious event of the evening was the distribution of the coal. Numbered programs were given to the patrons when they entered the theater. Frank Girard told the audience that a half ton of coal would be given to each person holding one of the programs, which were numbered. A large blackboard was placed on the stage and the lucky numbers were marked on it. The winners would receive the coal the following day. Not only was it a first for New York theaters but it was a highly desirable gift for Bowery families. Tony repeated the giveaway each Saturday night for the rest of the season.

When Tony made his appearance, he sang three songs. Before beginning the last one, he stated that the boys in the gallery should join in the chorus. The song was "You'll Never Miss the Water Till the Well Runs Dry." The gallery response of the first chorus was weak. Tony remarked that the boys must be getting their voices in tune. The next chorus was sung louder. Tony said to the audience that "people might talk of the Italian Opera, the German Opera and the opera buffers, but they were not a market for the Bowery buffers."[21] He received loud cheers from the gallery and for the final chorus, they sang with great enthusiasm. Tony smiled, winked at the crowd, did a little dance, and bowed his way off the stage.

Still, January and February receipts were average. At various matinees, sewing machines and bags of flower seeds were raffled off; at others, ladies received candy and flowers. Full houses were common when dress patterns were given out to the ladies at matinees. At the Valentine's Day matinee, every woman was given a valentine.

On March 13, the press reported that the Tony Pastor Opera House had been renamed the Bowery Opera House. The next day, a rumor suggested that Tony was going to manage a variety theater on Broadway for the 1875-76 season. To highlight his tenth anniversary at the Opera House, a benefit in Tony's honor was scheduled. Many performers from around the city volunteered to appear to pay homage to their old friend and mentor.

Leavitt had agreed to sell his lease at 585 Broadway to Tony for $8,000 a year for five years. On March 27, Tony played his last performance at 201 Bowery. The event was saturated with cheers and tears. Tony thanked the audience for supporting him all these years and hoped to entertain them again soon in his new theater.

Billy reopened the theater the following week for a summer season of variety. Within a few weeks, the theater closed. It was later turned into a beer garden with music and lager.

On July 31, Tony announced that he had become manager of 585 Broadway, the former Metropolitan Theater. He and his company planned to open the fall season in September. He assured his admirers that he would continue to feature the best in variety entertainment without regard to cost. Tony hoped that the new location would attract new patrons along with his ardent followers.

8

New Talent and Crowded Houses

Tony leased 585 Broadway for five years, from the fall of 1875 to the summer of 1881. His move to the new theater was facilitated by an old friend, M.B. Leavitt. From the beginning of his tenancy, box office receipts were satisfactory. They continued to improve each year as the country's economy gained momentum.

New York took the lead in the recovery. By 1878, there were unmistakable signs of a renewed prosperity. This was especially true along the Broadway corridor, with the expansion of the "Ladies Mile," new hotels, department stores, and retail boutiques, fine restaurants and theaters. A more gentrified class of people lived and shopped in this area. The streets were full of activity. Sidewalks and stores were crowded with shoppers and visitors. A variety of conveyances jammed the streets—wagons, carriages, push carts and horse-drawn omnibuses.

In contrast, the Bowery was home to thousands of immigrants from Ireland, Germany and Italy. Commercial areas housed factories and sweatshops, with cheap labor and long working hours. Tenements, row upon row, street upon street, were crowded with families. They were dirty, airless flats, engulfed with the smells of garbage and human waste. Neighborhoods were crime ridden, laced with saloons, gambling and prostitution. The few theaters that did business in the Bowery were known more for their bawdy entertainment than for anything else.

Tony initially called his new theater the Metropolitan, then Tony Pastor's New Theater, then Tony Pastor's. Patrons of the theater referred to it as 585. The theater was situated between Houston and Prince Streets. It was across the street from the Metropolitan Hotel, just south of the elegant St. Nicholas Hotel and north of the more modest Grand Central Hotel. Transportation to and from the area was frequent and convenient. The theater was within easy walking distance for many of the patrons and not so far away as to exclude many of Tony's long-time admirers. The location had its competition, however. A few blocks away was the Theater Comique, Tony's archrival for several years but now showing signs of neglect. Also nearby was the Olympic Theater, currently managed by John Poole, and the Globe Theater. All three were variety houses.

The 585 had about 1,100 seats, slightly larger than 201 Bowery. The theater was more elaborately decorated and had a large lobby and a pleasant welcoming entrance. During his stay at 585 Tony did little to enlarge the capacity of the theater, but he did redistribute the sections to reflect his operating strategy. More room was set aside for what he called "the family circle" for women and children. Admission prices remained the same, but Tony eliminated the giveaways.

Increasing prosperity was not the only factor in making 585 a profitable venture. The business of theater was maturing. Changes in customer tastes for entertainment were broadening

A billposting for the opening of Tony's new theater at 585 Broadway in 1875. During the period of his ownership of 585, vaudeville came into its eminence, developed and elevated by Tony.

the acceptance and growth of popular theater. Variety was now consciously accepted as a legitimate pursuit. It attracted entrepreneurs who were ready to invest, visualizing potential in its expansion. They opened theaters and sponsored traveling companies. Led by Tony's example, theater management became a skill, and financial decision-making a well thought out and calculated strategy. Amusements had become so business-like that city government recognized it as a welcome source of revenue, passing tax laws on theater ownership and box office receipts.

To promote his new theater, Tony introduced two tactics. He increased his advertising, and he began to use the word "vaudeville" as a way to separate himself from other variety houses. Advertising was not only increased by the amount spent on it but also in its descriptive content, projecting the kind of image and environment he wanted to create for 585. On October 4, 1875, Tony's ad in the *New York Times* heralded the grand opening of his new theater.

> Tony Pastor's Metropolitan Theater
> Grand Opening Monday Oct. 4 of
> Tony Pastor and his company of celebrated artists
> Brilliant array of talent, novelty and variety
> The people's favorite amusement
> Superior claims to patronage; splendid loyalty;

> Beautiful auditorium; and the finest company
> Of original humorists and vocalists ever seen together.
> Matinees Tuesday and Friday at 2 PM
> Popular prices $1, 50 cents and 25 cents.

The superlative proclamations continued in successive weeks. On October 30, the ads identified the kind of people Tony wanted to attract to his theater.

> The recognized and legitimate family theater of the metropolis
> established on a firm base. Representing more popular and
> celebrated stars than any other theater in New York.

On November 13, Tony added class distinctions to his ads.

> The acknowledged family theater in New York, nightly crowded
> With aristocratic and enthusiastic audiences.

Size, newness and a claim of superior talent were messages appearing in the December 18 ad.

> The only theater in New York that presents new acts and
> new stars every week. The best entertainment in the city.
> The largest company in the world.

The campaign was quite effective, with crowded theaters every week extending through the early part of 1878. And, with calculated affect, Tony introduced the concept of vaudeville, giving definition to the word. The first time he publicly used the expression was on January 8, 1876. It was the first time any theater manager in New York used the word in conjunction with their program.

The idea of vaudeville as a more refined and acceptable version of variety was in its infancy. Several theaters in the country called their bills vaudeville. Two traveling companies promoted their performing as engaging in vaudeville routines. The New York press soon began to use vaudeville rather than variety, as the latter word had taken on negative connotation because of its relationship to Bowery amusements. To audiences, vaudeville connoted a more professional show that featured talented artists. Because vaudeville's meaning was still new, managers built whatever imagery they could around the word, creating almost a mystique about it. Within a few years, vaudeville replaced variety as the legitimate description of popular theater. It also became an important part of the public's vocabulary as well as their favorite entertainment.

In a January 29, 1876, ad, Tony elaborated on his themes.

> Nightly crowded with the wealth, fashion and respectability of
> New York. The only recognized and legitimate vaudeville
> combination in New York.[1]

A March 4 ad spoke of the success of the theater with a description of vaudeville as an organization of headliners.

> The only theater in New York that turns people away.
> Always something new. Tony Pastor's gigantic
> vaudeville organization.[2]

In late March, a Pastor ad declared, "They said I couldn't do it, but I did." SRO crowds and generous profits attested to his boast at a time when the economy was not yet recovering.

Yet, Tony was astute enough to call his traveling company a variety troupe, aware that the vaudeville concept had not yet permeated the "provinces."

During the fall and winter season of 1875, Tony featured the stars of his traveling company and newcomers like Lydia Yeamans (her mother, Annie, had played for Tony a decade earlier); Jennie Morgan, a vocalist who was discovered to be a good actress and was added to the stock company; the Weston Sisters, banjoists and singers whose immediate success with audiences brought them back to the theater frequently; and Sam Devere, more a comedian than banjoist, who quickly developed a loyal following.

Sixteen theaters had opened the 1875-76 season in New York. Five were variety houses, two of which were new entries, the Globe Theater and Tivoli Theater. Only the Olympic seemed to be actively competing with Tony; the others were unable to attract top acts or advertise sufficiently. Tony's advertising campaign had overwhelmed everyone, and his strategy to be identified as the best house in town could not be disputed.

As the holiday season approached, Tony added several schemes to enhance his image even more. He announced that carriages could be ordered at 10:30 P.M. to accommodate people leaving the theater; chairs and private boxes could be secured six days in advance; and opera glasses were available for hire.

The usual Christmas pantomime was performed. A family of clog dancers, featuring a young boy, awed audiences with their endurance. A trapeze artist performed above the heads of the audience and elicited gasps of apprehension. Tony led the audience in carols, which were encored repeatedly.

The spring of 1876 was equally successful in filling the theater and establishing the theater as the best in the city. Tony discovered new performers and gave them a chance to appear before New York audiences. Some failed; others had potential but were not yet ready for the big time; still others did so well, by audience standards, that Tony kept them on the program for weeks. Having made a hit at 585, many performers were quickly picked up by other variety managers. Whoever Tony hired, whatever their talent, he never cut short their engagement. Instead, he took time to assist them with their acts as a father mentors his children.

The spring months of 1876 saw the return of old favorites like Jennie Engel, Sam Devere, Nat C. Goodwin (an accomplished mimic of dramatic actors), Harry Montague and Gus Williams. Future headliners, seen for the first time in New York, included Frank Cushman and Frank Mayo.

Billy was not doing so well. He occasionally appeared at variety houses in the area. He attempted to lease a theater in New Jersey but failed. He returned to New York when Tony asked him to manage 585 while he was on the summer tour. The theater had to close in June because of poor attendance.

On April 16, Fernando died of consumption at Tony's residence at 115 West 17th Street. His death was not unexpected. He was thirty-three years old and had been divorced. The funeral and burial two days later was attended by the Elks Lodge #1, of which Fernando had been a founder and charter member. Tony was with the traveling company in Baltimore, came back to New York for the funeral, and returned to the company the following day.

The Tony Pastor Combination opened its summer tour on April 3 at the Arch Street Theater, Philadelphia, for a week's engagement. The biggest event of the tour was a trip to the Far West, with a two-week run in San Francisco. Featured in the company were Harry Kernell, Gus Williams, Sam Devere, Harry Braham (English music hall singer and comedian), and Jennie Engel.

The company jumped from Kansas City to Virginia City, Nevada, playing at Piper's Opera House, then continued on to Sacramento and San Francisco. The stay at the Bush Street Theater was a revelation for both the company and audiences. Company members visited the city sites like Chinatown and the Barbary Coast, and attended performances at other theaters. Variety theaters began late in the evening and extended into the early hours of the morning. Audiences were struck by the skill and talent of the company, and programs were extended at each performance because nearly every act was encored several times and audiences demanded speeches from Tony and other stars. Tony's comic songs made a big hit with patrons who had never seen or heard any of the material. Most of the songs he rendered were old favorites, but to a neophyte audience they were fresh and funny. The local press quickly came to realize why Tony was so popular back East.

The tour was so profitable that Tony postponed the opening at 585 for two weeks, spending additional time in one-night stands in New Jersey and Connecticut. When the company returned to New York, Tony not only discussed the highly successful tour but also proclaimed in his latest ad that he had "the largest, best and most celebrated company of vaudeville stars ever engaged under one management."[3] When it was revealed that the tour had made more than $50,000, no one doubted Tony's swagger.

During summer and early fall, several events affected popular theater. Police raided a number of variety houses for giving indecent performances, and performers were fined or held for bail. A new law was passed preventing children under sixteen from performing in variety theaters. Those in dramatic shows, if not endangered, could perform. Variety managers disputed this distinction with police, to no avail.

Harry Miner, a former agent and promoter, planned to open a new variety house, the London Theater, at 235 Bowery. He promised to present first-class entertainment. Miner was beginning his management career, which would include ownership of four other theaters by the early 1880s. Although some considered him Tony's rival, they were friends and often shared performers. Miner helped in bringing respectability and professionalism to popular theater, following Tony's example.

Seventeen theaters were open in September 1876. Seven of them were variety houses, the most ever in the city. They included Parisian Varieties (16th Street and Broad-

Along with his brother John, Harry Kernell was one of the leading exponents of Irish and blackface comedy. The brothers were introduced by Tony and appeared often at his theater (Harvard Theater Collection).

way), Theater Comique (purchased by Harrigan and Hart to feature their own productions), Grand Opera House (8th Avenue and 23rd Street), Wood's Museum (adding variety acts to their oddities and freaks), Columbia Opera House (12th Street and Greenwich), Olympic Theater (John Poole, manager), and the Chateau Mobille Varities.

Attendance was SRO at Tony's opening on October 2. Most of the bill was made up of the traveling troupe. "Tragedy, comedy, vaudeville," claimed Tony's advertising, "the most famous company in the world." Along with the familiar favorites, Tony brought in new performers, like Harry Bryant, an excellent ventriloquist; Bobby Newcomb, song and dance; the Daly Brothers, clog dancing; and Fields and Hoey, who played many musical instruments and did grotesque dancing. Tony also brought in more established performers who would attract crowds. One of them, Denman Thompson, was a dramatic actor who had become famous with his Joshua Whitcomb character, performing the role for a decade. Thompson's Whitcomb skit was a hit and he played at 585 for four weeks. This suggested to Tony that serious material was acceptable to a better class of patron.

Variety theaters were attracting customers and enjoying profit. When Harry Miner opened his new theater the end of November, people flocked to his house to see what he was offering. They liked the programs and filled his theater. Still, when the *New York Times* surveyed the variety scene, it spoke glowingly of the increasing popularity of popular theater for all classes of people, but singled out Tony as the model for the genre. "The acknowledged vaudeville theater of the Metropolis," they said. "The resort most cherished by ladies, children and the cultured mass of amusement-seekers."[4] Tony could not have put it better in his own ads.

However, theater attendance went into dramatic decline in December with the burning of the Brooklyn Theater and the deaths of 295 people. Theater fires were a relatively common phenomenon, considering the amount of flammable material backstage, the dangerous gas lights and arc lamps, and the lack of adequate fire protection. It was estimated that thirty to forty theater fires occurred each year. When performers visited a theater while on tour, the first thing they did was seek out the fire escapes.

The fire began in the flies on the left side of the stage, apparently ignited by an open gas lamp. The scenery shifted and the audience noted confusion among the performers on stage. The cry of "Fire!" caused everyone in the audience to stand up. The manager quickly stepped to the footlights and claimed there was no fire, urging the audience to keep their seats. The flames spread rapidly across the proscenium, causing the audience to stampede for the exits. The panic caused people to fight for the doors, blocking the aisles. The main entrance became choked with people, and the pressure of the crowd pushed them over and piled them up four or five deep. The entire orchestra was lost when a stagehand closed the stage door and locked them in. Within a half hour, before the fire department was mobilized to fight the fire, the roof had collapsed and the entire theater was destroyed. It was the worst fire in theater history. An enquiry into the disaster revealed the lack of fire escapes and firefighting equipment in the theater. As a result, the fire department was commissioned to evaluate every theater in the city.

Twelve days later, a fire broke out in a photographic shop at 587 Broadway due to an open gas jet that ignited some chemicals. By the time the first alarm was given, Tony's theater was threatened. When the firemen arrived, they felt the chief danger was the theater catching fire and directed their attention to prevent the flames from spreading. Tony was informed and rushed to the scene. By that time, firemen had the fire under control. Tony was shaken, but relieved. He announced that there would be a performance that evening as usual. But business during the holiday season and into January was poor.

Fire department investigators found that the furnace at 585 was too near a retaining wall, and they instructed Tony to move it. They also admonished him for allowing too many standing room patrons in the aisles. New York theaters put on benefits for the Brooklyn fire survivors and their families. Tony ran his benefit for an entire week.

In February, the fire scare diminished and people slowly began to return to theaters. Tony worked hard to improve attendance by featuring familiar favorites, but patrons remained reluctant to attend. Talk of theater problems with lighting, lack of fire escapes and a push for fireproof scenery kept the issue in the headlines.

In late February, Tony ran afoul of the Gerry Society, the evangelist group checking on underage children in theaters. He presented an act called the Empire Children, musical prodigies. Tony claimed they were over sixteen, but the court disagreed. The act was prevented from appearing in New York and Tony was fined $100. A similar situation occurred at the Theater Comique where two midgets appeared. In court, the midgets proved they were adults. But the issue of a group of roving do-gooders unnerved managers and raised considerable debate in the city council about allowing such a group free rein to arrest would-be offenders. Little was done, and the Gerry Society continued its activities.

As if to demonstrate to patrons that his show had attracted a society audience, Tony changed his costume. He began wearing full evening dress, a tuxedo and opera hat, to introduce acts and perform his comic songs. The press remarked favorably on the change of dress and audiences accepted it with enthusiasm. Tony would wear this formal costume for the rest of his career.

With his emphasis on high-class shows, vaudeville as upgraded entertainment, and audiences made up of families and sophisticated patrons, the new identity for popular theater worked well for Tony. The March 17 *New York Clipper* affirmed his goals.

> That Tony Pastor has done much to elevate the variety stage is evinced by the character of his audiences. The private-boxes and highest price seats are generally filled with the class of our citizens who patronize our first-class theaters.[5]

Tony called his traveling company for the summer of 1877 "the best company ever organized." The troupe included established such headliners as Gus Williams, Harry and John Kernell, Fields & Hoey, Delehanty and Hengler and Frank Girard. It also included performers who had recently made an impression with 585 patrons: Watson and Ellis, Dutch comedians; the Delanos, society sketch artists; the Austin Brothers, sharpshooters; Harris and Carroll, blackface comedians; the Bennetts, a song and dance team; and Clara Moore, character vocalist. Tony's comic songs included something for everyone's taste. Colorful bill postings were printed and advance men plastered a city two weeks ahead of the engagement. Local newspaper advertising for the company was equally colorful in its hyperbole announcing Tony's appearance.

The tour began March 31 and concluded October 6, a total of twenty-seven weeks on the road. It included all the main cities of New England, New York, the Midwest and another excursion to the West Coast that not only included Sacramento and San Francisco, but also Oakland, San Jose and Stockton. Several weeks were spent in Chicago and Boston. For the first time, the company had its own train accommodations for the trip. Tony also announced that 585 would remain open during the summer, hosting a number of variety performers and traveling companies. Billy would manage the theater during this time.

The summer tour was another tremendous success even though five other traveling companies were covering much the same territory. Even with advanced prices, auditoriums were crowded. At the McVickers Theater in Chicago, the week produced a banner box office. The San Francisco visit was extended two weeks due to the demand for tickets. Near the end of the tour, weeklong stops in Baltimore, Philadelphia and Boston attracted full houses and netted sizable profits.

Of significant note was the initial appearance of the Irwin Sisters, May and Flora, with the company while they appeared in Boston. M.B. Leavitt had received a letter from an agent in Canada stating that the two young girls were seeking an engagement, and that they were good singers already successful in their part of the country. Leavitt passed the material on to Tony, who signed them for a week. Boston audiences heartily applauded their act and Tony had them return to 585 at the beginning of the season. Tony helped launch the Irwins on a successful vaudeville career. May Irwin, in particular, was later considered "the funniest stage woman in America."[6]

Prior to 585's opening, the theater was completely renovated and redecorated. In addition to the usual painting, reupholstering and carpeting, a large, ornate sign with a portrait of Tony was placed over the box office. The opening week featured the entire traveling company in their specialties and, as usual, people were turned away. Tony's advertising onslaught continued.

> The Great Show of New York.
> The leading vaudeville theater in America.
> The recognized and legitimate family resort in New York.

Tony retained most of the headliners through October, adding very few newcomers. Patrons crowded the theater to see their particular favorites, now well known stars thanks to the press. Theater sections in newspapers not only printed schedules, but also initiated feature articles about specific personalities and a gossip column on their activities. Avid readers sought out all the information they could about each personality. This began the phenomenon of star power.

When Tony returned to New York, he found Billy complaining of pain in his chest and shortness of breath. Upon examination, Billy was found to have a tumor in his chest. On October 23, Billy underwent surgery but little could be done for him. He died later that day. On October 25, Billy's funeral took place, at the "Little Church Around the Corner." Hundreds of performers were in attendance. Floral tributes were numerous. Billy was thirty-seven years old, had a wife, Adele, and a son, Henry. He was buried in the Pastor plot in Evergreens Cemetery. Billy was the second of the Pastor brothers to die within the past eighteen months. Tony did not appear at 585 for two weeks, mourning for a brother who had, over the years, become quite dependent on him.

The winter months featured programs filled with new performers: trapeze acts, contortionists, clog dancers, and acrobats. New acts also included Dutch comics (as the German population increased, Dutch acts were gaining in popularity), impersonators, club swingers, trained animal acts, sharpshooters (a sport that had become popular), and eccentric dancers. These acts were good for only one week since they did not change their routines. Tony was compelled to replace them with other similar performers. The afterpiece had fallen out of favor, and only a few skits were offered during the program, ably handled by the stock company. Each week, Tony appeared fourth on the bill, presenting new songs and delighting audiences with the usual encores.

The holiday program was intentionally filled with old favorites and acts attractive to families, like a ventriloquist, a trained dog and monkey act and a sketch about school. At matinees, ladies were presented with bouquets of flowers and all children received toys. The theater was well filled during the entire week and produced the largest holiday receipts on record.

Press reports of theater receipts from 1877 spoke of large gains for all variety theaters in the city, for the first time in history. Tony was said to have been the beneficiary of "many thousands of dollars" from the season at 585 and the summer tour.

For 1878, Tony began his advertising campaign claiming to be "always at the lead and will ever continue to be there." He added, "The endorsed and fashionable family theater in New York." In February, he featured themes like "the society vaudeville theater in New York."[7] Other variety theaters began using the word vaudeville in their own ads and programs. The word variety, it seems, was becoming a nasty word and the press refrained from using it in their theater reportage.

In February, Tony welcomed Harry Sanderson back as his treasurer after a three-year absence. Sanderson would not only oversee Tony's finances but would also be involved in auditioning and selecting performers. He would remain with Tony as his loyal assistant until Tony's death.

The spring season closed April 1 with the annual summer tour set to begin April 3 in Philadelphia. However, Tony became ill prior to the beginning of the tour. Neuralgia and rheumatism was the diagnosis, and the opening was delayed two weeks. That gave patrons additional time to purchase tickets, making the Philadelphia engagement SRO for the entire run. In Baltimore, the *Gazette* extolled the virtues of the company as "the best that has been seen here."[8] The company then returned to Brooklyn for one week and a rare engagement at the Grand Opera House for another week. A visit to the New York area while the spring season continued was a new strategy to attract large houses. The *Brooklyn Eagle* declared that "the audience was largely made up of fashionable ladies and gentlemen, who only turn out to see the opera or the very first dramatic attractions."[9] The week at the Grand Opera House was SRO with "hundreds turned away each evening." With these results, Tony's ad message about the tour boasted that it was "triumphantly continuing its prosperous course forcing rivals and aspirant institutions for public favor entirely to the background."[10] Big words; a flourish; but all true. The company was now ready to hit the road. Headliners in the company included Pat Rooney, Sam Devere, Harry Montegue, Georgina Southern and Frank Girard.

During the first few weeks that Tony was touring, 585 remained open under Frank Pastor's management, catering to various variety combinations. For the rest of the summer, it was rented out to both dramatic and variety companies.

The company spent a week in Boston where the press pronounced them "Tony's best company." In Chicago, at Haverly's Theater, the *Tribune* called the troupe "the greatest yet." Prior to traveling to San Francisco, Tony added Gus Williams, Kitty O'Neil and Billy Barry. The children in the company had to temporarily leave as California law prevented them from playing. Tony paid them while they waited to rejoin.

A week's engagement in San Francisco was extended to three weeks. Frisco newspapers offered high praise to Tony and his players.

> Mr. Pastor presents all the variety that can be desired — characters using the Irish, German, Yankee and Negro dialects, singing of various kinds and qualities, ingenious instrumentation, and short drama acts that serve as the vehicle for character studies and imitation.[11]
>
> The troupe is probably the best of its kind anywhere, and its success unfailing. The career of Mr. Pastor is something remarkable, especially considering the reception he invariably meets with, and the manner in which, throughout the East, the variety loving public swear by him.[12]

Harry Sanderson was hired as treasurer in 1878. He became Tony's business manager and counselor, and ran the theater during Tony's last years of management.

Returning East, the company made stops in St. Louis, Chicago, Cincinnati, Pittsburgh, Philadelphia and Boston for weeklong engagements, and the smaller towns in

The stars of Tony's company for the summer of 1878. They included Frank Girard, Billy Barry, the Kernell Brothers, the Irwin Sisters and Kitty O'Neil, an all-star cast of professional artists (Harvard Theater Collection).

between for one-night performances. Tony announced the 585 season would open about September 23 and would have a "new face."

However, the Eastern portion of the tour did so well that Tony decided to postpone 585's opening to October 14, giving the company three additional weeks in New England. The *Clipper* reported that the summer tour had netted more than $50,000 for Tony.

In the meantime, the entire interior of the theater had been overhauled and renovated. An extra 290 folding chairs were added to accommodate standing room patrons.

Several good years at the box office had made Tony a well-to-do entrepreneur. He spent lavishly on the theater, attending to the comfort of his patrons. No competitor came close to the amount of money Tony spent on advertising. As performer salaries increased, Tony continued to pay his artists well. He donated funds to charities, such as the Elks and the Actor's Fund. He owned several properties and purchased a home on 40th Street for himself and Josephine. Tony had a carriage take him to work in the morning and home after the evening show closed. Beginning with the new season, Tony started to invest in foreign performers, paying their way to and from the United States. He paid more for new songs garnered from both the U.S. and England. Tony also became known for his out-of-pocket assistance to destitute actors, whom he could never turn away.

To open the fall season program, the orchestra played an original overture by conductor H.T. Dyring, an innovation that other variety theaters quickly adapted. A comedy sketch introduced several members of the stock company. Next, the Irwin Sisters gave a song and dance; Bryant and Hoey performed on a number of instruments; Kitty O'Neil danced a jig and a reel; Tony sang some popular songs; Rogers and Vickers gave a skit full of imitations; and the French Sisters did a few eccentric dances. Watson and Ellis performed an Ethiopian skit, Bill Barry did his Negro specialty, the Kernells excelled in Irish songs and dances, Harry Kennedy, the ventriloquist, gave a dialogue with his puppets, and a Dutch skit by the stock company closed the show. Every act was encored, some several times. There was no intermission. (Tony did not believe in intermissions seeking, rather, a fast-paced show.) No act was more than fifteen minutes; skits ran about twelve minutes. The show normally ran for three hours, not including the encores. When audiences left the theater at the end of the evening, they were imbued with the excitement, intensity and boisterous merriment of the experience.

Flora Moore, a sweet singer from Ireland, was introduced to New York audiences. Charles Waterfield, an English character vocalist, lasted one week. Raymond and Murphy, with Irish character specialties, made an immediate hit with audiences. Henry Carney made his American debut with character songs and rapid changes of costume, representing three different types of Irishmen, a Scotsman and a Negro. Johnson and West, a Scottish pair, performed field sports. Only Flora Moore appeared for several weeks. Patrons found it difficult to understand the accents, jokes and imitations performed by these newcomers.

New acts by familiar actors were well received. John T. Kelly teamed with Thomas Ryan in a funny Irish skit. The Irwin Sisters combined comedy and dance. Louise Montague, a singer, who was on the threshold of entering comic opera, was extensively applauded. Frank Bush introduced a monologue using a Hebrew accent, likely the first to do it on the variety stage. Edwin French, an outstanding banjoist, added witticisms to go with his Southern renditions. Tony introduced new songs, singable with the gallery, and topical, like "The Elevated Railroad," "Tony's Choice for Mayor," and a combination recitation and song that described the types of people seen at the Catholic fair. His comic song, "Where Was Moses When the Lights Went Out?" was a decided hit, encored frequently, demanded often, and was later published in music sheet form.

On January 15, 1879, Gilbert & Sullivan's *H.M.S. Pinafore* opened at the Standard Theater. The show had made its first appearance in Boston on November 25, 1878, and in San Francisco and Philadelphia in December. The show came to New York with superlative reviews. A week later, a burlesque version of the production appeared on the variety stage. Copyright laws were so weak and confusing that the show was available to anyone wishing to present their own translation. A little over a month after *Pinafore*'s introduction to New York audiences, Tony's company produced a burlesque called "T.P.S. Canal Boat Pinafore," written by John Poole.

Gus Williams, in Dutch dialect, played the lead role of Sir Joseph Lager. Alice Seidler played Josephine; Deadbeat was performed by J. Lamont, and Neil Burgess, the great Ethiopian interpreter, was Little Buttercup. Nearly all of Gilbert & Sullivan's words and music were used, in spoken language rather than singing. Jokes and routines were interspersed into the dialogue. Costumes and scenery were copied from the original production. Instead of dropping the curtain to end the first act, twelve men attired in sailor's garb performed a clog dance. In between acts, various specialties were performed, including Tony singing several comic songs. By the end of the week, the theater was attracting SRO crowds. Tony advertised his new success in the *Clipper*, in glowing terms.

> Great success of Tony Pastor's Burlesque Pinafore. The most positive and legitimate success ever made with any burlesque in New York. People turned away. 100 artists. A full operatic company. A chorus of 40 voices. 12 clog dancers. 12 song and dance men. The Gilbert sextet. Tony Pastor and a full vaudeville troupe in connection with the splendid burlesque.[13]

The following week, at Tuesday's matinee, Tony had invited the cast playing *Pinafore* at the Standard Theater and those from other houses satirizing the play to watch his rendition. The theater was filled with professionals who were seen to be laughing and cheering like any group of patrons. Sanderson then announced that Tony had copyrighted his version of "Pinafore" and "any infringement will meet with speedy prosecution." People were unsure whether Tony was joking or not.

Pinafore was featured until the end of 585's spring season. The burlesque played for seven weeks and fifty-eight performances. Each week, new jokes, songs and routines were added or exchanged to keep the presentation fresh and exciting. Through this experience, Tony learned that audiences welcomed comic travesties on current hits. He planned to introduce more of them in the coming season.

In late March, Tony revealed the cast and route for the annual summer tour, to begin in Lowell, Massachusetts, April 7. His advertising said it all.

> Tony Pastor's Double troupe for the season of 1879 will commence its annual tour in April. Tony Pastor, always striving to make each succeeding company superior to its predecessors, feels confident of this season. Surpassing all former organizations. A company that has no equal in the world. Tony Pastor, America's own and the world's greatest comic vocalist, will appear at every entertainment. A feature of the performance will be the burlesque, "Canal Boat Pinafore."[14]

Headliners included in the summer company were the Irwin Sisters, Kelly and Ryan, Bryant & Hoey, Ed French, and the French Twin Sisters. Tony also convinced George Thatcher, a well-known actor and comedian of the dramatic stage to join the company. The composition was decidedly different from previous tours: no novelty acts, like acrobats and contortionists; no Negro dialect routines; heavy on comedy and dance; and most of the performers were new to a Pastor tour. The cast reflected in Tony's estimation, of changes in audience tastes.

Harry Sanderson remained in New York to manage 585, making sure that the best available performers appeared there. Frank Pastor assisted Sanderson; his job was unspecified.

The Irwin Sisters, May and Flo, were "coon shouters" from Canada when Tony introduced them to New York audiences. Under his aegis, they developed into versatile actresses. May went on to become one of vaudeville and musical comedy's best comediennes (Harvard Theater Collection).

After stops in New England, Boston and Philadelphia, the company returned to New York for a week at the Grand Opera House, managed by John Poole. It appears that Tony and Poole had worked out their differences. According to the *Clipper*, the company's recent successes were attributed to Tony's selection of new, lesser-known talent.

> The names in the company Mr. Pastor has with him this year are of less famous individuality than those Mr. Pastor has had. The entertainment they give is a stronger one, more generally satisfactory than any he has had in years. The fact is, during the winter he tried a number of people comparatively unknown and found an amount of talent he had not dreamt of in the eternal round of the same familiar names. From these, he carefully picked the best and got together one of the few variety companies to which the name "variety" can justly be applied.[15]

The company featured the burlesque of "Pinafore" which, being seen for the first time, delighted audiences. Three weeks in San Francisco, at the Bush Street Theater, was a "veritable bonanza," according to the theater manager, and Tony was persuaded to stay a fourth week. On the last night of the engagement, Tony was given a surprise benefit. Speeches, flowers, a proclamation from the mayor and a rousing audience completed an engagement that broke all records for the theater. However, after leaving Frisco, Tony swore never to return to the Bush because he was upset with its lack of sanitation and dirty dressing rooms. The ladies of the cast complained that they were compelled to pass through a "five-cent beer dive" to get to their dressing rooms. On several occasions, they were forced to make the trip with escorts to fend off the "intoxicated habitues."

On a return appearance in Chicago, the company played to a light audience, attributed to competition from a large circus. In Pittsburgh, the company nearly missed their train because the man in charge of baggage asked for more money. Tony paid it but later filed suit against the man. The more famous one became, the more people attempted to extract additional compensation for their work. Still, according to Sanderson, the books "looked good" and Tony made a "substantial profit."

The new season at 585 began November 1, the latest that Tony ever opened. The traveling company was featured on the bill the first few weeks. Then, Tony moved to change the entire bill each week, a mixture of old favorites and new people, with several introduced to American audiences from England. The new performers usually appeared only one week. They were primarily vocalists, dancers, song and dance teams and comedians. Few skits were performed. Business was good but not outstanding. Competition from seven other variety houses appeared to be affecting Tony's business but, more importantly, his competitors were enticing many of his favorites with higher salaries.

The holiday fare included a dog circus, marionettes and a pantomime on Humpty Dumpty, "great treats for the little folks." A special giveaway for ladies was *Tony Pastor's Almanac*, an illustrated booklet that included information on each day of the year, sun and moon phases, star phenomena and a listing of business law in daily use. The distribution of the attractive piece reflected Tony's perception of the type of audiences 585 currently attracted. On its back page was an advertisement. "A Vaudeville Theater! Devoted to Light and Amusing Entertainment. Elevated in Tone!!! Catering to Refined Taste and Emphatically A Family Resort."[16]

During the winter and spring of 1880, Tony continued his policy of introducing new performers each week; for every four new faces, one old favorite. Several new people scored decided hits and were retained for some weeks or returned weeks later. The St. Felix Sisters, a vocal quartet who also danced, were especially appealing. Lina Tettenborn was both a soubrette and a talented actress. Bonnie Runnells appeared in Dutch dialect specialties. Dan Collyer, Sam's now grown up son, did a song and dance and appeared in skits in various character roles. Hallen and Hart made their first appearance in New York in a funny sketch, the beginning of a long career in vaudeville. The biggest find was Jacques Kruger, who could sing, dance, tell jokes and act in whatever role was demanded of him. He quickly became a valued member of the stock company.[17]

Although Tony was looking for another Broadway show to burlesque, he settled for a long skit—several scenes—written by William Carleton. Entitled "Go West! Or, the Emigrant Palace Car in an Uproar," the loose plot portrayed a mixture of dialect comedians in one train car in a drama filled with absurdities and miscommunication.[18] More than any other Pastor skit to date, ethnic humor dominated. Along with a New York policeman and newsboy, the roles included Irish, Dutch, Italian and Negro characters. The skit was an immediate hit and played for two months, attracting SRO houses.

For the final two weeks of the season, Tony brought back "Canal Boat Pinafore," claiming the revival was better than the original. The annual summer tour had been announced in February and ads for it appeared each week in the theatrical newspapers; "the greatest company of specialty stars ever seen," headlined the ad.

The cast consisted mainly of familiar performers: Harry and John Kernell, Bryant & Hoey, St. Felix Sisters, French Twin Sisters, Flora Moore, Bonnie Runnells and Lina Tettenborn. The closing skit was the spring success, "Go West on the Emigrant Train." The skit would introduce a new kind of ethnic comedy to audiences around the country. As in previous years, 585 would remain open during the summer under the direction of Harry Sanderson and Frank Pastor. Unlike previous years, there were four other variety theaters open for the summer to challenge Tony's dominance of the market.

This year's route covered all the familiar stops except that it did not include a tour of the West Coast, instead concentrating on cities and towns in the Midwest. On the return portion of the tour, the "Emigrant Train" was dropped and a skit written by James Barnes, "Pastor's Evening Party" was introduced. In September, Ella Wesner was added to the cast, having just returned from Europe.

The summer tour scored a success although four other traveling companies were competitive. The company still dominated patrons' interest and box office receipts, "business being excellent and the overflowing audiences delighted at every stand," according to the *Clipper*.

The 585 had a gala opening on October 18. An excited audience cheered all the familiar favorites and demanded encores from each performer. Although Tony had begun looking for a new theater uptown, he renovated the theater once again. Entrepreneurs were seeking sites near Union Square and farther north on Broadway for both dramatic and vaudeville theaters. Rather than wait until his neighborhood showed signs of decline, Tony wanted to establish a theater in the heart of the business district where high traffic, good transportation and fine retail outlets were the attractions. Admission prices were raised: parquet, fifty cents; orchestra, seventy-five cents; and the five front rows, one dollar. Patrons were unfazed by the increase in prices.

The opening week featured the traveling company in their specialties as well as a return to the skit "The Emigrant Train." The following week, a revived skit, written by John Poole, "Fun on the Stage, or a Manager's Trials," was played. Poole updated the old script upon Tony's request. The skit was similar to "Emigrant Train" in that it served as a vehicle for several ethnic comedy performances, some funny scenes of verbal misunderstandings, and new songs and dances. The skit appeared for four weeks with new performers and new material added each week. Ads spoke of "the best, the greatest of all vaudeville shows on earth."

For the fall season, Tony introduced new performers each week while retaining a few favorites and select members of the stock company. Several new people were big hits with audiences. Lester and Allen did elaborate songs and dances, the beginning of their rise to vaudeville stardom. Charles Fostelle excelled in female impersonations. He became a noted actor. Ad Ryman gave burlesque lectures but later gained fame with Negro and Dutch comedy. Ferguson and Mack were eccentric Irish characters whose funny skits regaled audiences for two decades. On November 22, 1880, Tony introduced a pretty young lady named Lillian Russell, launching her illustrious career.[19]

Helen Louise Leonard's husband, Harry Braham (of the well-known family of orchestra conductors), persuaded Tony to give his wife an audition. At the moment, Tony was looking for singers to include in his upcoming burlesques of Gilbert & Sullivan operettas. With an accompanist playing the piano, Helen Louise sang an operatic piece and a popular song. For a few moments after she finished, the room was silent.

"Can you start next week?" asked Tony. Although stunned by the question, Helen Louise recovered her composure and readily accepted. Her salary would be twenty-five dollars a week. Before she performed, however, Tony and Harry Sanderson believed that her name had to be changed. Sanderson drew up a list of first and last names and pinned them on a board. They played with various combinations. Helen chose Lillian Russell because, she believed, the name sounded musical.

When Lillian began her career at 585, she was nearly nineteen, had been married for a year, had a five-month-old child, and three months of stage experience. Tony had to teach her stage presence, and she was required to learn new songs each week.

"Ladies and gentlemen," he announced to the audience, "I bring you the beautiful English vocalist, Lillian Russell." Tony made sure floral bouquets were available after she completed her act. The audience liked her signing and asked for an encore. The second week of her appearance, Lillian introduced an Irish love song, "Moonlight on Killarney," several encores of which were noted by the *Clipper*. By the third week, Lillian was not only singing, she was included in a skit, "Needles and Hairpins," playing opposite Frank Girard and Dan Collyer.

The holiday show featured the Kernell Brothers, Ferguson and Mack, Kitty O'Neil, the French Twin Sisters, Lillian Russell, Florence Merton and "Pastor's Evening Party" to close the show. "Best show on earth," claimed Tony's ad.

The shapely, nineteen-year-old Lillian Russell was signed by Tony in November, 1880. She appeared in his burlesques of Gilbert & Sullivan's operettas, which helped to launch her colorful career.

The year 1881 was going to be one for decisions and changes. While Tony was prospering at 585 and especially on summer tours, competition both in New York and on the road was getting fierce. Seven variety houses were open and most had incorporated Tony's ideas and signed many of his top performers. They were advertising more extensively, copying Tony's use of superlatives in their ads. Entrepreneurs were buying up or building theaters and locating them around Union Square. Performers' salaries were increasing as their star power helped to attract large audiences and considerable press coverage. Agents promoted their people vigorously with large ads in the theatrical newspapers. Popular theater was rapidly becoming the public's favorite amusement.

Tony continued his policy of bringing in new performers each week, supported by a few audience favorites and heavy advertising. An added feature was the distribution of bon-bons to ladies at every matinee. Pastor introduced a competition between Lillian Russell and Florence Merton. Who was the best singer? Who was the best actress? He used it to promote an upcoming burlesque of Gilbert & Sullivan's *Pirates of Penzance*. Which singer would play the lead? audiences were asked. In anticipation of the new burlesque, Tony added the Irwin Sisters, Lester and Allen, and Frank McNish, all versatile performers.

The Pirates of Penzance had opened at the Fifth Avenue Theater on September 30, 1879. It was another great hit for the composers but also another chance for American managers to produce their own versions of the piece. Tony's version, prepared by him and John Poole, followed the music closely but the lyrics and plot were localized and made into comic dialogue. When the new play was announced, entitled *The Pie-Rats of Penn Yan*, Lillian was given the title role; Merton played a minor character.[20]

In the program, the play was described as "an entertaining localization of the incident and burlesque on the action of "Pirates of Penzance" relating to the courtship, hardships, and want of ships of the Gentle King of the Prowlers and his apprentice Little Freddy." Little Freddy was played by Flora Irwin. Frank Girard played an Irish policeman. May Irwin was Ruthie, a prowler girl, and Lillian was Maria (Marie in the original play), a loving heart. The "finest police in the world," seven men, included Lester and Allen, Ferguson and Mack, and Dan Collyer. The prowlers of Penn Yan, fourteen men, included the above actors and stock company players. The daughters of Stanislaus, eighteen females, consisted of stock company members and others hired to make up the chorus.

From Scene One: a rocky pass near Penn Yan, the home of the Pie-Rats. In their grand chorus, called the "Prowler's Whiskey," they sang

> Hopping over muddy crossings,
> Petticoats so gaily tossing,
> Pretty little ankles showing;
> No policeman to assist us,
> Who before could ne'er resist us.
> And Susy Brown, the little dear,
> How very pert she does appear,
> When she is making down Broadway,
> To go to Pastor's matinee,

From Scene Two: a wood near Penn Yan, a chorus sung by the finest police in the world

> While we're standing on our beat,
> Scanning every face we meet,
> If we hear some little boys,
> Making an unusual noise,
> We march them off to jail.
> From them we never quail;
> And we make a great display,
> Taking girls across Broadway.

From Scene Three: Stanislaus brewery on the Hudson, a grand finale chorus of "A Copper's Life is Not a Pleasant One":

> They are not bummers of the common throng,
> They are all clergymen who have gone wrong.
> Let them all be married, those girls to me so dear,
> I am the pattern of a modern Deutsch Brigadier.

A reviewer for the *Times* observed that "it was no easy task and required peculiarly talented people to give full force to the fun. We are agreeably surprised that the company made as much of the piece they do. They are certainly at the happiest in the burlesque line."[21] Audiences left no doubt regarding their feelings about the production, with long applause, cheers and shouting for encores of songs at every performance. Lillian was particularly mentioned for her voice and acting in the *Clipper* review.

A month later, a burlesque of the operetta *Olivette*, playing at Daly's Theater, was presented, again featuring Lillian. She was costumed in a sailor's suit, cut to fit her form exactly. Her most important song, "In the North Sea Lived a Whale," had to be encored several times every evening. Audiences found both the voice and the figure equally attractive. "Olivette" closed out the season at 585, its last performance on April 9.

At the time, no one knew it would be Tony's last appearance at 585 Broadway.

The March 1881 playbill introduced the burlesque "Olivette," starring Lillian Russell. Audiences found both the voice and the figure equally attractive (Harry Ransom Humanities Research Center).

9

The Emergence of Vaudeville

In 1868, Tammany Hall opened its new headquarters and brought together politics and amusement. The building was located at 141 East 14th Street, two short blocks from Union Square. The Tammany Society kept one room for itself; the rest of the building was devoted to entertainment.

The Tammany Society was founded in New York in 1789. The colonial society was named after a Delaware Indian chief known for his wisdom. It had originally been a fraternal and charitable order, but became a political machine under the direction of Mayor Fernando Wood during the 1850s and William Marcy "Boss" Tweed in the 1860s. Tweed's corruption of city government led to cries for reform and in 1871, he and many of his colleagues were arrested and charged with defrauding the city.

Tammany Hall, the phrase, represented a political power for decades. Tammany Hall, the building, was a money producer for its owners, catering to the rapidly growing amusement business. The building contained two theaters, a larger one for meetings, special concerts and political gatherings, and a smaller one leased to various theater companies for performances. In the basement, the Café Ausant offered gymnastic exhibitions, pantomimes and Punch and Judy shows. The basement also included a bar, a bazaar, a ladies café and an oyster saloon, all of them open from seven in the evening until midnight for the combination price of fifty cents.

The smaller hall featured Dan Bryant's Minstrels (for several years), periodic classical concerts and opera, and the Germania Theater, with dramatic and musical productions in German.

By 1880, the Union Square area had become the heart of the theater district as well as a busy retail center. Women were attracted to the department stores and shops bordering the Ladies Mile. The Sixth Avenue elevated trains brought customers from other parts of the city to visit the stores, eat at the restaurants and attend the theaters. The Morton House was a favorite watering hole for actors and journalists. The Everett House attracted singers and musicians. Fashionable restaurants, like the trend-setting Delmonico's, appealed to the more sophisticated clientele. Brentano's and Tiffany's were favorite shops for books and jewelry. The *Dramatic Mirror,* a weekly theatrical newspaper, had its offices near the Square. Wallack's Theater, the epitome of dramatic entertainment, was a block away. The Academy of Music and the Germania Theater were only a short walk. The Union Square Theater was in the heart of this activity. Electric lights adorned the streets. In a nearby park, theater managers and agents made deals, signed contracts and hired performers. Actors frequented the park seeking employment. Surrounding apartments and boarding houses were home to people connected to the theater.

9. The Emergence of Vaudeville

In 1881, when the Germania Theater closed, Tony took over the 1,100 seat theater space at Tammany Hall. Although he had the choice of selecting from among a number of available theaters, he chose a smaller seating venue to retain the more intimate atmosphere needed in popular theater. Performers had to be close to audiences to gauge their temperament and exalt in their enthusiasm. Audiences wanted to be close to performers, to see their every expression, hear their dialogue and feel as a participant in the experience.

Performers were larger-than-life characters and the good ones became mythic to the audience. Acts were inexorable; there was no way of stopping their forward motion. That is why encores became such an important part of the stage relationship between performer and patron. Encores gave the audience a brief moment to recapture a pleasing song, an energetic dance or a comedy recitation. It gave the performer more time on stage and more adulation, the basic ingredient for success and career advancement. The communal experience of seeing a performance with a crowd was an irreplaceable happening, everyone sharing the same emotions of enjoyment or sorrow. The bigger the crowd, the greater the impact. A full house in a smaller theater was infinitely more exciting to participants than a larger theater with empty seats.

Tony Pastor's 14th Street Theater in Tammany Hall opened on October 24, 1881. In keeping with his ideas about seat configurations, he reduced the parquet section and increased the family circle. He added several rows of orchestra seats in the front and private boxes on each

The 14th Street Theater, also known simply as "Pastor's," was located in Tammany Hall. When Tony moved in, Union Square was the center of New York's theatrical community (Harry Ransom Humanities Research Center).

side of the stage. The entire interior was painted, the seats reupholstered and new rugs installed throughout. There was a ladies' lounge, and an inviting lobby with posters of shows to come. Admission prices were reasonable and competitive: family circle, twenty-five cents; parquet thirty-five cents; orchestra fifty cents; and children's tickets, fifteen cents. For one dollar a person could get a reserved seat. Tuesday and Friday matinees were retained, to attract ladies and children.

On opening night, the theater was filled with Pastor loyalists and admirers. Standing room only patrons filled the aisles. The company was made up of the performers who had been the stars of the summer tour. Tony sang five songs, the first of which was the old favorite, "Down in a Coal Mine." He had sung the song more than 1,500 times throughout his career and it had become his signature tune. When he announced the song, the audiences cheered and applauded for several minutes.

> I am a jovial collier lad,
> As blithe as blithe can be;
> For let the times be good or bad,
> They're all the same to me;
> 'Tis little of the world I know,
> And care less for its ways;
> For where the dog-star never glows,
> I wear away my days.
>
> (Chorus) Down in a coal mine, underneath the ground,
> Where a gleam of sunshine never can be found;
> Digging dusky diamonds all the season round,
> Down in a coal mine, underneath the ground.[1]

Tony sang five verses, the audience laughing or clapping at various allusions to social conditions or politics. They joined with Tony to sing the choruses. At the conclusion of the sing-along, the audience rose and applauded Tony for so long that he had to beg them to stop and allow the show to continue. At the end of the program, members of the audience refused to leave until Tony and a few of the headliners gave brief speeches. Assured that Tony was settled in at his new venue and promised to continue his high-class vaudeville for their enjoyment, the still effervescent patrons left the theater.

In his speech, Tony promised the audience that he planned to feature more artists from Europe, more new performers and several burlesques on current comic opera. Lillian Russell would be returning to appear in a travesty of Gilbert & Sullivan's *Patience*. She had not accompanied the summer company because Tony wanted her to get more seasoning playing with a group where performers played many roles. He loaned her to manager Col. McCaull at the newly opened Bijou Theater to appear in comic opera. In the *Grand Mogul*, Lillian was considered the show's "most attractive performer," but the show quickly folded. With revisions in the songs and dialogue, the production was reintroduced, this time called *The Snake Charmer*, and catapulted the twenty-year-old Lillian to stardom. However, her beauty, voice and provocative attire kept the play alive for only three weeks.

Gilbert & Sullivan's new opera, *Patience*, had opened in New York at the Standard Theater in September 1881, and continued to play to full houses throughout the end of the year. Considering Lillian's celebrity, Tony decided to delay the opening of his burlesque until she was available.

New York theatrical life was enjoying a splurge of prosperity. Twenty-two theaters were open and attracting good patronage. Nine were variety-vaudeville houses, including Tony's new theater. Four were new entries. Time would tell if they could sustain audiences and attract top talent. Competition was as fierce as it had ever been, and the demand for artists contributed to sizable increases in their salaries. Tony's policy of rewarding performers with return engagements and better salaries if they became local favorites captured many headliners' loyalty. Some performers stayed with Tony from four to eight weeks. Some obtained contracts that guaranteed them a place on the bill once every month. Others with a growing reputation joined the stock company and played for the entire season. Newcomers who did well their first week were asked back the following week. If they continued to do well, Tony signed them for periodic returns throughout the year. In this way, Tony ensured the availability of dozens of performers, supplanting the need for agents and offers from rival managers. Thus, Tony was able to present patrons with proven, appealing talent. He had developed this system while at 585 and would continue to use it effectively for the next decade.

Patience or the Stage Struck Maiden opened January 23, 1882, with Lillian in the title role. Supporting her were the Irwin Sisters, Dan Collyer, familiar man-for-all-roles Frank Girard, and a newcomer to the stock company, Jacques Kruger, a talented actor and comedian.

Although the music for *Patience* was retained, Tony localized the plot: twenty lovesick maidens became twenty stage-struck girls; soldiers became the Coney Island militia; and the male lead, originally a poet, became a despondent stage manager. Audiences rewarded Lillian "with the warmest marks of approbation." Kruger was cited for "quaint and extravagant drollery." The burlesque was a decided hit and was repeated for eight weeks.

Fresh from her success at comic opera and at Pastor's, Lillian demanded more recognition from Tony, going so far as to propose forming a separate company, with her as headliner, to open at his theater and go on tour. It was an unusual request by a performer and received an unusual answer. Tony appeared to agree with Lillian and even published an ad, talking about the new company and its star. Whether Tony was serious or not about the arrangement is unknown, for it was unlike him to agree to such terms. He was also reluctant to renegotiate her contract. For the time being, they were at an impasse.

The winter of 1881-1882 brought Tony several problems. Vaudeville theaters that were having difficulty attracting customers decided to lower admission prices. Tony refused to do the same. When theaters with lowered prices improved attendance for several weeks, Tony was forced to reconsider his decision. He again decided to hold the line on his prices. After the initial blush of success from his rivals, their receipts again declined and two had to close their doors. In contrast, Tony continued to attract full houses. The *Dramatic Mirror* astutely pointed out that "it is the man, not the location, which is the trademark of a lucky manager."[2]

With her brogue, booming voice and eccentric Irish dances, Maggie Cline, the "Irish Queen," had already been a success at Tony's theater.[3] Returning from a number of engagements where she received a larger salary, she demanded even more from Tony. He refused and played her only one week. She left angry and swore never to play for Tony again. Dyring, the orchestra conductor for some years, demanded a higher salary, going to court to claim additional compensation for his overtime work. He lost the case and Tony fired him. Both episodes were reported in the press, casting a slight shadow on the behind-the-scenes activities at the theater.

Fire inspectors reported that Tony's theater was in good shape except for the handling of standing room patrons. They recommended that Tony eliminate standing room altogether because these patrons blocked aisles. Tony did not entirely comply, but no further demands were made of him. It seemed that some pressure from Tammany Hall (the political machine) pardoned Tammany Hall (the theater) from enforcing the standing room requests.

Newspaper advertising for theaters had lost some of its hyperbole when the press refused to print statements thought to be boastful. Tony had to tone down his ad prose a bit, and he reduced advertising expenditures. This appeared to make no difference in attracting crowds to the theater. Tony did just enough advertising to remind people of the reasons why they should frequent his theater. Eighteen eighty-one was a profitable year; 1882 offered even greater promise.

In March, *Billee Taylor* replaced *Patience*, again featuring Lillian. Jacques Kruger wrote the travesty of an original play by Edward Solomon that opened in England in 1881 and had an excellent run. Both the *Clipper* and *Dramatic Mirror* praised the show and Lillian and predicted a long run. The production lasted only three weeks when salary warfare broke out between Lillian and Tony. She demanded a new contract; Tony refused. She left the company and never played for Tony again although she remained fond of her first manager.

To boost box office receipts. Tony rented the Academy of Music, conveniently located across the street, for matinee and evening performances on Washington's Birthday. The academy had more than 2,000 seats. The theater was filled at both times and the venture proved to be profitable. Tony then contracted with the academy for future holiday events, like Thanksgiving and Christmas, and even a weeklong engagement during the summer by his traveling company. These became annual occurrences.

In late March, Tony announced the cast of his eighteenth annual summer tour, to begin April 10 in Poughkeepsie, New York. The company included Jacques Kruger, Lester and Allen, the Irwin Sisters, the Watson Brothers, the French Twin Sisters, William Carroll and Frank Girard, all Pastor veterans. Newcomers were the Musical Four, a song and dance team; Mattie Vickers, a vocalist; Charles S. Rogers, a Dutch monologist; and Lizzie Simms, an Irish dancer. The orchestra and brass band was under the direction of Adolph Nicholls, the new conductor. In his ad, Tony promised "a truly superb combination of talent; a grandly artistic show; Tony Pastor and the best company on earth."[4] Frank Pastor would manage the 14th Street Theater during the summer.

Engagements in Brooklyn and Boston attracted large audiences. A week at New York's Grand Opera House was a big success. Appearing for several weeks in the New York area during the spring season was an innovation by Tony, who saw the advantage of playing to local audiences before the hot season. This worked so well that he planned to incorporate the idea into future tours, and to expand to theaters in growing areas like Harlem and Williamsburg.

A stop in Chicago for two weeks also proved to be a highly profitable engagement. A tour of towns in Michigan, Ohio, and into New England was also successful. But, in a dramatic break in routine, Tony announced that he and the company would take a brief vacation for two weeks at the end of July. Rumors suggested that something was wrong with the tour, that Tony was ill, that the claimed successes were really not true. In reality, Tony's wife had persuaded him to take a badly needed vacation, the first he had ever taken since managing a theater. They were seen relaxing at seaside resorts. When the tour began again, the company was the same. Those in the company that sought out other appearances during the break were allowed to pursue them. Tony paid those that elected to rest.

The renewed tour began July 31 in Newburg, New York, and repeated the route through Ohio, Indiana, St. Louis and Chicago. Business in St. Louis was average — an extreme heat wave was given as the cause — but the Chicago stop attracted large crowds. Pittsburgh, Philadelphia, Baltimore and a return to Hyde & Behman's in Brooklyn closed out the tour. Sanderson reported "large profits."

A meeting between M.B. Leavitt and Tony produced a new traveling company, the Leavitt and Pastor Combination, which began in Chicago in September. The plan was to have the company visit smaller cities and towns and continue to operate into the fall. They played in the Midwest only until the end of October. Leavitt and Tony vowed to continue the experiment.

The grand opening of Pastor's 14th Street Theater took place October 23, almost two months after all the other vaudeville theaters in New York had begun their season. Audiences were undeterred by the lateness of Tony's arrival. They had become familiar with his strategy and welcomed him with even greater enthusiasm. Said the *Clipper*:

> The name of Tony Pastor has now become a household name among seekers of pleasure, and he successfully strives to make his entertainment worthy of patronage.[5]

The gala festivities of the first week featured all the members of the traveling company. The following week, Tony promised "something new," in addition to Carroll, the Irwin Sisters, Kruger and Girard. Among the newcomers were the comedy team of Crandell and Eastwood, who gave Hebrew dialect impersonations, probably the first in popular theater to add Jews to the ethnic comedy repertoire. During the past several years, a large influx of German and East European Jews had arrived in New York and they were fast becoming a representative minority.

The fall season included the return of audience favorites like Kitty O'Neil, Prof. Parder's performing dogs, Lillie Western, Frank and Lillian White, the Daly Brothers, Frank Moran and Dan Collyer. The stock company players now included Kruger, Girard, Frank Budworth, Joe Buckley and Florence Bell. There were five or six new performers each week, but only a few of them were retained or asked to return later in the season. The number of new performers was rapidly expanding, but they had few venues in which to gain stage experience before appearing in higher-class theaters. The turnover was rapid as audiences expressed their opinions with minimal applause. Tony reintroduced circus acts again to fill in programs. And due to the inconsistency of high-class bills, Tony returned to more extensive and expansive advertising.

> Houses crowded. Standing room only.
> An entire new company this week, composed of
> The best artists on the stage.
> The best show of the season.[6]

With heavy lobbying by religious and evangelical groups, the city council finally passed what the press called the "blue law," forbidding the sale of alcohol and public performances on Sunday. Most theaters were already closed on Sunday but concert halls and beer gardens remained open. The sale of alcohol had been widespread. For the most part, the law was effective, if proving inconvenient to people seeking a drink on the weekend.

Theater managers, particularly those operating dramatic shows, later came up with the idea of free Sunday concerts. Well-known performers volunteered their time to appear. Audiences could donate what they wished for seeing the show. Tony turned the new law into a burlesque skit. Written by Kruger, "Blue Laws or Humors of the Penal Code" played for several weeks. The plot dealt with a family coming to New York and the father seeking a drink on Sunday. His confrontation with the police, the court and politicians were received "with roars of laughter." The skit also launched Kruger on a career writing humorous material.

The holiday show featured a Christmas matinee and evening performance at the Academy of Music, to full houses. Ladies and girls were given dolls at the matinee. A skit, "Muldoon's Picnic," a familiar Harrigan and Hart routine, was the feature of the program, which also included headliners from last summer's traveling company.

Tony spent the winter and spring of 1883 looking for skits that appealed to his audiences. With the diminishing popularity of afterpieces and with the introduction of burlesques on current Broadway shows, audiences wanted mini-plays filled with humor and songs. Skit writers were hard to find. Among the stock company, Kruger was the only actor who could prepare a script. In January, "Fun on the Stage" was brought back, featuring Kruger and the Irwin Sis-

Dan Collyer was a versatile actor who could play any role from blackface to royalty. He was the son of Sam Collyer, the boxer, who had played at Tony's theater a decade earlier. Dan was a stock company member at Tony's theater for several years (Harry Ransom Humanities Research Center).

ters. The skit played for one week, then was replaced by Charles Fostelle's "Mrs. Parrington." Fostelle impersonated a woman whose social demeanor was quite voluble, leading to many comic situations. The skit played for two weeks. Alf McDowell submitted a skit to Tony called "Who Owns the Baby?" which proved to be the most entertaining piece in some time. The skit played for two weeks, and Tony promised to bring it back for future performances. Kruger adopted a burlesque on Varney's *The Musketeers*, but the skit achieved only average response. In March, Kruger did a travesty of Audran's *The Mascot*. In spite of Kruger and the Irwin Sisters' comicalities, it played only one week. A revival of "Billee Taylor" was added to the program, with a newcomer, Rose Temple, taking Lillian Russell's part. It, too, lasted only one week. When Tony announced the opening of his nineteenth annual summer tour, he chose "Who Owns the Baby?" to be included in the program. For audiences outside of New York, the skit should prove to be funny and enjoyable.

Overall, spring attendance had been high. An examination of the treasurer's books for the 1882-1883 season showed a profit of $7,000.[7] An average week at the 14th Street Theater netted slightly more than $500. Performances at the Academy of Music garnered over $700. Of all the expenses, salaries took up almost 50 percent, averaging close to $850 a week. Top performers made $60 to $75 a week; newcomers earned $25 to $30 a week. Tony drew out $50 a week for his own needs. The profit balance was given to Frank Pastor to put in one of four banks Tony used. Marked on the ledger sheets were loans Tony made to actors, current and former, and charities. They often averaged over $100 a month.

Summer tours were decidedly more profitable. Larger theaters, higher admissions, lower salaries (actors signing on for a continuous run of six months generally accepted lower salaries) and lower advertising costs contributed to higher net receipts. However, the share of receipts had to be split with theaters in which the company appeared. The usual cut was fifty percent. Additional expenses were incurred because Tony paid for railroad fares and hotels. Still, a twenty-five week tour of more than 100 cities produced more than $20,000 profit in 1882.

Sanderson's ledgers included the name of the theater, the number of seats by price category, the date played, all admissions and expenses, salaries broken down by performer and notations on why the engagement was profitable or not: the weather too hot; returned too soon; too many shows here; always a good town; needed fewer musicians; and even such notes as "town dead" or "breakfast at hotel slow." Sanderson maintained this ledger from 1878, when he rejoined Tony, until the closing of the 14th Street Theater in 1908.

The 1883 summer company was the best to date, loaded with vaudeville all-stars. The cast included Harry and John Kernell, Jacques Kruger, the Irwin Sisters, Kitty O'Neil, Lillie Western, Kelly & O'Brien and lesser known but proven artists like William Carroll, banjo comedian; Harry Steele, roller-skating comic; sketch comedians Frank and Lillian White and grotesque comedians Bennett and Gardner. "Who Owns the Baby?" was the featured skit. Nearly the entire company emphasized comedy in all of its combinations.

When the company began its tour, there were nineteen other vaudeville companies traveling the country. Theaters in New York mostly closed down for the summer, the exception being the vaudeville houses. The 14th Street Theater, managed by Frank Pastor, featured a mixture of specialty acts. The theater closed June 23, partly because of low attendance but also because Frank was ailing. He was soon diagnosed as suffering from consumption.

Tony and M.B. Leavitt combined forces again to sponsor a summer touring company. The troupe planned to play at smaller towns in the East and Midwest while Tony's Combination appeared in larger cities for one-week engagements. The combination opened in Philadelphia, visited Hyde & Behman's in Brooklyn and then traveled to the Howard Athenaeum in Boston. Receipts were excellent and Tony used the occasion to proclaim his successes in the *Clipper*.

> Turning thousands away, an ovation everywhere;
> The country ablaze with excitement;
> Now en tour in New Jersey, Connecticut and Hudson River cities.[8]

This year, the tour took the company to Canada, New York, Cleveland and into Chicago for two weeks. The hot weather in Chicago generated only fair receipts. The company then traveled through Wisconsin and Minnesota (new territory), Michigan and a long jump back to Boston in early July, this time appearing at the Oakland Garden. Tony's next ad heralded their popularity.

> Absolutely, positively the best show on the globe, an American
> family entertainment appreciated by millions of the best people of
> the U.S. and endorsed by their patronage.[9]

Tony declared a rest of four weeks with a reopening August 6 at Saratoga to start a new tour of the western cities. During the hiatus, Tony joined his wife on a short vacation on the New Jersey shore.

Although they experienced some blank dates, the Leavitt-Pastor company appeared to be operating successfully if not profitably. The number of rival vaudeville companies on tour had dwindled to six by the end of July, making playing time easier to find. However, the company closed down at the end of August, reporting "some losses." Tony and Leavitt abandoned the idea of combining forces, at least for the immediate future.

After reforming the company and opening in Saratoga, the Pastor Combination toured through New York, Ohio, Indiana, Kentucky and Pennsylvania. In their final weeks, they played a week in Baltimore to "full houses" and Brooklyn to "large business." Frank had received another $7,000 from Tony to put in the bank.

New York theater began the new season in attractive fashion. They featured a new configuration of theaters, the appearances of important actors and actresses, and an increasing interest in vaudeville entertainment. The old Park Theater and Booth's Theater were torn down. The Metropolitan Opera House was under construction. Harry Miner expanded his theater ownership by building the People's Theater to present dramatic productions on the site of the old Volk's Garden. The Theater Comique opened the new season in early August with Harrigan and Hart's "Mulligan Guard Ball." There were now twenty-six theaters in the city, seven of them vaudeville houses; three theaters now operated in Brooklyn.

Famous actors and actresses highlighted the opening bills of dramatic theaters: Ellen Terry, Dion Boucicault, Edwin Booth, F.S. Chanfrau, J.K. Emmet, Joseph Jefferson, Margaret Mather, Helena Modjeska, Mrs. Langtry, Minnie Maddern, and Henry Irving. Audiences flocked to see these stars in action.

As usual, the opening of Pastor's 14th Street Theater on October 22 featured the headliners from the traveling company. The theater had been repainted and reupholstered. Professor Warner was the new leader of the orchestra. The auditorium was packed and the audience responded enthusiastically to every act that appeared on stage.

Tony's advertising had diminished in size as more theaters committed to advertising. Ads for song pluggers and products jammed the ad pages with information. Examining the ads shows the dramatic increase in the theater's support system, with displays of musical instruments, scenery, magic lanterns, costumes and makeup, even billiard tables and sport equipment. Ads by individual performers about their recent successes were a new self-promotion device. The fact that performers were spending their own money promotionally revealed the importance of past successes and future engagements. An appearance at Pastor's theater was heralded as a prime assignment; an announcement that the performer would soon appear at the theater indicated their specialty professionalism. In fact, mention of Pastor's theater was often used to jump-start a newcomer to the profession.

In the fall season, newcomers filled the bill with the usual backup of stock company players. Several European imports were introduced: Dermot and Doyle, Irish comedians, dancers and boxers (they played two weeks); Harry Rogers, English music hall artist (one week); and Little Tich, in a grotesque dancing and balancing act that sent audiences into roars of laughter. He was booked for only one week, but Tony signed him to return to the theater. Two new local performers, Harry Richmond, with songs and dances, and Bonnie Runnells, with Dutch character songs, became immediate favorites and were retained. However, Tony lost Jacques Kruger and May Irwin, two important stock company stalwarts. Kruger was loaned to Nat Goodwin to play a dramatic role. He never returned. Irwin's talent was noticed by Augustin Daly and he enticed her to appear at his theater as a comedienne on the dramatic stage. Flo, May's sister, remained with Tony.

Holiday programs were brighter than usual. The inauguration of electric lights inside the lobby and auditorium helped to attract crowded houses. Ladies and girls were again given dolls at the Christmas matinee at the Academy of Music, in what was becoming an annual event. Two skits were presented: a repeat of "The Pavements of New York" (by John Poole), and "The Mother Goose Party" with the stock company, in "special appearances" as Little Bo Peep, Red Riding Hood, Tommy Tucker, Little Jack Horner and other Mother Goose characters.

While all of this gaiety was taking place inside the theater, a confrontation had begun between theater managers and speculators, heretofore unmolested by the police. Speculators were buying up choice tickets and selling them at inflated prices, some even operating in theater lobbies. Chasing them away provided only a temporary victory. They came back, mingled with the crowds and plied their wares. At Tony's theater, speculators worked in the lobby. Patrons were incensed with the intrusions and price gouging. The press printed dozens of letters from patrons complaining about the harassment. Finally, theater owners persuaded the police to shoo away speculators. However, they could still be found on the sidewalk down the street from the theater. It would take several years of lobbying the city officials before an ordinance was passed against ticket speculators. For the time being, it represented a constant problem facing both managers and patrons.

Tony launched 1884 with a repeat of "Muldoon's Picnic." The skit played for only two weeks, attendance dropping significantly in the second week. Audiences were just too familiar with the skit, no matter how funny it was. Another skit, not dissimilar, "Mulcahy's Jubilee," lasted only one week. Charles Fostelle was brought back in "Mrs. Parrington" while Tony sought new ideas to offer his knowledgeable patrons. He staged an Ethiopian week, in which all performers and acts were in blackface, that was deemed mildly amusing. He did a travesty on Lillian Russell's current hit, *The Grand Duchess*, entitled "The Grand Dutch S," but no one could copy Lillian's persona. During the last month of the spring season, Tony hit upon a popular theme of boxing, a sport gaining a good deal of publicity, thanks to the larger-than-life antics of John L. Sullivan, the country's first sports hero. Tony brought in Dan Donnelly, the champion boxer from Ireland, to spar a few rounds, a routine that lasted three weeks. He then reintroduced the skit "Joe Kidd" that included a boxing match between the comedy team of Kelly and Murphy to end the season.

During the past season it had become increasingly harder to find new talent or retain proven talent because of the competition for performers from a growing list of vaudeville houses and touring companies. Broadway agents declared they were going to Europe to secure new acts because there were not enough good performers available to fill a vaudeville bill. Tony was not afraid to hire new people, but only a very few proved successful. Lester and Allen were big hits, but had already played at the theater. For the ladies and children, Till's Marionettes obtained great approval. Otherwise, Tony had to rely on repeat appearances for McIntyre and Heath, Lillie Western, the St. Felix Sisters and the Russell Brothers. Tony even persuaded Ella Wesner out of retirement to play for several weeks. The stock company now included Flo Irwin and Bonnie Runnells along with the regulars. Attendance was not the best, but Tony's reputation and that of his programs remained high.

There were a few highlights of the spring season. The Vanderbilts and a party of their friends paid a visit to the 14th Street Theater and were so delighted with the show that they had Tony and company play at their residence a few weeks later.

An Actors' Fund committee was formed, consisting of Tony, Edward Harrigan, John Poole, David Frohman, Harry Miner, Edward Aronson and others, to put together an annual benefit to assist ill and destitute actors. Their first effort was an evening in April in which five theaters, both vaudeville and dramatic, would feature a number of acts, with all proceeds going to the fund. The event was very well attended and several thousand dollars were collected. The Actors' Fund benefit would be held annually.

Tony's 1884 summer company planned to be on the road for six months. A change in this year's scheduling had the company concentrating on playing larger cities with weekly engagements, or other places that had proven in the past to be profitable. Heavy advertising was included in every place to be visited. There would also be a vacation break of five weeks in the middle of the tour. Tony was leaning heavily on the summer tour to replenish his bank account.

The tour began at Hyde & Behman's in Brooklyn, moved to Philadelphia and then to the familiar surroundings of the Howard Athenaeum in Boston. All three engagements produced "packed houses" and "immense business." Tony followed these results with advertising that ostentatiously boasted of his successes.

> Tony Pastor's Own Company. The blazing sun of American vaudeville shining in the bright light of popular favor. Grand in its success. Great is its merit. Crowding houses. Delighting thousands.[10]
>
> Tony Pastor's Own Company. The family entertainment of America. Catering to polite taste and inviting the attention of the refined public. A wholesome, pure and chaste vaudeville. Grandly successful everywhere.[11]

Part one of the tour covered the East and the Midwest and ended in early July with another engagement in Boston. Results to date were excellent. The company returned to New York and disbanded. Tony and his wife were seen at several local resorts and Tony himself was seen visiting other theaters. Part two of the tour began August 11 in Saratoga with the same cast of players. Engagements in Chicago, St. Louis, Cincinnati and Pittsburgh were synchronized to open each theater's season, bringing big turnouts and large profits. Stops in Philadelphia, Baltimore and Brooklyn closed out the tour. The second round of the tour was as financially successful as the first. Whatever lacked in profit from last season at the 14th Street Theater was more than made up by the summer tour. The press found Tony and Harry Sanderson "correspondingly happy."

The 1884–1885 season opened on October 27 and featured the usual array of traveling company artists. They garnered full houses, standing room only and many hundreds were turned away. Tony promised special programs for the fall, including new burlesques of current hits from the dramatic stage. But without a writer to prepare them, he was able to put together only ten skits for the entire season. Instead, Tony brought in other traveling companies for weekly programs to supplement his usual specialty performers. Extra matinees were given on Election Day and Thanksgiving, using the Academy of Music to attract larger crowds. The fees paid these visiting companies was less than salaries Tony would have been responsible for had he hired his own people. And it saved him the hassle of booking people for these bills.

Several new stars were discovered during this time. New to American audiences was Marie "Cissie" Loftus, a headliner from the English music halls.[12] She was a stellar impersonator of stage celebrities. Tony held her over for four weeks; it was the beginning of a successful career in the U.S. Hilda Thomas sang ballads and was so well received that Tony had her return frequently during the season. The Schrode Brothers were acrobats who also played a variety of musical instruments. They, too, were called back often. Regulars who appeared during the fall included Lizzie Simms, Frank Moran, the Dalys and perennial favorite Lillie Western.

Fire again came to dominate theatrical news. In late October, an unknown incendiary gained access through the 14th Street Theater in an attempt to burn down Tammany Hall. Just after the evening show closed, several workmen saw smoke coming from an unoccupied space near the barroom. The fire department was called and put out the fire before it could spread further. Tony and some of the performers were seen aiding the firemen.

Not so lucky was Harrigan & Hart's Theater Comique. On December 23, around seven in the morning, cleaners smelled smoke, and when they investigated, they found the stage in flames. The fire spread so quickly that firemen were unable to save the building; only the outer walls of the theater remained. No one was killed or injured. However, the blaze set off another inquiry into fire safety in theaters and caused a reduction in all theater attendance for almost a month, strongly affecting box office receipts during the holidays. The inquiry caused a flurry of visits by fire marshals, but nothing really changed the situation. Tony lent Harrigan his theater for rehearsals and assisted him in getting his company into another venue. Harrigan vowed to rebuild the theater.

In January 1885, an article about theater doings in New York noted that Tony was about to celebrate his 20th anniversary as a theater manager, a record unequaled in the history of the city. While not openly suggesting that Tony was an "old timer" in popular theater, the author used such phrases as "venerable showman," "established purveyor of amusement" and "career longevity" while describing Tony's influence on local entertainment. Brief summer vacations the previous two summers may have contributed to the observation. No other popular star had enjoyed such a long stage career and none served as performer, promoter, manager, agent and touring company impresario. Tony's answer to these remarks was an ad that claimed the winter-spring season at his theater would supply new adventures in presentations and business breakthroughs.

Tony's first decision was to book more traveling companies to appear at his theater, taking advantage of the increasing number that sought venues in the city. Some of the companies were managed by people Tony had originally introduced, like Sam Devere, George Knight and Harry Kernell. Tony also saw this as an opportunity to evaluate new performers without the need to recruit them himself. As vaudeville grew in popularity, some managers said that new performers with a wide variety of specialties were entering the business more rapidly than there were places to watch them. Tony still believed the best way to evaluate an act was to see it work in person in front of a discerning audience. He shunned booking agents for that reason. In the process, Tony discovered new artists that offered potential.

Tony also decided it was appropriate to reacquaint audiences, many of them new to popular theater, to vaudeville and variety old-timers, performers who for decades had been headliners. He selected several of them to head the weekly programs doing their unique specialties. They included Billy Birch, the circus and minstrel blackface singer and dancer; Kitty O'Neil, whose jig and clog dancing were unmatched; Frank Moran, in darky monologues; and Annie Hart, singing familiar love ballads. Audiences responded with excitement, participating in what was for them evenings of nostalgia.

Tony combined with M.B. Leavitt to lease the 3rd Avenue Theater. They would put in vaudeville programs similar to those Tony already presented, but with lesser performers at lower prices.

> As we go to press, we understand that genial Tony Pastor and M.B. Leavitt have formed a partnership, and will open the 3rd Avenue Theater January 26 as a combination house — combination of legs, beauty and high art.[13]

The 3rd Avenue Theater had fallen on hard times, due partly to poor management and partly to a transition in the neighborhood population. The theater had been closed for some months. After refurbishing the interior and lowering prices for the gallery to fifteen cents and the orchestra to twenty-five cents, the theater opened with a three-act comedy farce, "The Kindergarten," supported by a mixture of specialties. Initial reactions to the programs were encouraging, suggesting to the partners that there was a chance to resurrect the theater. However, by March, attendance was declining and Tony brought in more familiar artists to entertain. When Tony and the summer company began their tour, he booked them for a week at the 3rd Avenue, with good results. Nevertheless, immediately after, receipts dropped off substantially. By June 13, the *Clipper* reported that Tony and Leavitt's partnership had "expired by limitation." It was revealed that they had leased the theater for only nineteen weeks, an obvious hedge against possible failure.

Tony's 20th anniversary celebration was held at the Academy of Music on Sunday evening, March 22. Every seat was filled; standing room completely occupied; hundreds turned away. It was a gala event featuring previous performers, contemporaries, admirers, floral tributes, speeches, cheers of appreciation and tears of enjoyment.

P.S. Gilmore conducted the overture, with an orchestra of one hundred musicians, many of whom had played for Tony twenty years previously. John Braham, Tony's first conductor at 201 Bowery, came from Boston to lead the orchestra. A prominent lawyer made an address commending Tony on his career as a theater pioneer. Tony then sang a number of his favorite songs with the audience joining in. Lillian Russell followed, singing the songs that had made her a hit at 585, with Edward Solomon leading the musicians. She was followed by Henry E. Dixey, E.E. Rice, Pauline Hall, Barry and Fay, William Carroll, Chauncey Olcott, and John and Harry Kernell. City managers, headed by J.F. Donnelly, were receptionists and a number of lady professionals were ushers. B.W. Harvey, Tony's first ticket seller, presided at the box office.

The *Clipper* reviewer reported that Tony, "who has not grown old during his 20 years of management, looks as blooming as ever." The *Dramatic Mirror* put it another way. "Tony himself appears to grow friskier as he grows not so young."

In recognition of the favors he received from the profession and the press, Tony gave them a complimentary performance at the Academy of Music on April 9. He not only sang a number of old favorites but also surprised his audience with a dance, much to their delight. The *Clipper* reporter jokingly described the scene.

> Now, we all know that Tony can sing, but very few of us have ever dared to even fancy he could dance, especially of late years, since nature and good living, combined with a light heart and happy disposition, graced him with slightly larger than 22 waist. But upon the occasion Tony did dance, and danced so well that the house thundered with applause, recalled and recalled him, until, out of breath, he was obliged to excuse himself by pantomime.[14]

The annual summer tour began April 13 at Hyde & Behman's Theater in Brooklyn. The cast of the company featured Harry and John Kernell; the Watsons, a Dutch act; the Vivians, character change artists; Hilda Thomas and the American Four (Joseph Pettingill, Peter Gale, Peter Dailey and William Daly), a comic specialty group. After a week in Boston, the company

Dressed in his entrepreneurial finery, Tony celebrated his twentieth anniversary as a theater manager in March 1885. He was heralded as New York's foremost exponent of vaudeville entertainment (Harvard Theater Collection).

returned to New York for an engagement at the 3rd Avenue Theater, hopefully to build its flagging receipts. After a successful week in Philadelphia, they began a series of one-night stands in New Jersey, New York, and as far west as Chicago by early June. In Chicago, they played for three weeks at three separate theaters. On the final night of their stay in Chicago, Tony was given a benefit. In the audience was John L. Sullivan, heavyweight boxing champion, who was called up on stage. In tuxedos and with no gloves, Sullivan and Tony playfully threw a few punches while the crowd cheered their antics.

On June 25, Tony received a cable that Frank had died in San Antonio, Texas, where he had gone in an attempt to recuperate from his illness. While it was not unexpected, it was still a shock to Tony. He immediately called off the tour and disbanded the troupe (a first), returning to New York. It took five days for Frank's body to reach the city.

In 1873, Frank married the daughter of Blondin, the celebrated rope walker. Blondin had risen to fame by rope walking over Niagara Falls a few years earlier. Frank left the circus to become the agent for his father-in-law. In 1880, Frank joined Tony to assist in his ventures. When, in 1883, it was found he was suffering from consumption, Frank was sent to Virginia to recuperate. After returning in improved health, Frank caught a severe cold, causing a relapse from which he never recovered. Frank was forty-eight years old. He left no children.

Frank's funeral and burial in the Pastor plot in Evergreens Cemetery took place on June 30. Many former circus colleagues attended along with theatrical people who had worked with the Pastors. Obituaries were found only in the theatrical newspapers. Tony, clearly despondent, retreated into seclusion.

10

The 14th Street Theater

In the spring of 1885, an enterprising reporter from the *New York World* obtained a rare interview with Tony. He must have been frustrated by the results. All he was left with was a physical description of the man, some comments about his reputation and a statement that his private life was his own.

> Pastor is a short, dapper, well-dressed little fellow with a short grey moustache and a twinkle in his eye. In his dress, the old idol of the Bowery hangs onto some of the fashions of yesterday and they add rather than detract from his original personality. He still wears boots, shoes in reality wouldn't look just right on Tony. No links for his cuffs; big gold buttons the size of a half dollar, with a big "P" in diamonds set in each, and the fasteners for his sleeves. The dandified, swelled-head airs of the average successful theatrical folk are all absent. He is full of good hard horse sense. Tony Pastor is one of the most interesting and unique characters in the theatrical world. His work and success and the length of his service distinguish him from any other performers in the profession. He wears his laurels with the greatest modesty. You have to ask him for all the information you want about Tony.[1]

There is no doubt that Tony's personal life and that of his family were kept away from public scrutiny. Somehow, he had maintained a carefully controlled separation between his public persona and private life.

For example, back in the middle 1860s, at a time when high-visibility performers frequently found their names in newspapers, there was no mention of Tony's first marriage. A few years later, only a brief mention in a Saratoga newspaper let readers know that Tony's wife had died. His second marriage in 1874 was covered only by a Bridgeport, Connecticut, paper. At a time when Tony was considered the leading theater manager in the city, no newspapers revealed the marriage. The deaths of Fernando, Billy and Frank received brief mentions in the press, primarily obituary information and funeral arrangements. Only the theatrical press offered brief biographies.

Indeed, as the reporter duly noted, "you have to ask him" for information, and usually he only talked about theater related activities. The pattern was to continue throughout Tony's life. Only after he died did his wife reveal some of the tribulations he faced late in his career.

Immediately after Frank's death, Tony went into seclusion, for eight weeks. During that period, there was not one mention of Tony in any of the New York newspapers or in the theatrical weeklies. Only the *Daily Democratic Times,* Lima, Ohio, reported that "Tony Pastor is in New York resting."[2] One can only speculate why Tony withdrew from the theater upon Frank's death since, in contrast, he continued to perform and manage after Fernando and Billy died. Was Frank his favorite? Was it because Frank was the last remaining brother? Or, at age fifty-two, did Tony suddenly realize how finite life was? Possibly, all three reasons contributed to his emotional breakdown.

Tony reappeared in the public arena by announcing a return to the stage with an abbreviated summer tour. The tour would begin August 20 in Detroit and play all the major cities for a period of two months. All of the people who had been in the original company returned to continue the tour, a circumstance unprecedented in popular theater.

When they opened the Detroit theater's fall season, a reviewer reported the company was "exuberant," especially Tony. Everyone seemed happy to be back on stage. Audiences gave the company "a royal welcome."

A week at the Grand Opera House in Chicago brought out large crowds. The troupe was praised for its "high toned specialty entertainment" which was "perfectly clean and thoroughly enjoyable."[3] Weeklong visits to St. Louis, Cincinnati and Pittsburgh "pleased everybody." Noticeable in the reviews were comments about Tony's longevity in the business, as if marveling at his stamina. He was greeted as an "old-time favorite," said to have lost some of the "freshness" in his singing, but as a manager he remained "second to none."

Prior to their engagement in Philadelphia at the National Theater, Tony published one of his familiar ads boasting of the company's success.

> The ideal of fun. The mastodon of American vaudeville.
> Larger, greater, stronger than any other traveling entertainment in the new or the old world.[4]

The week was filled with packed houses. The *Press* reviewer called Tony "the perennial," and complimented him on his ability to arrange "good quality entertainment."

The tour ended with successful engagements in Baltimore and Brooklyn. All thoughts about Tony "having left something behind" had disappeared. Rather, audiences anticipated the new season at the 14th Street Theater featuring the traveling company. By the afternoon of October 24, seats were sold out and standing room sales were brisk. The evening was a typical season opener.

The theater sported new paint, red carpets, plush box-drapings (with Tony's initials on them) and a new drop curtain. Harry Sanderson and Tony were at the door greeting patrons. Floral arrangements already filled the lobby and the stage. The audience enthusiastically applauded every act and all performers gave encores. When Tony came on stage, he was cheered for several minutes before he began his budget of songs. He was also treated with six encores. The audience demanded a speech. Instead, Tony brought out the entire company who together took bows, waved to the audience and left the stage dancing and singing.

Tony again promised patrons that he would introduce new acts during the fall season and, this time, he fulfilled their expectations. P.C. Shorter presented banjo and violin solos. Juan Caicedo, in his first American appearance, offered a breath-taking high wire act. Hines and Remington, in their first New York engagement, were excellent eccentric dancers, one of the first male-female teams that excelled in ballroom dancing. Lillian Markham was a ballad singer whose diverse talents Tony employed in several skits. Harry La Rose, a juggler, was signed to return to entertain periodically throughout the season. Harry Thorne, the clown, shed his costume to appear in stock company skits for the season. All were decided hits. All returned often.

A coterie of familiar performers highlighted each week's program. They included Hilda Thomas, William Carroll, Lillie Western, Frank Moran, the St. Felix Sisters and Frank and Lillian White. Audiences never tired of these veterans, and Tony brought them back frequently. Rarely did other theater managers follow this strategy. It served as a trademark of loyalty between Tony, and his artists and patrons cheered each time one of the performers appeared. As usual,

Thanksgiving and Christmas programs were given at the Academy of Music. At matinees, photographs of the headliner of the week were given away. During the holiday season, ladies and girls received dolls.

Afterpieces were returned to weekly programs, many of them prepared by Harry Thorne. Another European import, singer and dancer Queen Vassar, performed her specialty with aplomb and also appeared regularly in the afterpieces. She attracted a great deal of audience attention, and she charmed fellow performer Harry Kernell as well. Since Harry was already married to Kitty O'Neil, strains in the relationship were about to arise. Vassar and Kernell later married.

During the winter and spring of 1886, Tony introduced a large number of novelty acts. When other vaudeville managers expressed reluctance to play them, because they demanded higher salaries for one week's work, Tony saw them as an advantage to diversify his bills. They included marionettes, a one-legged clog dancer, rope skippers, male and female weightlifters, acrobats, boxing teams, magicians, pigeon, dog and monkey acts, contortionists and, a new category of routines, imitators of celebrities. In a sense, Tony was repeating his programs of fifteen years ago. But these new patrons found the novelty acts as appealing as had earlier audiences.

Tony also concentrated on featuring women vocalists. Tony was said to have an eye for beauty, so they were all pretty, colorfully costumed and put across a song in provocative fashion. Queen Vassar led the singers for a month, her rendition of "Dancing with the Daisies in the Dell" a special audience favorite. She was followed by Evelyn Granville, a serio-comic soubrette; Flora Moore, one of the first in a long line of coon-shouters (the act had not yet been given that name); Maud Beverly, a ballad singer; Lulu Bryant, a comic singer who was quickly picked up to form a team; and the Gilmore Sisters, in neat Irish songs and dances.

Veteran Frank Girard had left to manage his own company. Stock company regulars were Maggie Willett, Harry Thorne, W.A. Melville, and Frank White. With the increasing number of team acts, short skits became a familiar routine and afterpieces were again dropped. In fact, the number of male-female teams, usually a combination of song, dance and comedy, was increasing and they were appearing at most of the vaudeville houses. At first, they were positioned as male acts with female accompaniment. In a short while, the women gained equal status due to their talent and audience appeal. A good male-female team had a variety of routines in their repertoire, making it easy for them to appear in several different New York houses in a season, or work in one theater for a number of weeks.

Tony's advertising had lost its uniqueness because so many other theater ads were appearing almost daily in newspapers. When newspapers created a column for theaters and their weekly programs, Tony was just another one in the list. The same was true for the theatrical weeklies as they jammed theater programs into a small section to accommodate large ads from traveling companies, performers, music publishers and product manufacturers. Along with a list of performers, Tony had only enough space for a sentence about their excellence and one saying "good reserved seats 50 cents." The era of hyperbolic ads was over, at least for the time being. Billboarding and programs were now the primary promotional pieces, along with press reviewers and critics, who now were becoming important players in the success or failure of a show. They were also flexing their powers regarding performers' careers.

Washington's Birthday was again celebrated at the Academy of Music. Along with the regular entertainment, the drum corps of the 71st regiment and the drum and flute corps of the Dalgren Post played martial music. John Martin, a dramatic actor, recited the Gettysburg Address. Tony sang several patriotic songs. The D.A.R. presented him with a gilded badge.

The spring program was filled with old favorites. Kitty O'Neil, Frank Moran, Lillie Western, Charles Fostelle, John T. Kelly and McIntyre and Heath appeared frequently on the bill.

The *Clipper* reported that Tony's theater was filled every week, often having to resort to standing room to accommodate patrons. Yet Sanderson's ledgers revealed that Tony was making only a minimal profit because of the significant increase in performer's salaries. In the current business climate, Tony could not lower his prices without losing money nor could he increase them and remain competitive. The summer tour again became his perfect vehicle for generating profit.

Competition was heating up. John Poole was about to open the Broadway Theater, featuring high-class vaudeville. The Comedy Theater, under new management, was about to reopen. Lew Dockstater was planning to open a vaudeville and minstrel house in September. The Bowery now had four vaudeville theaters, although of dubious reputation. In total, there were now nine vaudeville houses in New York, two in Brooklyn, and one each in Harlem and Williamsburg. Entrepreneurs were expanding their theater holdings. Jacobs and Proctor owned six theaters, two in the New York area; Harry Miner now held the leases to three theaters in New York; and Sam Harris managed theaters in five cities. When these managers signed performers, they promised appearances in each of their venues, a decided advantage over managers of single theaters. About that time, managers began to talk about combining forces to take advantage of vaudeville's increasing popularity, as well as the opportunity to obtain top acts with extended contracts. So far, no one could agree on the governing parameters.

In early April, Harry Sanderson was given his annual benefit in his eighth year as Tony's business manager. Many performers volunteered to appear and the program highlighted many of Tony's previous and recent discoveries.

Tony's annual summer tour opened April 12 at the 14th Street Theater, advertised as loyal patrons' first look at the traveling company. The house was filled with an enthusiastic audience. The *Clipper* called the company "about as strong as any the popular manager has ever sent out." However, except for a few familiar headliners, the members of the company were first-timers. It was a decision Tony was forced to make because of the salary costs for mounting a tour when there were five other vaudeville companies covering the same territory. Nellie Farrell, an English music hall star, was supposed to head the company. At the last moment, she had to cancel because of illness, depriving Tony of a European crowd-pleaser. To replace her, he signed Harry Morris, a Dutch comic.

The tour was divided into two parts, the first running to June 20, the second commencing August 2 and continuing to October 24. The six-week interval was called Tony's vacation. It was rumored that Tony was planning a trip to Europe to look for new acts, but the trip did not take place. Instead, Tony and his wife enjoyed some time at local resorts. In between, he visited other theaters and conducted business in his little office behind the stage. The initial part of the tour included visits to Brooklyn, Boston, towns in New Jersey and New York, and a long jump to Chicago the early part of June. The jump took fifteen hours by train from Buffalo to Chicago, said to be a record run.

Back home, the 14th Street Theater remained open for the summer under Sanderson's management. During the first few weeks, the theater hosted Harry Kernell and Company (John was ill and placed in a sanitarium), McIntyre and Heath, and the Dan Sully Company. Sully then rented the theater for the entire summer.

When the first part of the tour closed in Milwaukee, Tony was reported to be "well pleased with financial results." Sanderson declared that the "season has been much better than he himself had anticipated." At the time, there were only two other traveling companies on the road. Upon his return to New York, the *Clipper* observed that Tony "is looking extremely well as to indicate that his season on the road was a beneficial one, financially and physically."[5] Tony stated that his business was the best he had known for four years, but Sanderson's ledgers disputed that boast. Even his summer tour receipts were not as good as in previous years.

Part two of the tour began August 2 in Rochester, New York. From there, the company had engagements in Albany, Detroit, a repeat in Chicago, St. Louis, Baltimore, Washington, D.C., and Philadelphia. For early October, Tony arranged a week's engagement at the Grand Opera House, New York, a break in the usual pattern but advantageous in that the company played in the city at the same time other vaudeville theaters were opening their seasons. Tony also added several new acts imported from Europe to appear at that time.

The 1886-87 season featured a total of twenty-eight New York theaters, nine of which were presenting vaudeville. Brooklyn had eleven theaters, two of them vaudeville houses. Five of the New York vaudeville houses had been in business for some years and were managed by veteran people: Koster & Bial's; Harry Miner's three houses, the 8th Avenue Theater and Bowery Theater; the London Theater; and Tony's. One new theater, managed by Lew Dockstater, featured minstrels primarily and vaudeville only occasionally. Three new theaters promised to offer high-class vaudeville entertainment: Huber's Prospect Theater; the Globe Museum; and John Poole's Theater. According to critics, there were too many vaudeville theaters open and some fallout was anticipated. No one seemed to recognize the growing popularity of vaudeville at this time.

On October 24, the 14th Street Theater opened with the usual gala celebration. Unlike previous openings, the majority of the performers were not from the traveling company. Fisher and Lord began the program with dance eccentricities. Isabel Ward sang songs. George Murphy gave a Dutch act. Van Gofre and Ardell performed comic acrobatics. Hilda Thomas, Jolly Nash and Frank Bush were holdovers. Byrnes and Helene, with crayon drawings, were admired. Slebb and Tepp, from Vienna, pleased with high-wire antics. Regarding Tony, the *Clipper* reported:

> When Mr. Pastor's genial smile and expansive shirt front entered the stage, he received the usual tribute of cheers.[6]

Old friends and admirers gave him a royal welcome. Floral bouquets were handed him and he responded with a short speech. His songs went with his old-time zest.

The fall season featured a mixture of familiar faces and new acts, with a few imports from England. The Julians, John T. Kelly, Frank Bush, Hilda Thomas, Joe Hart and the Schrode Brothers were already proven performers. New acts were Capitola Forrest, a comic acrobat, the Mephisto Electric Orchestra, and the Harvey Brothers. A unique act, the Electric Orchestra had all of its players and instruments wired to display lights as they performed. Twenty-eight miles of wire, the program stated, gave a hundred novel effects of electricity. The Harvey Brothers, direct from the English music halls, offered a comic musical set. Others who dropped in periodically, as contracted with Tony, were Pat Rooney, Willett and Thorne, and Till's Marionettes.

Both Thanksgiving and Christmas shows were held at the Academy of Music to crowded houses. The holiday programs were again slanted toward family fare. They featured a dog circus, skip-rope dancers, an Irish comedian, acrobats and a school farce, "A Red Hot Stove," with the entire company.

One of the special events during the holidays was the first annual presentation of a benefit for the Roman Catholic Orphan's Home. Under the direction of Augustin Daly, the event was staged at the Metropolitan Opera House. Tony was among the performers asked to appear, and he sang some topical songs. Tony also donated money to the home, and was to do so for decades.

Eighteen eighty-seven began with a flourish of patron exuberance. Theaters were filled. Managers reported profits. Going to the theater had become the city's top leisure time activity. Amusement was being sought by all classes of people. Warnings about vaudeville theaters being too numerous had vanished. Instead, there were reports that more were in the planning stage. To demonstrate the burgeoning vaudeville business, it was reported that twenty-three travel-

In the later 1880s, Tony was known not only for his high-class vaudeville but also for his acts of philanthropy and charity. He never turned away the needy.

ing companies were crossing the country with great success. A few years before, only five dared to travel. The total number of performers had exploded as well, barely keeping up with the venues available. Newcomers who did well were hustled for engagements. Many of them, having received good reviews, advertised in the theatrical newspapers, not only stressing past successes but future dates. Tony's theater seemed to be the center of this activity. A good showing at the 14th Street Theater was invariably used in ads as an expression of success. The story repeated was that any performer who did well at Tony's theater was headed for a long career. It happened often enough to gain credibility. But this also meant that Tony lost performers after a few weeks and was forced to continually seek new ones. So competitive was the signing of acts that, throughout the season, Tony brought back familiar performers to fill bills. They had become a very important part of his program planning. He also began advertising good seats at twenty-five cents.

Dramatic theaters were prospering as well. They attracted the best actors and actresses in dramas that often ran for more than a hundred performances, a rarity until this time. Dramas starred such well-regarded performers as John Gilbert, Fanny Davenport, Robert Martell, Margaret Mather, Mrs. Langtry, Denman Thompson and Richard Mansfield. When Sarah Bernhardt announced her first appearance in America, scheduled for March, 10,000 tickets were sold. Tony had seriously considered parodying some of these dramatic plays. It was even reported that he had put one into production. In March, a news release said that Tony had abandoned the idea. The lack of a writer appeared to be the reason. But the costs for producing had risen so high that Tony chose to use his money on a high-class summer company.

In November of the previous year, Tony hosted a guest from London, William Riley, manager of the Royal Cambridge Music Hall. Riley had been responsible for sending Tony many English performers. Riley's advice was for Tony to come to Europe and see them for himself. Considering the current competitive climate for both performers and patrons, the idea had merit. Several English acts that Tony introduced in the spring convinced him to make the trip. The Three Phoites, an eccentric dance group, was a big hit. Tony immediately signed them for the summer company. Lizzie Hughes was a serio-comic vocalist. May Howard sang popular ballads. Harry Braham, an English music hall veteran, was an accomplished singer of character songs. Braham later supplied Tony with many comic songs that had originated in England.

During the spring, Tony again brought back his best artists to head the programs each week: Lillian Markham, Joe Hart, the Julians, Jolly Nash, Frank and Lillian White, Queen Vassar, Isabel Ward, Frank Bush, Jennie Yeamans and Harry Thorne. They appeared in their specialties and in skits. Tony increased his advertising presence once more, with an emphasis on admission prices. And in an uncharacteristic public display of personal opinion, Tony wrote Mayor Beekman, commending him on his move to close "immoral" concert halls. Was this a serious concern or image building?

For months, theater managers had discussed consolidation. Some of the managers owned or leased theaters in different cities. Some were single theater owners, like Tony, who held high positions in their respective locations. They did not view one another as competitors. At first, they discussed combining forces to lower their costs for printing and bill boarding. Discussion then came around to performers and the potential advantages managers might have by being able to offer artists up to sixteen weeks of work if they agreed to appear. Since these theaters were already featuring high-class vaudeville, why would any performers turn down the opportunity? This was the first time that theater managers formed an association to reduce production costs and develop a network offering performers long-term contracts.

The new combination was made up of William Harris, Boston; Harry Miner, New York; James Donaldson, New York; James Kernan, Baltimore and Washington, D.C.; H.W. Williams,

Pittsburgh; Thomas Grenier, Chicago; Fred Waldman, Newark; William Gilmore, Philadelphia; and managers in Paterson, Cincinnati, Providence, Buffalo and Louisville. Tony was among the Board of Managers of Vaudeville Theaters (B.M.V.T.).

Theaters were available for those managers that sponsored traveling companies during the regular season. For Tony, the arrangement was a boon. In a twenty-eight week tour, Tony would have access to at least fifteen weeks of solid engagement time. And since Tony visited a number of these cities twice during the summer, the vast majority of his engagements would be pre-booked. When he set up this year's summer tour, Tony would be appearing in all of his colleagues' theaters. Incidentally, they were all larger than Tony's theater, but none of them had the prestige or the reputation. Tony's performers also saw the arrangement as an opportunity for long-run assignments.

The company for the 1887 summer tour consisted of Harry and John Kernell (John had supposedly recovered from his illness); the Three Phoites; the Clipper Quartet; Joe Hart; the St. Felix Sisters; Adams, Casey and Howard, duets and trios on musical instruments; Topack and Steel, gymnasts and comedians; and William De Bar, contortionist. Because of the break in the tour, some of the performers were not returning for the second part. The 14th Street Theater was scheduled to be open the entire summer, catering to traveling companies visiting New York. One of these groups was Gus Hill's World of Novelties who, in their cast, featured a young team of Dutch comics, Weber & Fields.

On April 11, the company opened in Philadelphia to a full house. In Boston, "Tony Pastor's Company couldn't have opened to another dollar if they wanted. The Howard was packed thicker than any New York 4th ward primary ever dared to be."[7] Newark attracted "crowded houses." The St. Felix Sisters left for England. Tony hired Frank Dumont, the minstrel veteran, to write a skit; it was titled "Two Fine Ducks" and was a welcome addition to the bill.

Toronto and Buffalo attracted large audiences. Detroit had "top heavy houses." The Three Phoites returned to England and the Julians joined the company. Chicago was the final stop for part one of the tour. As always, enthusiastic audiences in Chicago welcomed Tony back. The Kernell Brothers left for an engagement in Cincinnati. The Pastor troupe returned to New York where Tony and his wife prepared for their first trip on a boat bound for London and Paris. Joining them was M.B. Leavitt, also on a booking trip. Leavitt's account of Tony's first voyage was humorous but questionable. He claimed that Tony was so afraid of the water, he stayed in his cabin the entire trip. The story is unverified. Tony later declared that the voyage had been a wonderful experience and he would do it again next year.

While Tony was preparing for the trip, his mother became ill. At age seventy-six, she retained a clear mind but had been suffering from a variety of physical ailments. Tony decided to sail for Europe, confident that Cornelia was well cared for.

On June 18, Tony and Josephine sailed for Liverpool. The *Times* reported that they received a "large display of affection in the form of flowers for the occasion."[8] They included floral bouquets on their dining room table and in their cabin. On June 25, Tony and his wife arrived in London and he immediately began visits to music halls, seeking possible performers for his theater.

Cornelia Pastor died Sunday, July 10, at 246 East 40th Street. The doctor's report indicated that she died of a stroke and ensuing paralysis. News of her death was cabled to Tony. He was unable to leave England until July 23. Cornelia's remains were temporarily placed in a vault in Evergreens Cemetery, awaiting Tony's return. It appeared that Tony's two sisters deferred to him the responsibility for preparing a funeral and burial.

Tony arrived in New York July 31. Cornelia's funeral took place August 3 at the cemetery. Close friends and relatives attended as well as a number of theatrical professionals. The ceremony, led by a local priest, was simple and Cornelia was placed in the Pastor plot, joining her three sons.

Two weeks later, Cornelia's will was filed for probate. Tony received the house and lot at 521 Broom and his sister, Caroline, the house at 246 East 40th Street. Delores, the oldest sibling, was given $1,500 from the proceeds of the house at 443 West 77th Street, the residue divided between Tony and Caroline. The remainder of the estate was divided among the three children after paying $2,500 to Henry Pastor, Billy's son, and $1,000 to Adele Pastor, Frank's wife. Tony and Caroline were the executors of the estate.

Cornelia had fared poorly during her marriage to Antony, although it had begun with promise. After Antony disappeared, she was forced to operate a saloon for almost ten years. When Tony became a successful performer and theater manager, he bought property for her and supplied her with sufficient funds to live comfortably.

When asked about his plans, Tony stated that the second part of the summer tour would begin August 15 in Saratoga with an almost entirely new company. He planned to return to New York for an October 24 opening of his theater. He also mentioned his enthusiasm over the new people he had engaged in Europe, believing they would "make a sensation" in America. There was no mention of his mother's death. The will would have been kept private except that the probate court was required by law to publish the information.

The revived company featured Harry and John Kernell and the Julians, both holdovers. Joining them, were the Donnells, dancers and comedians from England; Harry La Rose, acrobat, also from England; the Sisters Coulson, dancers; Rice and Barton, blackface comedians; Alfred Clive and his acrobatic dog; the Brantfords, imitators and vocalists; and Little Tich (Harry Relph), the eccentric comic already a hit in Europe. In an ad about the new company, Tony boasted about his American and European stars. The *Clipper* reported that Tony and his wife "had a fine vacation, and another journey to the other side is among the possibilities for the future."[9] The comments seemed incongruous considering recent events.

Engagements were confined to towns in New York, New Jersey and Pennsylvania. Results were reported to be successful, but with seven other traveling companies appearing in the same cities, there were no sellouts. John T. Kelly joined in Pittsburgh. The Kernells left in September. Tony seemed happy to be back in New York after a so-so tour. Sanderson, however, called the tour "prosperous."

Tony opened the 14th Street Theater on October 24, to a packed house of loyal admirers. The traveling company was on hand for the first week. There were now thirty-one theaters in New York, ten of them labeled vaudeville houses. Seven of them had been in business for more than one year: People's Theater, London Theater, Poole's Theater (second year), Miner's Bowery Theater and 8th Avenue Theater, Koster & Bial's and Eden Musee. New vaudeville theaters included the Alexander Musee, Harlem Pavilion and Dockstater's Theater. Those located in the Bowery had questionable futures, not only due to the class of neighborhood clientele but because of recent actions by the city to close them. The Musees combined freaks and oddities with specialty acts. Dockstater's promised minstrels but gave vaudeville when minstrelsy was unavailable. They all offered comparable price and were housed in respectable buildings. However, they were unequal when their entertainment was examined. Only six of the houses could rightly claim to offer high-class acts. The remainder were secondary venues, later to be given the derogatory name of ten-cent vaudeville by patrons.

Next to Tony, Little Tich was the star of the evening.

> There was no question as to his success. His make-up alone was sufficient to set the people in a roar but when he danced with shoes almost as long as he is high, the audience went wild with delight. He is the greatest little man the vaudevilles have had in many a day.[10]

The fall season included a few regulars, some interesting newcomers and visitations by various traveling companies. New people came from Europe, the result of Tony's recruitment trip. Herr Pitrot, a character impersonator, was well received. He later went on to become one of the most sought after impersonators in vaudeville. Amy Boyden, a soubrette, sang pleasing songs, but her accent was hard to understand. A local couple, Fred Huber and Kitty Allyn, did sketches and their comedy presentations were audience pleasers. The couple was soon viewed as one of the best and most popular sketch teams on stage. In the next few years, sketch teams would be found on most programs, the act becoming an attractive addition to the usual bill.

One of vaudeville's most renowned Irish comedians, John T. Kelly gained fame appearing repeatedly at Tony's theater for more than a decade. He later became a star in Weberfieldsian travesties and burlesques (Harry Ransom Humanities Research Center).

For the holiday programs, Tony advertised reserved seats for twenty-five cents. A family bill filled the theater at each performance. Dolls were again given away to ladies and girls. As usual, Tony sang Christmas carols and had the audience join in, making the entire experience a festive one.

All questions about Tony's future were set aside when it was announced that he had renewed the lease on the 14th Street Theater for ten years, at an annual rental of $11,500. Tony predicted that he would celebrate his 35th anniversary in 1900 at this theater, a boast that few took seriously.

The winter and spring of 1888 was similar to previous periods. Tony featured new performers and returned familiar headliners. Artists from Europe were included in the lineup. But unlike the previous year, most of the performers were novelty acts, from high wire to contortionists to trained monkeys. None of them remained more than a week, and audience attendance lagged. In contrast, song and dance teams and comedians excited audiences. When Tony selected the summer traveling company, he stocked it with English performers, but made sure they were comedians first and dancers or singers second.

Spring programs appeared to be experimental in nature. In February, Tony devoted an entire week to minstrels, highlighting blackface veterans Dave Foy, Billy Birch, Frank Moran and E.N. Slocum performing their storied routines. Minstrelsy was no longer the top amusement, and the number of minstrel theaters and companies had declined in recent years, but audiences still enjoyed the songs, dances and jokes given by a blackface minstrel troupe.

The return of Maggie Cline was a noteworthy event. She and Tony appeared on the stage as old friends, obliterating whatever might have happened between them previously. Maggie was given standing ovations. Upon the conclusion of her act, she and Tony hugged and the crowds cheered their reconciliation.

When some of the novelty acts failed to gain patron approval, Tony brought in several traveling companies to play weeklong engagements. Kernell's Company, the Howard Athenaeum Company and Dan Sully and Company featured familiar stars, many of whom had appeared at Pastors before, and drew large crowds.

The constant fear of theater fires, always an undercurrent in people's minds, were reinforced once more when, on February 28, the Union Square Theater burned to the ground. Close to the 14th Street Theater, it served as a reminder to Tony of the dangers inherent in such cataclysms. No one was hurt because the fire occurred in the early morning. But attendance at surrounding theaters were reduced for a few weeks. Owners of the Union Square promised to rebuild the theater and incorporate all of the newest in fire safety equipment. But because of the actual cost of reconstruction, the promise was not entirely realized.

Tony's twenty-third anniversary as a manager and Harry Sanderson's benefit were going to be celebrated together on March 22. Many performers volunteered to appear and the speaking program resembled that of a political convention. Actually, Tammany Hall was the sponsor of the Democratic Convention in September and candidates were out in full force, taking advantage of every public opportunity. Since his anti-war position during the Civil War, Tony had become an active supporter of the Democratic Party and the candidacy of William Jennings Bryan. (Bryan lost to Grover Cleveland.)

Tony also participated in annual benefits given by the Roman Catholic Church, especially those devoted to children. Each spring, the orphan asylum ran a benefit and Tony not only appeared on stage but also gave large donations as well. In the fall, a benefit for the children's hospital was another occasion for Tony's benevolence. According to friends, Tony was a serious Catholic. He had a cross hanging in his office and was said to have installed a small shrine backstage. A poor box had been installed in the lobby of each of his theaters. It was also reported that Tony had placed a sign backstage warning people not to take the name of the Lord in vain. Some historians credit Tony's religiosity to his business practices, his care of performers and his charity and generosity to people in need. An equally likely reason could be his family's poverty and his own early years as a performer.

Tony did not use profanity himself, at least not in public. It was reported that the worst expletive he ever used was "Geminetty" and sometimes "so help me Bob." But when people heard these words used, they knew Tony was very angry and stayed out of his way.

A "crowded to the rafters" audience greeted Tony and Harry Sanderson on March 22. More than fifty performers gave a few minutes of their specialties to honor the popular theater impresarios. Floral tributes covered the stage and lobby. Local dignitaries praised the recipient's efforts. Entering the stage in his dress tuxedo, Tony popped his top hat, bowed to the wildly cheering audience, and quieted them long enough to give a short speech, thanking them for their loyalty and appreciation. After six encores and a hoarse throat, applause and cheers went on for another five minutes. The press claimed that Tony was at the acme of his career and was one of the most popular and respected men in the theatrical business. Some declared that Tony had "made the business."

The annual summer tour began in Philadelphia April 2. Except for the eccentric comic, Little Tich, the rest of the company was new, five of them appearing in America for the first time. The roster included Annie Oakley, in her first appearance in vaudeville after some years as a sharpshooter in Buffalo Bill's show; the Two Armstrongs, knockabout comedians; Beane and Gilday, comedy sketch artists; Revene and Athos, grotesque vaulters; the Sisters St. Albert, dancers and actresses; the Donnells, duet singers and dancers; Farrell and Willmont, Irish dancing comedians; the Musical Lindsays, instrumentalists and acrobats; and Max Pettingill, blackface with his acting dog. It was a decided risk by Tony to introduce new people, knowing audiences were expecting old favorites. And Tony had already planned to break up the tour to return to Europe and sign up more performers.

The company did well in larger cities. When they visited the smaller towns in New England, they received good reviews but attracted only fair audiences. On June 2, the tour stopped in Buffalo and the company returned to New York.

During the early morning of June 6, a fire at Tammany Hall completely gutted Tony's theater. Tony was on hand to sift through the ruins. Newspaper headlines asked, Would he rebuild? Would he continue in theater management? Or would the venerable performer and theater manager retire?

Apparently, the fire had only slightly interfered with their arrangements. Mr. and Mrs. Tony Pastor sailed on June 9 for a ten week tour of England and the Continent.

The theatrical world was astonished at Tony's apparent disregard for his theater, his "livelihood" as they called it.

11

"The Most Popular Theater in Town"

A day after the fire, Tony and Harry Sanderson surveyed the damage to the theater. They found the auditorium was completely destroyed, seats scorched, rugs reduced to ashes, walls burned to the base boards, the ceiling covered with soot. The stage fared no better. The wings and flies crumbled at the touch, curtains and scenery were reduced to cinders, and the proscenium was devoid of paint.

Tony's office behind the stage had suffered only slight damage. His old desk was scarred but refinishable, as were the chairs and shelves. Sadly, most of the old programs, some dating back to his days at the circus and at 444 Broadway, were incinerated. Only a few of the photos could be salvaged. The safe, housing the ledgers and all of Tony's music and lyrics, stood strong, only its surface removed of paint.

The dressing rooms, which had been filled with costumes, props and makeup, were totally burned out. The only part of the theater that was relatively untouched by the blaze was the lobby. The fire had been put under control by the fire department before the flames entered the lobby. Estimates of the loss from the fire and water would reach $50,000.

That same day, Tony notified an architect and builder to meet with him to discuss rebuilding the theater "as quickly as possible." Tony wanted the theater to be completed by the time he was ready to open the fall season, the middle of October. No theater had ever been rebuilt that quickly. The press believed the task could not be concluded in the time Tony allotted, and suggested that Tony consider buying a new theater. There were some available in prime sites, and at much less cost. Tony responded that his theater served a class clientele and he did not wish to disappoint his loyal patrons.

In reality, the theater had been leased from Tammany Hall, so Tony lost nothing on the building itself. The Tammany Society valued its property at $350,000. It was insured by thirty-two companies for $100,000. The actual loss was evaluated at $30,000 to $40,000, paid for by the insurance companies. Tony actually lost only $5,000 due to the fire. Money was available to begin repair on the theater almost immediately.

Another reason for a fast recovery was political. On July 4, 1888, Tammany Hall would play host to the Democratic National Convention. All outward signs of the fire were to be removed by that date. Leaving the rebuilding in the hands of Sanderson, the architect and builder, Tony felt free to sail on June 9, bound for England and Ireland. Sanderson would keep him informed of progress almost daily. Tony planned to be back in New York early August to launch an abbreviated summer tour. He had plenty of time to design the new theater as he wished.

Tony's trip across the Atlantic on the Cunard steamship *Etruria* was uneventful. Among the passengers accompanying Mr. and Mrs. Pastor were the Bradfords, Bells and Goulds of New York society, Joseph Pulitzer, and several members of the British Parliament. As soon as Tony arrived in London that he and "Pony" Moore, owner of music halls in several British cities, began to visit theaters in London. Within a few days, Tony signed Bibb and Bobb, musical clowns; Tom Costello, an Irish comedian; and Tom Barrett, a singer of considerable popularity. Tony and his wife were also guests of theater managers and patrons.

The social highlight of the trip was music hall star Peggy Pryde's 21st birthday party and the christening of his baby boy. Tony stood as godfather to the child. Tony and his wife were also invited to Jenny Hill's farm for a party. Hill was one of the music hall's brightest singers, and Tony was attempting to sign her. He presented her with a silver server and an offer to appear at his theater. She demurred, being already booked for the next two years.

Tony signed more than ten acts while in England. Along with his friend, M.B. Leavitt, Tony was the most active manager in New York using foreign entertainers. It would be several years before rival managers realized the appeal and drawing power of foreign artists. When they did, the race for talent became a highly competitive exercise, to the point where English music hall managers complained that America took their best performers away from local audiences and affected their box office receipts.

The Pastors left Liverpool on July 23 on the *Etruria*, arriving in New York July 30, a very fast voyage of six days and a few hours. Since several artists were on board, they gave an impromptu evening of entertainment and Tony sang a few songs.

Before beginning the short summer tour, Tony examined his theater's reconstruction. He found the theater near completion, When finished, it would "rank among the finest vaudeville in the city," according to the *Clipper*. "It would be thoroughly fireproof, decorated and finished in the highest style," they continued.[1] Automatic sprinklers were installed, the first time these were used in a New York theater.

All lighting in front of the theater and in the lobby, auditorium and backstage was by electricity. Boilers for heating were placed in a vault under the sidewalk. The retaining beams were made of iron and the floors were covered with marble. Tony added boxes, orchestra seats and especially wide seats "for portly people." In effect, by adding boxes, he reduced the number of seats from 1,100 to 948. He believed that the higher admission prices for the boxes and orchestra seats would offset the smaller audience capacity. The strategy worked for almost five years. All the seats were made of cherry wood and upholstered with blue plush. Walls were hung with velvet and lace, and the auditorium floor carpeted with India rugs. "A handsome theater," remarked the press.

The short summer tour began August 5 in Long Branch, New Jersey, a town which was fast becoming a venue to launch new shows. Visits to towns in New Jersey and Connecticut culminated in a gala week late in August in Boston. Tony's company opened the fall season of the Howard Athenaeum. Full houses persuaded the *Globe* reviewer to say that "Tony and his capital coterie carted off heaps of coin."[2] With successive stops in Rochester, Buffalo and Cleveland, the company opened each city's fall seasons "turning people away every night." The remainder of the tour included playing at theaters in Pittsburgh, Philadelphia, Washington, D.C., and Baltimore. Business on the tour was said to be so successful that Tony's profits more than paid off any losses he incurred due to the fire.

The opening of the new 14th Street Theater on October 22 was a festive event. Tickets went on sale a week earlier and were sold out in a matter of hours. In front of the theater, patrons waited in long lines for the box office to open to sell standing room. "A fairy palace," one reviewer called the theater, and patrons agreed.

The big posters in front of the theater shouted, "Mr. Pastor and his own company of European and American artists." Six of the performers had come from Europe but would play only two weeks before returning to England. Nevertheless, Tony had other replacements for them. Also on the bill were the familiar favorites Harry La Rose, Ella Wesner, Lester and Allen and Ryan and Richfield. Prior to the English performers ending their engagements, Tony gave them a luncheon party and presented each of them with a turquoise ring. The *Clipper* reviewer noted that "it was a graceful compliment from one of our most popular managers."[3] What other manager treated his artists so well? they mused. No wonder Tony held a monopoly on introducing new foreign acts as well as local newcomers.

The successes of the fall season added to the prosperity of the Pastor organization. Tony was involved in every theater-related activity—a promoter of programs, a donor to charitable groups, and a mentor to his artists. He arrived at his office each morning at 9:30, accompanied by one of his dogs, cheerful little animals that befriended everyone who came through the office door. A superstition arose that if the dog licked the hand of a new performer, that performer would be a hit.

First of all, Tony looked over his program and selected the various songs and skits submitted by the performers as well as his own repertoire. He made sure that advertising was in place, paying particular attention to correct spelling of the artists' names. He then went on stage to observe rehearsals and was not hesitant to make suggestions to artists. He stood at the back of the auditorium and in the gallery to make sure that the orchestra did not overwhelm the singers and that every word was heard. Back in his office, he wrote new lyrics for his songs or poetry to be included in his monologues.

Lighting had to be adjusted for each performer, and Tony supervised the backstage crew. After a brief lunch, he and Harry Sanderson met to select artists for future dates. Sanderson kept a list of every performer who had played for Tony and the results of their performances. They chose mixtures that would complement one another and score well with audiences. They placed new artists in advantageous positions on the bill depending on their act. They often called on already proven artists to heighten a bill's excitement.

Tony and Sanderson examined the ledgers and decided what monies were to be spent, paying particular attention to salaries. During the past few years, salaries had escalated with the growing public interest in vaudeville and its stars. Salaries ranged from $40 a week for a newcomer to $120 a week for people like John T. Kelly and Frank Bush. When Maggie Cline first appeared for Tony, she earned $25 a week. Now, she commanded $100 a week. Salaries would continue to rise in coming years.

A few season's earlier, Tony had stopped introducing each act. Instead of personal and boastful introductions, there were musical preambles for each act, along with heavy billboarding and colorful programs describing each performer's routines. On those days that featured a matinee and evening program, Tony remained at the theater, reviewing acts, discussing changes in skits, or assisting performers with their acts. Tony had food brought in, primarily for orchestra members, but often for the entire cast if a matinee ran longer than usual because of numerous encores. Payday was Saturday evening after the show. Tony personally gave out the pay envelopes, usually with a few complimentary words. The most important compliment for a new act was an offer to return.

In November, Tony performed at the annual benefit for the Catholic Orphan Asylum and at the Actor's Fund benefit. When other managers raised the issue about foreign performers taking the place of Americans, Tony came out strongly in favor of foreign appearances in New

York theaters. Why not be open to any good artists, he declared. Did dramatic theater and opera forbid actors and actresses from another country? Tony felt that vaudeville should not be so chauvinistic. Entertainment is universal, Tony said, and performers come from all classes of people. The issue died when other managers reluctantly agreed to book acts from outside the country. In a few years, the issue would reverse itself. Many American performers would travel to Europe and local managers would bewail their revenue loss.

Thanks to a committee of women, headed by Josephine Pastor, Mrs. Fernandez and veteran stage actress "Aunt" Louisa Eldredge, a Christmas party for children of the theater, that is, children who perform in theater, was planned for December 30. The program would consist of a matinee at which the children would perform their specialties. The show took place at the 14th Street Theater with Tony as host. After the performance, a dinner was given for the children and their parents and gifts were distributed to them while they all sat around a large Christmas tree. The event was a unique way to honor these children.

The force behind the celebration was Louisa Eldredge. An outstanding actress for forty years, widowed, with two children, she devoted much of her time to supporting children's organizations. She was a leading member of the Professional Women's League (and its president for a decade), the Actor's Church Alliance and Rainy Day Club (assisting destitute widows with children.)

At this time, children under sixteen were not allowed to perform on vaudeville stages in New York. To honor those youngsters who were forced to play elsewhere while vying for a stage career, the committee planned a special day to help inspire them to continue their careers and expose their talents to agents. Tony was in full support of the committee's goals. He underwrote this first of annual events and appeared as a "father" to all of them. More than thirty children participated, a few of them destined to become vaudeville stars, like Irene Franklin, the Clifton Sisters, and the Widmark Brothers, who later gave up performing to become one of the leading popular music publishers during vaudeville's heyday. The unique event was a great success and received good coverage from the press and theatrical weeklies.

The spring season of 1889 brought much improved business over the previous year. Thanks to a run of headliners and loyal patrons, Tony's theater was packed to standing room each week. The fact that the theater was always crowded was not overlooked by reviewers. References to the new theater as "cozy," "little," and "close" due to the reduced seating actually promoted Tony's philosophy of intimacy between performer and patron.

Three traveling companies, two of them with familiar stars like Harry Kernell, Billy Birch and Frank Moran, occupied most of February. Very few new people were introduced. Instead, Tony relied on the drawing power of his perennial headliners. Maggie Cline appeared four times; Edwin French, Lillie Western and Lester and Allen three times; and Harry La Rose, the Inman Sisters, the Julians and Harry Kennedy twice. Even popular novelty acts had multiple appearances; Max Pettingill and his canines played three times and Prof. Abt, purveyor of art pictures, twice. The results of this billing strategy could not have been better. The *Sunday Dispatch* summed up Tony's success in very complimentary terms.

> Tony Pastor is rightly the Dean of the Variety Stage. He has done more to preserve the good repute of that branch of amusement than any other living man.[4]

The *Times* declared that "time and age" had in no way affected Tony's unique performances.

> Time seems to be unable to make any impression on either the spirits or the popularity of Tony Pastor. He was received last night with the most rapturous applause, and he sang three new songs with such energy, vocally and physically, that the audience encored him again and again, and was

then loath to let him go. Mr. Pastor was so appreciative of these manifestations of favor that he indulged in several graceful dancing steps to the surprise and intense delight of the people in the auditorium.[5]

It was not surprising then, that when Tony announced the cast of his summer tour, the names were familiar: John Kernell, the Julians, Lillie Western, the Inman Sisters and Prof. Abt. Several additional dancing, singing and comedy teams were also included, all of them newcomers to the summer company. This year's tour began in Brooklyn, at Hyde & Behman's Theater, then moved to Philadelphia, Boston, through Massachusetts and New York, Toronto and Cleveland with a closing in Detroit. It was a familiar route to familiar theaters and accustomed audiences. The first part of the tour was more profitable than the previous year at home had been, netting more than $6,000.

The Pastors left for Europe on June 11 for a ten-week tour of England and the Continent. Already in negotiations with headliners he had courted last year, Tony was ready to finalize some important engagements. The people he planned to introduce to American audiences during the coming season would place vaudeville in the top echelon of popular entertainment.

On July 31, Tony returned from Liverpool. On August 5, the traveling company reopened their tour at Long Branch, New Jersey. Several newcomers had been added to the company, all as a result of Tony's visit to England. Lizzie Collins, a serio-comic singer, the Sisters Graham, dancers, Millie Hylton, and Revene and Athos all agreed to perform for the entire tour. However, the biggest news that Tony revealed to the press was the signing of Bessie Bonehill, a leading star of English music halls. Knowledge of her fame had already reached America and managers had been vying for her attention. Tony captured her and he planned to make Bessie the star vaudeville attraction in New York.

The second part of the tour duplicated the cities visited with the same successful results. Theaters were crowded and receipts were profitable. Tony's idea of helping to open the fall season at many of his August and September engagements complemented the pocketbooks of both the theater manager and the company. Audiences jammed the theaters to help inaugurate the new season, made even more exciting by seeing the Pastor troupe.

On October 21, the 14th Street Theater opened. All other theaters in New York had been playing for almost two months. No matter. Seats were sold out in advance and the buzz of the town was Tony's American introduction of Bessie Bonehill. She did not disappoint.

Entering the stage for her first appearance in America, Bessie was greeted with a standing ovation. With a soft, sympathetic voice, an attractive personality and a magnetism that quickly captured her audience, she began to sing. She was frequently interrupted in the middle of a song. He first two songs were done in full evening male attire, her third in a newsboy suit and her fourth dressed as a naval attaché. Her expressive face and lithe form were in accord with the song lyrics. Audiences quickly discovered that she was a singer, an actress and a dancer. At the conclusion of her set, audiences were on their feet applauding for a full five minutes. Floral greetings were numerous and lavish. The best news followed when Tony announced that Bessie would play at the theater for six weeks.

The remainder of the cast, including such stalwarts as Frank Bush, Frank and Lillian White, Lillie Western and fellow English imports Millie Hylton and Jennie Williams, were welcomed but by already exhausted patrons. Unnoticed on the bill was Susie Russell, Lillian's younger sister, making her debut in vaudeville.

It made little difference who was on the bill with Bessie. She had become the "talk of the town." SRO signs were posted at every performance. "London's Idol" was now "New York's Idol." To highlight her appearances, Tony revealed that Bessie would again appear at his 14th Street Theater next year. He also mentioned that another great English star would come to

Tony brought Bessie Bonehill from the English music halls to star at his theater. She filled the theater at every performance. Her vast repertoire of character songs and magnetic personality captivated audiences (Harvard Theater Collection).

America after the first of the year to entertain the theater's audiences.

During the last week of Bessie's engagement, the *Clipper* described her outstanding success.

> She once more captured the house and her cleverness was never more brilliantly seen and appreciated. She has made the most substantial and deserving success of years in our vaudevilles, and she easily could remain many months more with the same gratifying results. The audience demanded five numbers from her at every performance and still want more.[6]

On the last night of her appearance, Bessie was given a testimonial. She began by singing a new song by Arthur West entitled "How I Like America." She responded to innumerable calls for encores and finished with a speech of thanks to her friends, the press, the public and the profession. She also thanked Tony "for untold kindnesses as a manager and as a friend." Floral offerings came from Mrs. Pastor, Tony and Harry Sanderson, Jennie Yeamans, Mrs. Frank Bush, a box of handkerchiefs from Mrs. Harry Kernell, exotic bouquets from Ross and Fenton, Maggie Cline and many others. Sanderson, on behalf of Tony, gave Bessie a medal adorned with diamonds, bearing the inscription, "A souvenir of esteem to Bessie Bonehill, presented in testimony to her worth as an artist, a lady and an ornament to her profession, from Tony Pastor." She received the medal and pinned it to her dress, tears of thanks in her voice. A case of champagne mysteriously appeared and toasts were drunk all around. "Auld Lang Syne" closed the festivities, everyone clasping hands and singing.

One other event of interest closed out the year. On December 29, at Tony's theater and under his direction, the second annual festival for children of the stage was given. A committee of women, led by "Aunt" Louisa Eldredge, Josephine Pastor and others had planned the event, for weeks collecting toys, candies and money for the little performers. After the performance, the children were given a Christmas dinner and gifts. Included in the long list of child entertainers were the Widmark Brothers, the Clifton Sisters, Evie Evans (Charles "Honey Boy" Evans' daughter), Annie Bishop, and little Irene Franklin.

The years leading up to 1890 had seen an explosion of multiethnic popular culture, the commercialization of entertainment as a business enterprise and the emergence of competitive amusement forms.

The new immigration to America featured Jews, Germans and Italians in large numbers. Like their forebears, they began their habitation in the Bowery. The Bowery, situated at the low end of Broadway, was filled with mixed ethnic neighborhoods and cheap amusements. Melodrama and variety appealed to the newcomers. Venues like the London Theater, Miner's Bowery Theater and the Globe Museum featured a potpourri of ethnic comedy and novelty acts at cheap prices, their audiences responding with enthusiasm at the "down-to-earth" presentations. Yiddish and Italian theater were born here. It was also the training ground for performers-to-be.

Show business, as the phenomenon was now being called, was big business, involving bankers, investors, speculators and politicians. They backed theaters, managers and traveling companies. They supported headliners and publicists. Some already owned or leased strings of theaters in different cities and gave long-term contracts to top artists.

Union Square was the center of the theater industry, home of the best in vaudeville and popular music. Surrounding neighborhoods housed producers, writers, actors, backstage people and others connected to the profession. Commercial businesses that supported the industry were close by. Chief among the contributors to the area's dominance as a theatrical center was Tony Pastor. In spite of the immense competition, Tony was still its impressive leader. But, while he was a great influence in the city, he expressed little ambition beyond his own theater. The ruling clan of entrepreneurs was still in their infancy, not yet ready to industrialize the business. They would be arriving in a few short years.

Coney Island had become one of the world's most famous beaches, full of cheap entertainment for everyone. The city's moral arbiters named it "Sodom by the Sea." On any given day, the beaches and amusements were filled with a diverse cross section of New York's population. It was the only place in the metropolis where such a marvel occurred.

Resorts like Brighton and Manhattan Beach catered to better classes of people, with race tracks, gambling, large hotels and fine restaurants. They represented a constellation of amusement that favored the cultural elite.

Eighteen ninety was also a banner year for theater, both legitimate and popular. Theaters were filled; profitability was widespread. Competition among managers was fierce as they attempted to attract the best and most popular performers. The cost of producing shows was increasing due, primarily, to the escalation in artists' salaries. Yet admission prices remained the same, managers afraid that by raising prices they would lose patrons. Still, business could not continue in such an environment. Some things had to change.

Tony began the 1890 winter and spring season by introducing Jennie Valmore, an English music hall performer similar to Bessie Bonehill. Valmore was best known for her character changes, costumes, style and song selection, and scored a hit with patrons. But, unlike Bonehill, Valmore appeared for only three weeks and returned to England. No testimonials, no medals, no floral bouquets; she just left the country.

Instead, Tony depended on familiar performers who were already audience favorites as he had done innumerable times before. Maggie Cline, the Whites, the Julians, Ad Ryman, Prof. Abt and Lester and Allen appeared on bills several times during the spring. Flora Moore, Frank Bush, the Russell Brothers, James F. Hoey, Lottie Gilson, Lillie Western and Jennie Yeamans each had their special week. Birch and Moran did a minstrel engagement. The Harry Williams Company, a traveling troupe, played a week in early March.

When Tony talked about the prosperous season he was enjoying, the *Clipper* repeated his comments and praised him for his management style.

> This has been a great season for popular Tony Pastor, and his cozy theater has held fine audiences since the opening. This is as it should be, for the management never catered more popularly than has been the case this year. Nothing is too expensive to give manager Pastor's loyal and large clientele, and the result has been as stated above.[7]

The compliment was followed by an ad from the Pastor organization about Tony's 25th celebration as a theater manager, to take place March 21.

"It should be a gala occasion," the ad stated, "and one of magnificent proportions, to do full justice to Tony Pastor's popularity as manager and caterer to the best of public patronage." Indeed, it was to be a milestone in Tony's life, likely the apex of his career.

For the event, Tony wrote a poem that was published in the theatrical newspapers and also appeared in the program for the event. It was Tony's way of thanking his public.[8]

Tony called Lottie Gilson "The Little Magnet" because she was a guaranteed draw at his theater. Her renditions of comic ballads and tearjerkers made her one of the most popular soubrettes in vaudeville.

"A Welcome!"
Twenty five years ago your bright
And cheering smiles greeted my sight;
A hearty welcome, true, sincere,
To all my friends assembled here!
'Tis pleasant to look back once more
Along the road we've traveled o'er;
So please indulge a passing rhyme,
From me about the olden time,
When first as Manager I sought
To please the Public.

Time has wrought
Full many a change in those few years;
The world a different world appears.
Changes have come to State and Stage;
New fangled notions are the rage.
Then, our own Mary Anderson
Her road to Fame had not begun.
The Actress of Society
Was something then we did not see.
Baseball was not the People's craze;
And men did not the Ante raise
At Poker, as they do now days.

The ladies, bless them! Didn't care
To flaunt the huge hats now they wear;
Chicago hadn't got the fair;
In spite of what Chauncey Depew
And other Yorkers tried to do!
In those days, people would have sat
Upon our great and only Platt!
'Tis pleasant now, to give a line,
In memory of "Auld Lang Syne!"
The pleasure of my life has been
Ever your kind applause to win.
In future years, as in the past,

> Still may our genial friendship last,
> Success to attend you everywhere!
> And I in my heart I still shall bear
> Your smiles, striving to more deserve
> The praise of those whom here I serve!
> That good fortune may keep you, thro' life, from disaster,
> Is the heartiest wish of your friend,
>
> Tony Pastor!

Besides the souvenir program, every member of the audience was given a medal bearing on its face a likeness of Tony inscribed, "March 22, 1865, Tony Pastor, March 21, 1890." The reverse side bore the words, "Presented by Tony Pastor, as a souvenir of remembrance, and in commemoration of the completion of his 25th year of management in New York City."

A.H. Hummel, a lawyer well known to the theatrical community for his high profile celebrity divorce cases (and Tony's legal consultant), presented Tony with a gold medal inset with ten large blue-white diamonds, upon which was inscribed, "To Tony Pastor, from his brother managers on the completion of his twenty-fifth year as a manager, March 20, 1890." The medal was given by Messrs. Williams, Stetson, Harris and Gilmore, all members of their theater combination. Tributes came from Rudolph Aronson, Augustin Daly, James Donaldson, T.H. French, Daniel Frohman, Harry Miner, Proctor and Turner and other managers. Words of esteem and thanks came from such familiar headliners as Evans and Hoey, Harry Kernell, Denman Thompson and Gus Williams. Floral offerings were sent by Edward Harrigan, Ad Ryman, the Julians and others. Telegraphic congratulations were received from across the country and Europe. The performers and the audience, sang "Auld Lang Syne" to end the program.

After the evening performance, Tony was taken to the Four A's Club to receive his friends, the reception being tendered to him as well as his colleagues and invited guests. A large portrait of "Our Own Tony," decorated with club flags, was hung at the front of the large parlor. The tables were set with silver and floral decorations and the banquet "reflected great credit on the club's coterie."

Following the dinner, Chairman Charles W. Thomas called upon members of the profession to offer toasts, highlighted by de Wolf Hopper's zany impersonation of Tony. When Tony rose to speak, his voice choked several times as he thanked his hosts for their compliments. As he ended his speech, the club rose, and at the end of their cheers, took their boutonnieres from their coats and bombarded Tony with violets.

Along with theatrical managers, performers, politicians and businessmen in attendance were Gen. George A. Sheridan, F.W. Sanger, Marshall P. Wilder, W.A. Lackaye, John Drew, J.M. Hill and W.S. Mullaly (Tammany Hall representatives) and members of New York's social elite.

As the attending reporter from the *Times* wrote:

> Thus ended a day never to be forgotten by all present, and an evening of such good fellowship seldom if ever seen before. It is little wonder that Mr. Pastor went to his home with his heart filled with pleasure and gratitude toward the public, the profession and the club who gave such a glorious ending to his twenty-fifth year as a manager.[9]

The writer could not know that his phrase "glorious ending" might well be applied to Tony's career. In the coming years, dramatic changes in popular theater would challenge Tony's ingenuity, determination and management style.

12

Business Challenges and Changing Audiences

At the same time he was contemplating his future, Tony was enjoying the benefits derived from vaudeville's increasing public popularity and his stellar reputation as the city's best showman.

The annual summer road tour began on March 31, 1890, without traveling a mile. Since many of the performers were new, Tony wished to try them out at home to make sure they were up to his standards and those of his discerning patrons. Sheridan and Flynn, Frank Bush and Isabell Ward were already local favorites. But Henri Cazman, Rose Sullivan, Vonare, Flora Gillimore and Marzello and Millay had never appeared before American audiences. It was somewhat of a risk to bring over new acts based on the recommendation of "Pony" Moore, but the veteran English music hall impresario was reliable and knew what Tony sought in performance.

Moore had chosen well. Audiences gave resounding approval to the newcomers. On the final performance prior to launching the tour, Tony thanked his patrons for their affirmation of his program. He was confident that the upcoming tour would be as successful as previous ones.

The summer company opened April 7 at the Central Theater in Philadelphia. A rainstorm deterred no one, and the theater was filled to greet Tony and his all-stars, as they were being called this year. The European performers were especially singled out for their stage work. A jump back to Brooklyn for the second week at Hyde & Behman's Theater was equally successful. Tony added Maggie Cline, the Julians and Lottie Gilson to the cast, and the old favorites packed the house. The tour moved to cities in New York.

Buffalo now warranted a full week's engagement with Albany and Syracuse three-day stops. These cities now had more than one vaudeville house, and patrons filled them continuously. A week in Detroit played to "large business." Tony worked hard with his newcomers to add to their repertoire of routines, to vary their acts and keep them fresh. Apparently it was not customary in Europe to deviate from familiar formulas, and a few of the performers were having difficulty modifying their routines.

Chicago was the last stop before Tony took a recess to make his now annual trip to Europe. While in Chicago, the company appeared at three theaters in each of three weeks. The *Tribune* reported that "they had all the business they could accommodate." The company disbanded when they returned to New York.

The *Clipper* reported on Tony's planned trip to Europe.

> Tony Pastor will sail for Europe June 14, and will spend about six weeks abroad, returning to open with his new company in August at his home theater.[1]

An entirely new company was selected for the remainder of the summer tour. Rumor suggested the starting company had not performed as expected. In a break from past summers, Tony revealed that the new company would not only continue the tour but would play at his theater during the fall season.

> He will once more have some new faces to introduce to America and, as usual, the shining lights of foreign and American vaudevilles will be with him. Bessie Bonehill returns with Mr. and Mrs. Pastor and will be the bright particular star of the company next season until November.[2]

The six weeks in England passed in a whirl of theater visits and parties. Tony was an honored guest of the musical hall managers and performers everywhere. During one special program at the Washington Music Hall, London, "Pony" Moore presented Tony with a warm and engaging testimonial. "To my old and valued friend," said Moore, "it is a pleasant task to present this testimonial."[3]

> Mr. Pastor came over to England to engage talent, and an engagement by Tony meant "safety." The artist was sure to get his money and to be treated as a friend and brother. If any English artist got stranded in New York, Mr. Pastor came on the wings of friendship, and at once assisted him.

Tony was presented with a silver dessert service and, in accepting the gift, was received with loud acclamations. He declared his thanks and said that so long as he lived, he intended to keep open house for English artists. It was reported that English performers enjoyed playing for Tony because of his knowledge of knowing how to "work" them with the American public. When Bessie Bonehill was announced, she came to the stage wearing the medallion Tony had given her the previous year. She spoke of her successful run at the 14th Street Theater, the scene of her greatest triumph, and said that Tony had booked her for this year and next to appear for several months. Moore, Bonehill and others joined hands and sang "For He's a Jolly Good Fellow," with the audience joining in on the second chorus. Together, the entire theater sang "Auld Lang Syne" and the audience cheered as the curtain descended.

While Tony was in England, his theater closed for the summer to get a complete refurbishment. At the same time, Hyde & Behman's Theater in Brooklyn, Tony's yearly stop, burned down. An early morning fire caused no loss of life, but the building was totally destroyed.

Tony, Mrs. Pastor and Bessie Bonehill arrived in New York on July 27 on the *Umbria*; "The trip had been fraught with pleasure," he told reporters. The second half of the summer tour began in Long Branch, New Jersey, on August 5. An entirely new company, headed by Bonehill, was to complete the tour and also open the new season at home. With Bonehill as headliner and Maggie Cline and the Russell Brothers as backup, the tour guaranteed crowded houses and sizable box office receipts. In Boston, the stars "were greeted by an audience that lined even the stairways." In Washington, D.C., people were turned away. In Baltimore, the SRO sign was out at every performance. Of course, Bonehill was making her debut in each city and was expected to duplicate her last year's feat when she opened the season at Tony's theater.

When reviewers summed up the results of Tony's summer tour, particularly the second half, they extolled his artist list as "having no equal in its field."

> Tony's company has won unlimited commendation during their travels this season. The veteran actor/manager has certainly tightened his grip on provincial playgoers who have grown to like the man fully as well as what he does for their amusement. His company this year was a remarkably good one. It contained some vaudeville stars of the first magnitude and several novelties of unusual merit.[4]

October 27 was this season's opening night. The theater was packed "from top to bottom and all round" with Tony's admirers and friends. "There seemed no end to the good cheer, hearty well wishes and rousing endorsements expressed by Mr. Pastor's loyal legions," reported the *Clipper* reviewer.[5] The opening act featured the Turles, grotesque aerialists; Edith Vincent, rope dancer, in her first appearance in New York; Kelly and Ashby, as Chinese laundrymen in comic tumbling; the Sisters Hardwicke, English character duettists, making their initial metropolitan appearance in songs and dances; and the only Tony came on stage to "thunders of applause."

> The inimitable Tony was in his best element, and never did he sing with more eloquence, gesture with more emphasis, or contort his features with more expressiveness than on this gala night. Mr. Pastor is assuredly a genius in his way and, like old wine, he seems to grow better with age.[6]

Seeley and West made harmony on all sorts of musical instruments; with her usual vociferousness, Maggie Cline rendered her ballads; the Sisters Coleman did some fine songs and neat dances; the Russell Brothers, in their sketch of the "Irish Servant Girls," received a good welcome. Then came Bessie Bonehill, who was accorded a standing ovation.

> Comely in feature, graceful in movement and invested with a strong magnetic individuality, it is small wonder that she makes hosts of friends at her every appearance. She is honestly entitled to shine as the vbrightest star, and will long remain a thorough favorite of New Yorkers.[7]

The performance concluded with a pantomime by the Haytors, acrobats and contortionists. All the acts were encored repeatedly and the floral offerings filled the stage. The same company played for more than a month, by popular demand.

The 1890-1891 theater season actually began in late August. As usual, Tony opened well after the season had settled down. The city now contained thirty-three theaters, eleven of which were vaudeville houses, and four were museums, which showed a combination of curiosities and variety acts. This represented the greatest number of theaters to date and also the largest number of vaudeville houses. Competition among them was ferocious, both for patrons and high-class performers. It was not uncommon for a good performer to appear in six different vaudeville theaters in a season, drawing large crowds in each of them. Still, Tony's theater remained the most popular and most desirable place to visit. When tourists came to the city, amusement guides noted the 14th Street Theater as "shouldn't miss."

Bessie Bonehill played through the end of November to large and demonstrative audiences. During her last week of performances, she gave a special dinner, and Tony put on a final night testimonial. Both were gala events. Since Bessie had just married William Seeley, the events became special celebrations. The dinner, at the Hotel Hungaria, included a reunion of the summer company as well as current performers at Tony's. A midnight dinner was served, an elaborate feast laid out with the best of wines, cordials and cigars available. Bessie spoke of her great friend Tony, her "wise governor," as she called him, and ended with a toast to the members of the company, which was drunk to shouts of hurrahs. A short entertainment followed with Tony as master of ceremonies. Bessie ended the festivities singing "How I Long for England Dear." She and her husband were on the boat for England the next day.

Several new acts were introduced during the fall season. Marguerite Fish, the former Baby Benson now grown, performed a comic skit. George Murphy was a Dutch comedian of high merit. Kamochi, a female Japanese magician, drew enthusiastic cheers with her tricks. Of greater significance, however, was Tony's announcement that he had signed the English music hall star Jennie Hill, and that she would appear early in the new year.

In December, a small notice in the newspapers mentioned that Tony had purchased a residence at 72 West 94th Street for $19,000 as an investment. It was his fourth property purchase. Also of note was a meeting of ladies at Tony's theater to plan the annual Christmas festival for the little children of the stage. "Aunt" Louisa Eldredge was named president of the group and Mrs. Pastor vice president. Tony would again serve as host. Harrigan's new theater at 35th Street and 6th Avenue opened December 22 to perform plays produced by the owner. And Hyde & Behman's opened their rebuilt theater in Brooklyn by borrowing several of Tony's stalwarts, and one night of Tony's time, to inaugurate their reopening.

On December 28, the Christmas festival was held at Tony's theater for 400 children and their parents. After the children performed, they were feted at Tammany Hall with dinner and gift exchanges. The committee had collected $1,500 and all of it was spent on the event.

The winter and spring season of 1891 continued to attract full houses and SRO audiences to Tony's theater, as it did to other high-class vaudeville houses in the city. Managers spoke happily about profitable box office receipts and the public interest in vaudeville entertainment. B.F. Keith, who had recently opened a theater in Providence, Rhode Island, was looking for an opportunity to expand his flourishing empire into New York. F.F. Proctor had opened a theater on 23rd Street presenting legitimate attractions but he too was seeking a place in the vaudeville business. The ultimate entrance of these moguls into New York vaudeville would jolt popular theater, and Tony as well.

Tony's plan for early 1891 was to corner the time of his reliable favorites and book them for extended periods. While he filled in programs with novelty acts, he featured headliners like Maggie Cline, Harry Kernall, the Russell Brothers, Harry La Rose, the Julians, Edwin French, the St. Felix Sisters and Prof. Abt. Loyal audiences packed the house weekly to cheer their "own" favorites. In late February, Jennie Hill arrived from England for a six-week engagement. Like Bessie Bonehill before her, Hill electrified the patrons. The *Dramatic Mirror's* reviewer called her audience "as brilliant as it was large, and as enthusiastic as it was Anglomaniac."

Hill was called "The Vital Spark" by English audiences. She pleased Tony's patrons with magnetic life and restless energy. She bounded on the stage attired in a conventional street costume looking trim, neat and attractive. Small and slender of stature, although known to be more than forty years old and a grandmother, she had pretty features with eyes that snapped with fire and a nervous vitality. Her transformations from gay to serious were rapid but natural. Descriptive songs, of which she was said to have been the originator, best displayed her versatile talent. Her forte was the depiction of London types, complete with a Cockney accent. Audiences had become so familiar with English singers that accents no longer bothered them.

Her first song was an impersonation of a lower class girl from London who had just returned from a tour of the Continent. Her next rendition was a comic song, "The Coffee Shop Girl," in which she dressed as a waitress in an East End eating house. "Masks and Faces," a descriptive song, was well received. Hill concluded her act with "'Arry," a burlesque impersonation of a London swell. Applause shook the house. A mountain of flowers was passed over the footlights while the audience continued to cheer. In response to repeated calls for a speech, Hill thanked the audience for their cordial greeting.

> I had heard and read of an American welcome, but I had no idea that it could be so generous and thorough. This occasion is really and truly the red-letter day of my career.[8]

She thanked Tony for persuading her to come to America. Of course, Tony was very pleased with Hill's reception. He had the most attractive vaudeville performer in New York; he would have her for six weeks; and the box office would be huge.

In April, Tony gave Hill a benefit, which included many complimentary speeches, a flood of floral bouquets and a medallion studded with diamonds from the entire company. Hill also appeared at the annual Actors' Fund benefit along with Gus Williams, John T. Kelly, Edward Harrigan and Tony. Harry Sanderson's annual testimonial took place on March 23 along with a celebration of Tony's twenty-sixth anniversary as a manager. On a special program were Edward Harrigan's company, George Thatcher's Minstrels and the Pastor company.

The press wanted to know whether Tony could outdo last year's list of performers for this year's summer tour. Tony claimed they were the best yet, although five of the acts had never before played in America. They included Minnie Jeffs, character vocalist and dancer; Hector and Lorraine, in acrobatic eccentricities; ventriloquist Captain Slingsby; Evans and Livermore, grotesque comedians; and the Brothers Ali, Arabian boxers. Highlighting the traveling company were stars Maggie Cline, the Russell Brothers, Marguerite Fish, the Daly Sisters, and Sam Dearin. As usual, the 14th Street Theater remained open during the summer to various traveling companies and specialty acts, all under the direction of Sanderson.

The company opened at the Howard Athenaeum in Boston on March 30. Large audiences attended every performance. All of the new performers were well received and settled in as fixtures, at least until the break in the schedule to accommodate Tony's trip to Europe. The engagement in Philadelphia produced "a rattling good week." At Hyde & Behman's in Brooklyn, Tony added Weber and Fields to the company, producing "a barrel of money to all concerned."

Tony and his wife sailed for England July 10. His schedule included the usual run of theater visits, auditions, social gatherings and, for the first time abroad, a few days of relaxation. In all, he signed twelve acts, some of them returning with him to appear in the second part of the summer tour. No New York manager was recruiting and signing foreign performers like Tony. The artists that Tony brought over were as good as, if not better than, their American counterparts. They fit in well with the changing audience tastes for music, dance and social satire. Audiences could easily laugh at the impersonations of working class Londoners without being embarrassed about their own accents. This coming season, however, there would be no Bessie Bonehill or Jennie Hill to entertain.

The couple sailed from Liverpool on July 25, arriving in New York August 1. The second part of the summer tour began August 10 in Long Branch. Thanks to Tony, the town was being selected by other managers to try out new plays and rehearse companies. A second theater was built there to accommodate the increased business. Included in the traveling company was the demonstrative Maggie Cline, veterans John E. Drew, Sam Dearin, the Haytors and newcomers Lina and Vani, the Sisters Le Blanche, and Williams and Griffin. Harry Kernall would join the company midway through the tour.

The profits from the past season must have been good, because Tony purchased another house at 49 West 94th Street for the large sum of $27,500, the second on that block in the last year.

Tony opened the 1891-1892 season at his theater on October 26. The theater had been newly refitted with carpets, scenery and backdrop. The cast included Maggie Cline, whom the audience anticipated with feverish expectancy. The *Times* reviewer aptly described Cline's appeal.

> Miss Cline is a dramatic rather than a musical artist. As a singer she does not rank even with Mr. Pastor. Her voice is large, but not beautiful. She was a splendid sight in her handsome evening dress, and looked every inch an Irish Queen. She was greeted with cheers, tigers and vocal rockets. She handed her fan to the leader of the band, asking him to be careful of it as it cost $3 and performed a song called "When Hogan Pays the Rent," which is a misleading title, because it is disclosed that Hogan never pays the rent and hence the excitement in his neighborhood on rent day, which Miss Cline set forth with photographic accuracy.[9]

Londoners appearing for the first time were Conroy and Fox, song and dance; the Le Blanche Sisters; Griffin and Williams; the Schallers, grotesque acrobats; and the Leonards, English vocalists. The next week, Tony introduced Nettie Lingard, a music hall singer; Herbert Albini, slight of hand; and George Beauchamp, comic singer. In fact, the entire fall season featured several foreign performers on every week's program. Tony hoped that his French acquisition, Juniori Valarez, a character vocalist, would become the star of the season, but her introduction in early December fell flat. She proved an ordinary singer. Her beauty and costume elicited the most comment. What got reviewers' attention most was her body language, twists and kicks, which they considered vulgar. After "cleaning up" her routine, Tony kept her for a month. She became mysteriously ill the last week of her engagement.

The fall season through December attracted top-notch business. In observation of Tony's continued success, the *Clipper* compared the various vaudeville houses with the 14th Street Theater. While they were all thought to be doing well, Tony's was at the top of the list.

> The audience on Monday as on every night for the past season was large in size and brilliant in make up. This latter phrase is used advisedly for it has become a noteworthy fact that the character of the audience at this gilt edge vaudeville house will compare favorably with those in attendance at any one of the town's places of amusement. Fashion has put her seal of approval upon the leading entertainer appearing under Pastor's banner, and the results are highly gratifying to the management.[10]

The annual Christmas festival for children of the stage was held December 27, with Tony as host and "Aunt" Louisa Eldredge as leader of the sponsoring group. Along with the usual coterie of parents, there were a number of theatrical agents and managers seeking young talent. New members to the women's organization this year included Mrs. Neil Burgess, Mrs. Edward Harrigan, Queen Vassar and Julia Arthur. The event was becoming one of the anticipated, fashionable gatherings during the holiday season.

The year 1892 heralded discernable changes in popular theater, the beginning of a decade in which a clearer definition of the various amusement forms—vaudeville, comic opera, musical comedy and revues—was being realized. Audiences became more interested in content rather than spectacle. Oddities and novelties were less desired. Thanks to the maturity of ethnic comedy, audiences were able to identify with everyday people in everyday situations. Minstrel companies had all but disappeared. The performers became specialty acts in vaudeville. Music publishers and vocalists teamed up to sell songs. Publishers sold more sheet music, and vocalists were identified with certain hits that increased attention to their act and their career.

European themes and plots continued to dominate legitimate theater, but the American influence on farces and travesty was setting the foundation for homegrown musical comedy. For the growing number of fashion-oriented theater patrons, comic opera with its elaborate plots, scenery, costumes and semi-operatic music, satisfied their desires. Vaudeville was now a full-fledged business made up of bottom-line entrepreneurs looking to expand their hold on one of the country's most profitable enterprises. The era of individual managers was in decline. Tony, however, continued to reap the benefits of reputation and high-class entertainment for a while longer.

The winter and spring of 1892 saw a continuation of crowded houses for Tony. While he loaded his bills with familiar headliners like Maggie Cline (she seemed almost a member of the Pastor family), Harry Kernall, the Julians, Edwin French, Lillie Western (now in her 50s), Sam Dearin and Frank McNish, he also introduced New York audiences to several new artists who went on to become star performers. Thomas O'Brien, a comedian, was assisted by Clara Havel when they first appeared. By the third week, they were billed equally. Clara sang and danced as well as playing straight person, thanks to Tony who modified their act. Women in the audience loved to see Clara upstage her partner and cheered when she delivered the comedy punch line. Lydia Yeamans reappeared; after three years out of the country, her versatility as a performer had matured. She received hearty applause, floral tributes and several feature appearances at

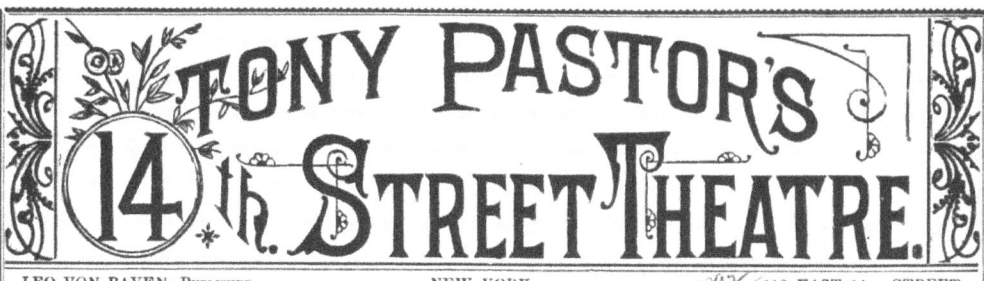

The 1892 playbill demonstrated the array of high-class artists Tony presented. Any one of them could have headed a vaudeville bill. It was Tony's commitment to give his patrons the most value for the money (Museum of the City of New York).

Tony's. Lydia was now assisted by her husband, F.J. Titus, a handsome and accomplished pianist. William Jerome, a composer of popular music, put on a comedy act in which he parodied his own compositions. The parodies were better received then the original songs. He went on to become one of the period's most prolific songwriters. Capitola Forrest, the dancer and high kicker, was an immediate crowd pleaser with her eccentric moves and became a Pastor favorite for years.

This season's English music hall vocalist, Nellie Maguire, came without the fanfare of her predecessors. She appeared February 15 with a minimal introduction but became an immediate hit.

> From the moment that she bounded upon the stage in the fulsome apparel and vigorousness of a hoydenish Hibernian maiden and throughout her respective changes into a racing tout's rollicking sweetheart, the slatternly garb and devil may care jollity of a rough Irishwoman, the elegant attire of an English girl, until she had tripped the last step in a lively dance, she was highly interesting and wholly agreeable.[11]

Audiences responded enthusiastically with cheers and applause for Maguire's work. Tony had signed her for only two weeks; she stayed until the end of March, attracting large audiences each week.

F.F. Proctor had been running the 23rd Street Theater for several years. In conjunction with the Frohman brothers, legitimate drama was presented. However, Proctor was interested in vaudeville, and when the arrangement with the Frohmans expired, he changed his theater into a vaudeville house, with a new strategy. Copying B.F. Keith's Boston theater operations, Proctor's became a "continuous vaudeville" house; that is, there were no interruptions in the performance that ran from noon to 11 P.M. For one low price, patrons could come to the theater when they wished, leave when they desired, and stay as long as they wanted. Matinees, obviously, were abolished. Artists were now required to perform their act three times a day as the cycle for each program was about three and a half hours. (Headliners performed twice a day or were paid larger salaries for three appearances.) Regular performers had fifteen to eighteen minute stints but were paid no differently than before.

The response from audiences made continuous vaudeville a success. They embraced the idea of coming and going at will or staying for an extended time. Proctor's theater was an immediate winner. His strategy threw vaudeville mangers into confusion. What would this new presentation form do to their business? Should they emulate Proctor? There was no doubt that continuous vaudeville changed the way vaudeville, and variety before, had been managed since its inception.

Tony was also concerned, since the new operation had implications for his own business. But because Proctor's theater was located quite far from his neighborhood, Tony decided to simply monitor the situation. He and Sanderson kept a close eye on Proctor's, paying particular attention to the composition of the audiences.

Tony was also aware of the movement of theaters uptown. Most of the houses recently built were located above 35th Street, some even beyond 40th Street. The area was becoming the new commercial location for retail businesses. After the Theater Comique was destroyed by fire, even Edward Harrigan saw the value of moving his new theater near Madison Square. The relocation of vaudeville theaters was slower than dramatic theaters because many managers believed that vaudeville audiences were more likely to come from immigrant neighborhoods. Talks among vaudeville managers suggested future moves but, for the time being, opening a theater in Harlem or Brooklyn offered more potential.

Since Tony's move to 14th Street, he had demonstrated that better classes of people would travel to Union Square to see a high-class show. For the immediate future, he saw no reason to move.

Within two years the situation would change enough to persuade vaudeville managers to consider the move uptown. Part of the reason was the apparent decline in the neighborhoods south of Union Square. Part was due to the increasing legitimacy and drawing power of vaudeville among the higher social classes. An emerging middle class sought "refined" entertainment, classier-looking theaters, established performers, more sophisticated acts and the development of a strictly American-style vernacular. They supported the gloss and fantasy of comic opera and the farces, the forerunners to musical theater.

Tony was quite sensitive to audience tastes and the changing face of Broadway. In 1892, he considered making a move uptown when a dramatic theater closed near 35th Street. the predecessor of the Herald Square Theater going bankrupt. But the move seemed too far from his loyal legions, almost two miles beyond 14th Street and even a mile north of Madison Square. There were no vaudeville houses in the area and the neighborhoods were in transition (actually for the better). More importantly, Tony believed he would have left behind his loyal friends and admirers and had no wish to disappoint them. Tony decided to stay where he was. It was probably one of the poorest business decisions he would ever make.

The spring season saw Tony's increased involvement in the Actors' Fund. Members of the Fund committee were concerned that the demands on their benefits were greater than their resources. What to do about it? Led by Tony, they agreed to not only to increase the prices of their annual all-star show in late March, but also to solicit money from a theater fair being held at Madison Square Garden the following week. The plan worked and the fund's coffers were replenished for the coming year. They assisted more than 400 performers who became ill or destitute, or who died and left widows in poverty.

Harry Sanderson's annual benefit was held March 23. Volunteer performers from various theaters appeared at Pastor's to honor the treasurer, now in his fourteenth year as Tony's alter ego. He was keeper of the finances, manager of the theater during the summer, scout for new talent and Tony's personal advisor. Sanderson received accolades from the audience, and also from performers who considered him as fair and honest as Tony.

The twenty-seventh annual summer tour began April 4 in Philadelphia. The company consisted of several familiar headliners—the Russell Brothers, Weber and Fields, Monroe and Mack, Lydia Yeamans-Titus (and her husband), and a group of popular European stars: the Sisters Flexmore, song and dance; Herr Grais, juggler and animal trainer; the Phantos, acrobats; Major Newell, roller skating dancer; Mons. Visto, instrumentalist; and Professor Thornburg, cartoonist and ventriloquist. A reviewer noted that Tony's foreign contingent consisted of circus and novelty performers, the kind of people he had hired in earlier years. Yet audiences still enjoyed their exploits.

The tour included the usual visits, Brooklyn, Providence (now for a full week), Boston, Syracuse, Rochester, Detroit and a three-week engagement in Chicago at three theaters. Although the regular season had not yet ended and there were still twenty traveling companies on the road, Tony continued to draw full houses and SRO. At the end of the Chicago run, Tony and the company returned to New York, he to prepare for his European trip, many in the company to appear at his theater.

Tony and his wife left for England on June 18. On the trip, Tony divided his time between visiting theaters and signing up talent and relaxing at seaside. Most important, Tony had again captured Bessie Bonehill to appear with his traveling company and open his fall season in New York. He would follow her with the first appearance of Vesta Victoria in December. She was as popular in England as Bonehill, and Tony believed she would be equally successful with his audiences. Tony, his wife, and Bessie returned to the U.S. on August 2. He formed his new company and they traveled to Long Branch to open August 8 for the second part of the summer tour.

One of the best comedy teams in vaudeville history, Joe Weber and Lew Fields, appeared at Tony's theater early in their career. Like Tony, they became managers who never forgot what it was like to be a struggling performer seeking stage recognition (Harry Ransom Humanities Research Center).

Bonehill, of course, was the star attraction. She was supported by Americans Maggie Cline (who never had a problem playing behind Bonehill), Lizzie and Vinni Daly, Seeley and West, Ward and Vokes and the Glenroy Brothers. Foreign performers included Birdie Brightley, a banjoist; Mr. and Mrs. Nawn, sketch artists; Fred Malburn, concertina; and Ida Howell, singer and dancer.

The tour took the company through towns in New England, Boston, Montreal and Toronto, Cleveland, Pittsburgh, Baltimore and Harlem. According to Sanderson, this was the most profitable summer ever.

The fall season at Tony's theater opened October 31 and featured all the members of the traveling company. Soft, rhythmic music ushered in the star of the bill, Bessie Bonehill. The *Clipper* reviewer declared she was "the best character singer ever imported to these shores."

> In a quiet, appropriate little prelude, she announced that he initiatory song was prepared especially as a greeting to her friends, and her excellent rendition called forth vociferous applause. Miss Bonehill was in her element. Her audience was with her, and, artist that she is, she felt and showed that she was aware of the happy relations. New character songs were at her fingers' ends, and were sung with all the effective dash and skill which had made her a favorite with New Yorkers.[12]

Along with the enthusiastic cheering and applause, Bessie received a wealth of floral tributes, enough to fill the stage. Tony appeared to be the most animated that admirers had seen him in years.

> The orchestra banged and twanged, and Mr. Pastor, as buoyant and rakish as of yore, followed with a collection of catchy songs, the best of which was "The Law Won't Allow Me to Do It."[13]

Maggie Cline, showing the audience she was in no way intimidated by Bessie Bonehill, established the fact that her "well wishers are still legion in number and staunch in spirit." "The Broadway Brunhilde," as she was called, had a new song that was well received, and she finished amid the slam-bang and hurrah of the familiar "McClosky."

The crowd was ecstatic over the program, and continued so as long as Bonehill and her colleagues remained on stage. Additions to the bill in successive weeks kept the audience on edge, in anticipation and exuberant enjoyment. Katie Lawrence, from London, a ballad singer, had an uncertain first week, but, under Tony's tutelage, she showed her talent and won patrons. John W. Kelly had become one of the cleverest monologue artists in vaudeville. Lillie Western, the accomplished instrumentalist, played on two banjos at one time. Monroe and Mack did their funny Negro character studies.

In late November, Tony was unable to appear at the theater for two weeks, the victim of "la grippe" as Sanderson described it to audiences. It had been many years since Tony had missed a show and audiences missed him. A reviewer suggested that it was amazing Tony was as durable as he was, considering his long career as a performer and "he was almost sixty." The comment was brief and seemingly went unnoticed, but Tony understood the reality of the situation nevertheless.

After Bessie Bonehill sang her last song and returned to England, having guaranteed Tony several months of full houses, he prepared to greet his next great English star, Vesta Victoria. Victoria, a singer and comedienne on the English music hall stage, was Tony's next hope to bring in large crowds. She more than fulfilled his expectations.

When Tony introduced her, Victoria was received with enthusiasm. By the end of her set, her reception was warm and adoring and she was encored repeatedly.

> Miss Victoria is young and talented, and possesses a charming stage presence. She is as versatile as she is artistic. One moment she is sprightly and volatile, the next she is grave and sedate. She

has fully mastered the art of blending pathos and humor on the canvas of character singing, and the pictures she turns out are well nigh perfect. There is no denying the uniqueness and vigor of Miss Victoria's work.[14]

Victoria remained on the program until February and made Pastor's house "the place to go during the holiday season." Her appearance concluded Tony's best year of profit as a manager, even against increased competition and higher salaries for performers. Victoria introduced a particular character song, "Papa Won't Buy Me a Bow-Wow," that was a hit and became her signature song for the remainder of her career. With an extensive repertory, she introduced new songs each week, a truly Pastor-style artist.

The holidays featured the annual Christmas festival for stage children at Tony's theater. Close to 400 children attended and thirty of them performed. The usual banquet and gift exchange topped the evening. A score of well-known women artists now supported the program and attended the event.

Eighteen ninety-three began with Victoria, Bonnie Thornton and a new import, Pacquerette, to entertain Tony's audiences. Victoria continued to mesmerize patrons with her character singing. Thornton showed a new sophistication, thanks to her husband writing her songs. Her rendition of "My Sweetheart's the Man in the Moon," a new ballad, pleased audience so much they had her repeat it several times. Another new song, "After Dark," had the audience joining in the chorus. Mlle. Pacquerette, a contortionist and singer from France, both awed the audience with her caricatures and somewhat appalled them in their vividness. Her arms and legs were long but, instead of minimizing them, she strove to lengthen them. At the climax of her act, she hugged herself. Posing with her back to the audience, she wrapped her arms behind her until her hands touched, then shuffled sideways off the stage.

> Yet there is no denying her cleverness as a burlesquer, and her ability to get the most grotesque results from her freakish form. She makes up her face in the most outlandish way imaginable, even stepping beyond the bounds of the conventional clown, and she wears a wig that resembles a lot of wet, frizzled bagging. But all her theatrical agenda is used with the purpose of heightening her grotesqueness of figure and comic mannerisms, and she achieves her end successfully and creditably.[15]

Tony had promoted Mlle. Pacquerette as "different from any French artist that has ever visited America and that her entertainment is very refined, neat, clean, humorous and faithful in its portrayal of French provincial character."[16] She must have been well liked, because she remained on the bill for ten weeks.

Tony had already singled out the summer of 1893 as a special event, one that would modify his usual touring plans. The World's Fair would open in Chicago in May and remain open until October. Many performers and traveling companies were already planning to appear there to hopefully reap the benefits of large crowds. Tony believed this would be an opportunity for him as well. He sought to hire the best troupe ever and scheduled a summer long engagement at one of Chicago's downtown theaters. His intent seemed reasonable; however, actual events would cause unexpected problems.

The winter and spring programs were highlighted by Victoria and Pacquerette. They were ably supported by John W. Kelly, Bonnie Thornton, the Dalys, Russell Brothers, James F. Hoey and Annie Oakley. Tony seemed to have no need to add new people to the bill during this period. Receipts were outstanding, the profit excellent, and the immediate future rosy.

Two significant events of financial and social consequence occurred at almost the same time: the opening of the Columbian Exposition (Chicago World's Fair) and the Panic of 1893.[17] On May 3, stock prices fell dramatically, particularly among industrials. Rumors spread from Wall Street about major losses among big companies, a wholesale wiping out of small entrepreneurial funding and failures at several brokerage firms. Repercussions from the stock debacle spread across the country. Over speculation, wildcat enterprises and the government's creation of trusts and monopolies the previous year contributed to the financial failures.

Within a few weeks, businesses and factories closed, forcing thousands of workers into unemployment. Those lucky enough to hold a job found their wages cut. The consumption of goods declined precipitously. At first, financial institutions believed the market decline to be temporary, but then they discovered that banks held less assets than originally thought and that coin was in short supply. Banks announced a thirty-day notice for the withdrawal of all accounts of more than $100 and sixty days for withdrawal of all accounts of more than $300, creating a rush that totally overwhelmed them.

Among the retail business, amusements were particularly hard hit, the number of customers attending theaters dropping off dramatically. Vaudeville houses in New York remained open, but they attracted only small audiences.

Tony had begun his summer tour on April 3 in Boston, with overflow crowds at the Howard Athenaeum. The summer cast included such headliners as Lydia Yeamans-Titus, John W. Kelly, the Russell Brothers, Ward and Vokes and four new acts from England. Stops in Williamsburg, Brooklyn, Harlem and Detroit were sell-outs. While the company was making its way to Chicago for the World's Fair, the Panic broke out.

The Chicago World's Fair officially opened the first week of May. Only three years before, Chicago had beat out New York for the right to represent the U.S. in its 400th anniversary celebration of the discovery of America. They outbid New York with an offer of an additional $5 million, which they in fact did not have, to win approval. One of the important components for the fair was popular entertainment and its ability to attract visitors.

The Panic hit the fair a resounding blow. Attendance fell well below expectations. Attendance figures were so poor that planners considered closing the fair. Several traveling companies came to Chicago counting on the popularity of the fair to make substantial profits. They included Tony's company, Weber and Fields, Gus Hill and Lillian Russell. Tony was able to eke out sufficient box office receipts to play to June 10, far short of his contemplated stay. The others had closed their engagements before him. The company returned to New York, somewhat chastened by the experience. Tony and his wife prepared for their trip to Europe.

In mid–June, two decisions by the fair planners saved the exposition. They decided to open the fair three nights a week until 11 P.M.; and, after a bitter dispute with religious authorities, they got approval to open on Sundays. Attendance immediately improved, and by July more than 100,000 people were visiting the fair each day. It seemed the Panic had little effect on Midwestern fairgoers.

Tony's trip to Europe was quite successful. Instead of his seeking out performers, they were coming to him. He engaged Nellie La Strange, a character singer, to join his summer company in August. He persuaded Bessie Bonehill to play two weeks for him before she embarked on a tour of the U.S. with her own company. He also signed the great Vesta Tilley, the acknowledged English music hall star, to come to America during the coming year for an extended stay at his theater. Others he obtained for fall engagements were the Sisters Preston, Mlle. Langtree and Katie Lawrence. Tony had discovered that foreign female stars did better than their male colleagues.

Opening day for the new summer company was August 10 in Albany. Considering the current economic climate, deciding to tour was a sizable risk. The Panic had caused many theaters to close, traveling companies to return home and had put many performers out of work. In those theaters remaining open, attendance was poor.

The opening in Albany featured Nellie La Strange and caused an immediate uproar. In her act, which included a number of comic songs, La Strange took out a flask and appeared to drink out of it. While Tony was taken by surprise, the audience and reviewers were decidedly upset. He solved the problem quickly, but the residual unease when La Strange performed continued. It was all overcome when, two weeks later, Bessie Bonehill appeared, and all eyes and ears were upon her. In spite of the attractive program, theaters in New York, Ohio and Michigan were only half full and Tony was losing money nightly. The company then returned to Chicago; with the fair now running profitably, a four-week engagement recouped Tony's losses and made enough money to cover the entire summer tour.

From Chicago, the company visited Pittsburgh, Philadelphia, Harlem and Brooklyn before returning to the 14th Street Theater. When Sanderson reported that "business registered at an even and satisfactory degree in the box office thermometer,"[18] it meant Tony had likely broken even on the tour. However, New York had suffered more than any other city due to the Panic. Business was slow and unemployment high, with thousands still living in distress.

While Tony was busy keeping his tour afloat and planning for the upcoming season, the enterprising B.F. Keith entered the New York market. He already owned vaudeville theaters in Boston, Philadelphia and Providence. Just before Tony left on his summer tour, Keith began negotiations to lease the Union Square Theater, only two blocks from Tony. In early April, Edward Albee, Keith's business manager, was in town to close the deal. When Albee announced that the Union Square would be totally renovated and would feature drama, Tony was temporarily relieved. Nevertheless, it was a departure for Keith to favor drama over vaudeville, and the press expressed skepticism about the announced intentions. It seemed an odd time to open a theater in New York, especially one featuring drama. Tony believed that Keith would become a competitor in the near future. The "near future" came more quickly than Tony had planned.

In late August, Keith announced that the Union Square, once refurbished, would open in September as a vaudeville house, offering first-class programs in a continuous vaudeville format. Proctor was already using a similar format, but Keith was only a short walk from Tony's theater. Sanderson informed Tony of the news while he was in Chicago. Real competition was now at his doorstep, and he would have to meet the challenge for the first time in twenty-eight years.

Thanks to the loyal legions of Pastor admirers, the opening on October 23 was a huge success. Every performer was loudly applauded upon entrance and frequent interruptions of the specialties showed the kindly feelings of those on stage.

> It was indeed a royal welcome to the manager of New York's bon ton vaudeville theater. The lobby of the theater resembled a hot house, both in color and appearance. Against the wall stood baskets, bouquets and stands of flowers, the fragrance of which permeated the farthest part of the auditorium.[19]

Tony was received with the usual greetings, the applause deafening. It was some minutes before he could proceed with his songs, and it took a half dozen of them before he was finally allowed to retire, again to loud cheers of approval. The *Clipper* observed that "the scarcity of money does not seem to be felt at this high-class vaudeville theater, for the friends of Mr. Pastor are always willing to risk their money on his program in the race for amusements."[20]

For the next several weeks, full houses were the standard. Keith's Union Square, meanwhile, was just beginning to attract customers. Tony used the introduction of English music hall stars to gain attention, and it seemed to be successful. Mlle. Duclerc, a tall, slender, graceful singer, sang all her songs in French. But audiences could judge from her actions what the songs were about, "those actions given with such abandon and cash that the meaning was readily understood." Within a few performances, she had become accustomed to the wishes of the patrons and was well received.

A few weeks later, Tony introduced Lillie Langtree, "the pearl of the English music halls." No relation to Mrs. Langtry of dramatic fame, her name nevertheless conjured up images of fine acting. (One Pastor ad actually spelled her last name Langtry. Mistake or promotion?) Langtree had been engaged for three months, and she continued as the featured attraction for the entire engagement.

By the middle of November, however, attendance at Tony's theater was gradually declining. The Union Square was now a firm competitor and its lower prices were drawing people away from Tony. He attempted to compensate for it by bringing back old audience favorites, but the strategy failed to boost attendance. During the holiday season, business picked up, with programs designed to attract women and children, Tony singing Christmas carols, acrobats and pantomime.

But Christmas was not a happy time for many thousands of New Yorkers. Unemployment remained high. Retail business continued to suffer from a paucity of customers. Churches complained that they had run out of food and clothing and went house-to-house seeking donations. "Hundreds of families starving in our midst," headlined the *Times* in early January 1894.

Theaters were severely affected by the weak economy. Many reduced their admission prices. Performers' salaries, likewise, were lowered. There were nine vaudeville theaters in New York and all were suffering from a loss of patrons. The near future looked bleak as city officials reported only slow progress in getting people back to work.

Tony appeared to be holding steady. His philosophy of keeping good people or bringing them back frequently and his determination to present a high-class show continued to attract his loyal patrons and admirers. The addition of the Rogers Brothers; Bonnie Thornton; Mlle. Valerez, a French singer and dancer; and comic opera star Helen Mora helped to bring in patrons, but sellouts were rare.

With weakened attendance, intense competition from Keith and higher performers' salaries, Tony was losing money. Pondering this situation, Tony wondered what he could do about it.

13

Continuous Vaudeville and Shrinking Profits

When Vesta Tilley appeared at Tony's theater in April 1894, she saved his season.

Her presence also allowed Tony to begin his annual summer tour on time, while she ruled the 14th Street Theater's stage until early June.

Theater patrons knew that Vesta Tilley was coming because of an extensive advertising campaign and word of mouth that spread across the Union Square area like wildfire. Tilley was England's most popular performer, a male impersonator whose comedic interpretations captured audiences. More than a performer, she had a magnetism that exhilarated patrons. Her stage presence was exciting. Off-stage, she was even more personable. Tony's persuading Tilley to come to America and play at his theater was the theatrical coup of the year.

When she made her debut April 16, SRO signs had been out from early in the day, and still hundreds of people were on the street hoping to get a glimpse of the star. She gave a turn of thirty-seven minutes, long for a vaudeville act, but not long enough for her audience. Her first song was "The Rocketty Club," sung in a red coat and black knickerbockers. The *Clipper* reviewer reported that "she acted the character in such a pleasing manner that it could be seen that her heart was in her work."

In her song "My Friend, the Major," she appeared in long trousers, a long frock coat and jaunty cap. She also appeared as a yachtsman.

> In action, speech and manners Miss Tilley is more like an American than an English woman and she is sure to make many friends in this country.[1]

Tilley followed with six weeks of stellar performances, with sellouts every night. Each time she appeared, audience greetings were deafening. She was unable to leave the stage until she had sung at least six songs. With an enthusiasm rarely given a vaudeville performer, the *Clipper* extolled her virtues.

> To see her once imbues one with a desire to see her again. Miss Tilley not only sings the words and music to her songs, but she acts the characters perfectly. Few foreign music hall people have ever met with the success on Tony Pastor's stage as had his latest importation.[2]

The rest of the bill was equally attractive. Lottie Gilson, Frank Bush, Billy Carter, Annie Hart and the Russell Brothers appeared on the same bill with Tilley. None of them felt slighted by playing opposite her. Audiences left the theater knowing they had witnessed much more than any admission could buy.

Tony began the summer tour on April 2, scheduling the company into Williamsburg and Brooklyn so that he could return to his theater to personally introduce Tilley at her opening. The company then moved on to Boston, Philadelphia and Chicago (for three weeks) to complete the first half of the tour. The cast was of the usual high quality, including such headliners as the Rogers Brothers, Russell Brothers, J.W. Kelly, Ward and Vokes and lesser, but no less talented performers like Dan and May McAvoy, Musical Dale, Nellie Harris and Hasker and Lester. In Chicago, Tony picked up a local vocalist who had collected a following and featured her while they played in the city. Reported the *Tribune,* "Tony Pastor and his following of clever vaudeville entertainers packed the house to the doors at nearly all performances."[3]

Tony also made sure that he was back in town to help celebrate Tilley's last performance on June 1. She was the recipient of many gifts and a stageful of floral bouquets. Tony presented her with a gold medal encrusted in diamonds. Sanderson gave her a banjo, and the company presented her with a black lace parasol. The next day, Tony and the company went down to the dock to see Tilley off; she received another floral gift before boarding the ship.

Thanks to Tilley, Tony eked out a small profit of $5,400 for the 1893–1894 season. Tilley was paid $300 a week, the largest salary Tony had ever given to a performer. Salaries had increased substantially the past few years due primarily to the competitive demand for headliners by the various vaudeville managers. When Lottie Gilson first played at Tony's, she earned $25 a week; she now received $150. Weber and Fields formerly earned $75 a week; they now were paid $250. Other performers receiving high salaries included Frank Bush, $150, J.T. Kelly, $200, Rogers Brothers, $125, James F. Hoey, $150, and Bessie Bonehill, $250. Salaries would continue to escalate, putting additional pressure on vaudeville managers.

Not wishing to lose the box office momentum, Tony signed Bessie Bonehill to follow Vesta Tilley. She appeared

Vesta Tilley, the great English male impersonator, gave Tony's box office a lift every time she appeared. Tilley captured audiences with her vitality and vivacious personality. When she appeared for Tony, the press called her "the star of New York."

for three weeks, until Tony closed the theater for the summer. It was the first time in more than twenty years that Tony's theater had been closed. Due to the currently poor economic conditions, theaters were attracting small audiences and as long as they stayed open were losing money.

Tony, his wife, Frank Moran, Joe Weber and Thomas Grenier left for Europe on June 16, with a planned return to the U.S. July 28. Tony was actively seeking new acts but also pressing those headliners who had recently starred at his theater. Bidding for their services had become ferocious. This time, Tony lost out on most of his previous headliners, with the exception of Vesta Tilley.

The roots of Tin Pan Alley were formed during the 1880s when music publishers served as distributing houses for established songwriters. With the rise of vaudeville, publishers began producing "songs written to order." In 1886, Witmark and Sons, a Jewish company like most of the new music publishers, changed from commercial printing to selling sheet music and song production. Both Julius, a boy soprano, and Isadore, an aspiring songwriter, had appeared at Tony's Christmas festival for children of the stage. They now were the leading music publisher in town. As new companies entered the field, selling songs became "ferociously competitive."

> Rival song "pluggers" stalked popular vaudeville vocalists, snared them on street corners, and sang them their songs amid the passing throng. To get real stars to work their ditties into an act, pluggers would buy them drinks or dinners in Union Square restaurants, pay their board bill, purchase their railroad tickets to distant cities. They also wooed bandleaders, managers, and waiters, hired boys in the galleries to take up the chorus, and got organ grinders to spread their melodies throughout the city. In addition, they cultivated the growing number of vaudeville agents who worked in the Union Square area booking agencies supplying acts and songs to theaters across the country.[4]

Vocalists were known to put "plants" in the audience to shout out songs to be sung. Some singers were given royalties for all the sheet music sales they could generate. The biggest advertisers in the theatrical weeklies were music publishers, highlighting their newest songs and recent hits.

The combination of publishers, songwriters and vocalists pushing the latest in popular music turned the enterprise into a million-dollar business. Songs like "After the Ball" by Charles K. Harris, "The Sidewalks of New York" and "The Band Played On" became big hits. Successful waltzes had memorable choruses that made it easy for the audiences to sing along. Every vaudeville theater had to feature a favorite vocalist on the bill. The vocalists needed a large repertoire of songs to use in an act that often required them to sing several encores. And their repertoire had to include the latest songs.

Most of the music activity congregated around Union Square, the city's theatrical neighborhood. In the late 1890s, the Witmark Brothers moved uptown to West 28th Street, closer to the newly built theaters. Other publishers soon followed, forming a new center for popular music, soon to be labeled Tin Pan Alley.[5]

Tony knew the value of featuring bright vocalists and fresh material. Beginning in 1865, he made sure every bill had a female vocalist, since they were the best song pluggers. He did not permit "plants"—Lottie Gilson tried it once—nor did he permit singers to talk about purchasing songs. At the same time, he encouraged his singers to visit music publishers to look for new material. He often featured more than one singer on a bill. When Bessie Bonehill and Vesta Tilley appeared, local favorites like Lottie Gilson, Bonnie Thornton and Maggie Cline shared the program.

Tony reopened the summer tour on August 20 at West End, New Jersey, to play through September and October. The cast included the usual headliners: J.W. Kelly, Rogers Brothers, Will

H. Fox, Russell Brothers, Annie Hart, McAvoy and May and Musical Dale. Also in the cast were two imports, the Hengler Sisters and the Nawns, and a new male-female song and dance team, Clifford and Huth.

The short tour traveled through New England and visited Cleveland, Chicago, Pittsburgh, Philadelphia and Harlem. Even with heavy advertising and promotion, there were few sellouts, the trip barely breaking even.

Tony opened the new season October 29. As usual, it was a festive evening, the theater filled with Pastor loyalists and admirers. At the rear of the theater was a mass of flowers, all Tony's tributes to his company. As each one performed, the floral offerings were brought forward and presented, accompanied by cheers from the audience. Tony, of course, was heartily welcomed and "sang several times in his old-time style, as if enjoyed being home again as much as the audience liked to have him."[6]

The opening cast featured the Nawns in a skit, Billy Clifford and Maud Huth in Negro melodies and dancing, and Princess Pauline, from England, in acrobatic work. Tony followed with his usual budget of songs, with two minutes of bows and thanks; McAvoy and May, wooden shoe dancing; Annie Hart, vocalist; Musical Dale, instrumentalist; the Preston Sisters, also new from England, in songs and character changes; Rogers Brothers, Dutch dialect comedians; J.W. Kelly, monologues; and the Harbecks, juggling and contortions.

Tony had discarded afterpieces, primarily at the request of performers, who did not like the additional time on stage or the loose skit normally presented. Instead, Tony installed non-vocal, action-oriented routines to end the program — jugglers, animal acts, for example — which were soon labeled "chasers" by reviewers because they were designed to empty the theater.

During the fall season, Tony featured many new acts, primarily because they could be signed at lower salaries. He advertised "good seats downstairs, 50 cents" and "society's only specialty house" to attract a more select audience. He succeeded in getting good-sized audiences but few full houses, even as business began to improve. Dramatic theaters were the first to see the improvement and they responded by raising admission prices back to the level they had been before the Panic. But vaudeville houses were not yet in such a position.

A little observed but notable event occurred in November when the first Negro performers, a choral group, appeared in a popular vaudeville house. They were politely received. More Negro performers were waiting in the wings.

Tony's holiday show headlined old favorites Maggie Cline and Annie Hart; newcomers the Fortesque Sisters, character singers, and Kitty Nolan, Irish ballad singer; and a group of acts—acrobats, jugglers and pantomimists—to entertain the women and children. At several matinees, all ladies and children received dolls. Tony himself made a surprisingly sprightly presentation, as noted by the indulgent *Clipper* reviewer.

> Mr. Pastor was evidently pleased with the way those in front enjoyed the performances, for he appeared to infuse new life into his songs and made the audience feel as though they were listening to a younger Tony Pastor than the one who has amused them for so many years.[7]

In early 1895, several events occurred which, while attracting little notice at the time, would later prove significant. Oscar Hammerstein purchased a plot of land on Broadway between 44th and 45th Streets to erect a music hall and theater. Its cost was estimated to be over $900,000. More importantly to observers of the theatrical business, it was a decision that initiated the rapid movement of theaters uptown.

In another first, the comedy team of Negro actors Williams and Walker broke the racial barrier with ads in both the *Dramatic Mirror* and *New York Clipper*. A few weeks later, they were seen at Proctor's 23rd Street Theater, far down the list of performers on the bill but, nevertheless, the first Negro comedy song and dance team to play before white audiences in a heretofore white theater.

During the middle of January, Tony introduced to New York audiences a husband and wife team, the Houdinis, in "mystifying and mind reading illusions."[8] Actually, they had appeared at Huber's Museum along with the usual oddities and freaks that made the theater unique. E.A. Albee, Keith's business manager, looking for new talent, attended one performance at Huber's. He was impressed by the Houdinis' handcuff act but, when he presented the idea of having the actors at the Keith house, was turned down. At the same time, the Houdinis were asked to audition at Pastors. They could hardly believe it!

Arriving in New York, the Houdinis immediately went to Tony's theater. They found their name on the poster at the bottom of the list, in small type. They were positioned as the opening act for the program, usually reserved for non-speaking performers new to patrons. For their first show on Monday evening, patrons were just entering the theater. Houdini recalled that "the cleaning-women had hardly finished, and were still in evidence with their pails and mops." In reality, the theater was filled with people who always came to Pastor's on Monday evening to see the week's new show.

After performing, they waited anxiously to find out how management liked the act. When Tony entered their dressing room, he was reported to have said, "Well, you kids do a fine act. I'm going to give you a better place tomorrow." Maggie Cline, also on the bill, liked their routine and wished them well. Tony wrote them a recommendation dated February 4, 1895. "The Houdinis act as performed here I found satisfactory and interesting," signed Tony Pastor, on his personal stationery.

With attendance still lagging, in March Tony began advertising "good reserved seats for 25 cents and 50 cents." Business improved slightly but, without familiar headliners on the bill, he was unable to fill the theater. For several weeks, he featured former circus performers. Then, he introduced a new strategy to improve attendance, intended to compete directly with Keith's Union Square Theater's continuous vaudeville. He offered matinees on Monday, Tuesday, Friday and Saturday. The strategy seemed to work, so in early April, Tony offered matinees six days a week. He had persuaded performers to appear twelve times a week instead of eight, with only a slight increase in salaries. The move appeared to work, as he attracted larger audiences. Again, the arrival of Vesta Tilley for a six-week engagement put Tony's profit in the black.

Tilley opened on April 22 to a vociferously cheering audience. Dressed in attractive costumes, she sang five songs, with the audience applauding her throughout. Floral offerings were handed over the footlights during her performance. "She still maintains her work at a standard justifying the highest praise and commending immediate recognition," reported the *Clipper* reviewer. Tilley's stay at Tony's theater was a financial bonanza for him.

On March 22, Tony celebrated the thirtieth anniversary of his theater management to a full house loaded with performers and managers showing their respect for

This photograph of Tony appeared in the *Dramatic Mirror* on his thirtieth anniversary as a theater manager. Tony was sixty-two years old. Although he had curtailed his performances, he still ran the theater, as he had for three decades (Harvard Theater Collection).

the "venerable gentleman." Upon the completion of his act, he was inundated with bouquets. Harry Sanderson came on the stage carrying a photograph album and, in a brief speech, presented it to Tony with compliments from his associate managers. On the cover of the album was inlaid a gold medallion surrounded by figures, all in gilt. The medallion was inscribed: "Presented to Tony Pastor, to commemorate his thirtieth anniversary as theater manager, by his brother managers of the city of New York." Tony, with tears in his eyes, thanked the entire audience for their heart-warming display of sentiment.

On April 1, Tony launched his annual summer tour in Brooklyn. While in Williamsburg, Tony returned to his theater to make the introductions for Tilley. The company then proceeded to Boston, Detroit and Chicago, completing the first part of the tour in early June. When Tony returned to New York, he, his wife and Tilley boarded a steamer for England. His theater remained open one week after Tilley closed and reopened August 19, featuring several traveling companies. Tony returned to New York July 13 and began the second portion of the summer tour August 5 in Long Branch. Vesta Tilley's appearance gave Tony a small profit for the 1894–1895 season amounting to slightly over $5,000. It had been a hard-fought year made up of business decisions that actually netted Tony very little.

The summer tour cast featured the Russell Brothers, Will H. Fox, Fisher and Caswell, John and Nellie McCarthy, Travelle and M. Layman, not all headliners but familiar enough to draw crowds. The company struggled through Massachusetts, Ohio and Michigan on its way to Chicago. In Chicago, Vesta Victoria joined the company and box office receipts vastly improved, remaining so for the rest of the tour. Prior to opening the fall season, the company played in Brooklyn and the addition of Pacquerette contributed to crowded houses.

The new season at Tony's theater opened on October 28. A packed house, audience enthusiasm, large quantities of floral displays and an atmosphere of good cheer highlighted Tony's return home. Members of the road company were supplemented by several new performers whom the patrons embraced. Led by Victoria and Pacquerette, the program was filled with professional entertainment. Tony received extended applause when he entered the stage, sang a full repertory of songs to the point of hoarseness, and retired to shouts of approbation.

Through November, the programs were well received. But even with the appeal of Victoria and Pacquerette, patrons did not fill the house. When Victoria and Pacquerette left, they were replaced by Bessie Bellwood, another English music hall star whose act was similar to Bonehill's. Bellwood stayed until the end of December and garnered good box office receipts. But, regardless of the foreign stars' successes, the results were still not enough to challenge Keith's Union Square dominance of the area.

The holiday fare consisted of the usual entertainment, tilted somewhat to appeal to ladies and children. With songs and dances, roller skating, banjos, Swiss bells, juggling, bicycles, magic and Tony's Christmas carols, audiences went home happy and satisfied. Tony gave away one thousand dolls to ladies and children attending the matinees. The annual Christmas festival for children of the stage was held December 29, administered by "Aunt" Louisa Eldredge and Mrs. Pastor. Tony acted as host and announced each children's act. Performers like Lotta, Cora Tanner, Neil Burgess, Bonnie Thornton and others served the children at the banquet. For the first time, Tony was not involved in the planning of the event; Harry Sanderson had taken over his responsibilities.

Tony was reminded of the changing face of vaudeville when Hammerstein's Victoria Theater opened at Long Acre Square and Proctor opened a theater at 58th Street. Both featured family-style vaudeville. Now Pastor's was not the only clean, high-class house in town; other managers had adapted the same policy with good results. The emphasis on headliners and professionalism made bidding for performers difficult with the result of another increase in actors' salaries.

Tony and Sanderson were debating the effect of continuous vaudeville on their business. Competition from theaters with the new format was affecting box office receipts, but the costs of operating a theater for eleven hours each day and paying higher salaries seemed prohibitive. Besides, would Tony's loyal patrons accept the new system and continue their visits as often as before? And would new patrons be attracted by the change of operations? Their debate continued for several weeks; Tony even consulted some of his favorite performers and old friends Robert Grau and lawyer Abe Hummel to determine their opinions about the new format.

On January 13, 1896, Tony made a special announcement that gained headlines in the press. He was changing his format of thirty-one years to that of continuous vaudeville. The press noted that it was the first time in Tony's role as theater owner that he followed a rival manager's business decision. And he took the change one step further by lowering the prices of seats to 20 and 30 cents. The *Times* suggested that Tony had applied the new format due to the neighborhood in which he was located. The intense competition from Keith's continuous house went unmentioned.

> Tony Pastor, the veteran theater impresario, has joined the forces of "continuous" performance managers, and tomorrow his theater will become one of the regular all-day performance houses, 30 cents securing the best seat in the house and 20 cents a seat in the balcony. Mr. Pastor has decided to change his policy after long thought. He believes that the continuous performance is the only one required in the section where his theater is situated. Mr. Pastor proposes to give just as good a performance as ever, only his performers will have to work a little harder for the money.[9]

The *Clipper* seemed more nostalgic and generous regarding Tony's pivotal decision.

> Monday, January 13, marked the beginning of the end of the policy which had made this house a local favorite, and a resort well-known throughout the whole field of amusement. In keeping with his well-known qualities of enterprise and business sagacity, Manager Pastor has determined to keep pace with the current trend of fashion, and will therefore inaugurate continuous performances with the beginning of next week. In making this move the genial manager has sprung a genuine surprise, but to those who know him best there will come no doubts as to the soundness of his business logic.[10]

Patrons were confused about the change in admission prices, especially those people used to occupying the best seats in the theater. Tony was forced to explain the new pricing policy, assuring them that the "best seats" remained higher.

> There seems to be an erroneous impression aboard that I have reduced my prices down to a level that the highest price of admission to my theater is thirty cents. I desire to correct this error by explaining that my prices are one dollar, seventy-five cents, thirty cents and twenty cents, the latter being the lowest price in the house. We have plenty of seventy-five cents and one dollar seats for the accommodation of our old patrons.[11]

Actually, Tony was reluctant to change the format but he believed he had no choice. He did not want to lower his admission prices but had to be competitive. Would the change be beneficial? He would know in a few months.

Somewhat surprisingly, Tony saw attendance improvement in a matter of weeks. Box office receipts were higher. But so were out-of-pocket costs, including salaries. The attentive *Clipper* observed that Tony's policy change was successful, judging by the increased patronage and "an air of determination that seemed to prevail" at the theater. But real profit was not yet discernible.

Tony followed the change by dropping the number of orchestra players to two pianists during the day. The orchestra returned for the evening performance. He also introduced the stereopticon to his act, by showing pictures while he sang. Koster and Bial's were already using the new picture machine but they used it as a chaser at the end of the program. Audiences seemed well disposed to the instrument and quickly expected it at every performance. Another alteration drew consternation from Tony's loyal patrons. He withdrew from performing during the second show, which ran from about 4 to 7 P.M. To see Tony required patrons to adjust their visiting schedules. Tony gave as an excuse the wear and tear on his voice.

Yet, contrary to Tony's fears, audiences packed the theater throughout the day and evenings called out the SRO sign. The new format appeared to be a hit with patrons, particularly with the loyalists. And many new people attended as well.

> Manager Pastor's cozy house has rarely fallen into recognition as a non-stopping vaudeville resort, and its new patrons have proven as loyal as were those in days agone found their weekly amusements in the excellent bills he maintained, and they are equally fortunate in having presented for their edification entertainments as thoroughly worthy as of yore.[12]

Receipts improved, as did profits. To assist in his drive for profitability, Tony had persuaded many of his favorite headliners to appear at their former salaries. A mixture of familiar faces and newcomers seemed to satisfy audiences and kept expenses in line. Those who agreed to Tony's terms were the Russell Brothers, Ad Ryman, O'Brien and Havel, Lillie Western, Lydia Yeaman-Titus, Frank Moran and George Evans. Among the new performers who warranted return engagements were Kitty Mitchell, a Quaker vocalist; Josephine Sabel, a ballad singer new to the local stage; Cora Routt, one of the first coon-shouters; and the Elinore Sisters, in funny sketches. Some of them played for three weeks in a row, with offers to return later in the season.

The *Dramatic Mirror* predicted that lower prices at Tony's would improve business. The *Clipper* noted that attendance at Keith's Union Square had declined since Tony went continuous. In March, Sanderson acknowledged that business at Pastor's was "looking up," but real profit remained elusive because of the combination of higher overhead and lower prices.

Tony welcomed the summer tour as an opportunity to improve his finances, with higher admission prices and large crowds at all of the familiar stops. But Tony's road company was no longer alone. More than twenty other companies were visiting the same towns and cities and competing for the audience dollar. Nearly all of them featured at least a few headliners and spent lavishly on advertising. Theater managers in smaller cities could now count on high-class companies appearing at their houses even during the summer when they were normally closed. Large cities now had several vaudeville houses open and it was not uncommon to have separate troupes playing in the same city at the same time.

Due to financial constraints, Tony's road company had no top headliners. Only O'Brien and Havel and Fields and Wooley were popular outside of New York. In contrast, Tony's theater, open during the summer as usual, featured top favorites like the Rogers Brothers, the Donovans, Katie Rooney, Maud Raymond, Bernard Dyllyn, the Elinore Sisters and a new star-in-the-making, Charlotte Ray, a vocalist and avowed "new woman." Tony believed he had to keep stocking his theater with first-class people to compete against the other vaudeville houses and maintain the size of his audience even during the normally slow summer months.

In another decision that surprised the theatrical world, Tony announced that his summer tour would continue to October. No break for the company this year since Tony was not traveling to Europe. In fact, he never traveled to Europe again. The likely factors in his decision centered around finances, according to the theatrical weeklies. The fact that other managers were actively involved in signing foreign performers may have also played a part in Tony's decision.

While in the middle of the tour, Tony unexpectedly returned to New York. Rumors suggested that he and Sanderson were discussing their financial situation. Actually, Tony was aching from a combination of arthritis and rheumatism, ailments that had bothered him for years but not to this extent. After two weeks' rest he was back leading the company.

Another possible reason for Tony's New York visit was the introduction in his theater of a moving picture machine, the kineopticon, which showed brief features that ran for a minute or more. The device was positioned at the end of the show to give a separation, or finality, to each complete program. It was an immediate hit. Pastor's audiences, used to new programs each week, expected the same from the moving pictures. In effect, the pictures reduced the number of performances on a bill but it cost additional money to purchase new material for each week's presentation. Several weeks later, Keith introduced the cinematographe to their bill. The biograph was already showing at Koster and Bial's. The events marked to beginning of the invasion of moving pictures into vaudeville, not as a chaser as originally intended, but as a distinct act on the program.

October 26 saw the opening of the 1896-1897 season at Tony's theater. As usual, it was a grand and gala affair. The primary feature was the appearance of electric lights for the stage and dressing rooms, with a Pastor promise to the audience that the entire theater would be "electrified" soon. The theater was crowded to SRO, the cast filled with all-stars: Clifford and Huth; Lew Dockstater, the veteran minstrel star; the Rogers Brothers; the Donovans; Maud Raymond; the Weston Sisters and others. As the *Clipper* observed:

> Monday night was given over to hits at all stages in the bill, and floral offerings and cheers for the favorites as they passed in review, making the night seem like an old time Pastor opening, with a stage as full as ever of performers of the highest class.[13]

Accompanying the cast was the kineopticon, in its twelfth consecutive week showing moving pictures.

In the fall of 1896, there were thirty-seven theaters operating in New York. Twelve featured vaudeville; three were museums with a mixture of oddities and variety; one was a minstrel theater. In Brooklyn, there were now thirteen theaters, five of which presented vaudeville programs. Of the twelve vaudeville houses in New York, five were located north of Tony's theater. The *Clipper* estimated that there were more than 10,000 performers in the country, half of them on the East Coast, and more than 2,000 in New York alone at any time. The number of new acts was proliferating; vaudeville bills were filled with newcomers; concert halls, beer gardens and ten-cent variety houses had become the proving ground for new people. Most never made it beyond that point.

The amusement industry continued to grow at a rapid pace and as it grew, innovations in production, diversity of acts, theater operations and enterprising entrepreneurs grew with it. While Tony was fully aware of these business conditions, he had to be more focused on his own theater and its survival. The *Times* discussed the rapid movement of New York entertainment and postulated that a few old-timers found it difficult to keep up. Tony was viewed as one of them.

Through the fall, Tony continued to present high-class programs. Dockstater, Raymond, Sabel and Western returned often. Houdini appeared in October. Hoey, Dyllyn, Evans, Arthur Sidman, of comic opera fame, and William Sweatnam, an old minstrel star, headlined weekly bills. The theater was continually crowded and the SRO sign was often seen hanging outside the lobby door. Finding that Keith's cinematographe was better than his own kineopticon, Tony adopted the machine also. Movie subjects now included news events and sports.

December 27 was the date of the annual Christmas festival for children of the theater. It had become one of the premier social events of the holiday season, attracting members of the city's social elite and prominent actresses. "Aunt" Louisa Eldredge and Mrs. Pastor were in charge of the activities but it was Harry Sanderson who oversaw all the details. Tony acted as host. An added feature of the event was the presentation of a silver dollar to each child, courtesy of an anonymous donor.

Early in 1897, the *Times* remarked about the increased popularity at Tony's theater.

> The attendance showed no falling off in the remarkable run of prosperity which has been the gratifying portion of Mr. Pastor since the introduction of non-stopping performance.[14]

Tony noted the renewed success of the theater. The ledgers showed a substantial profit during the previous six months. To his surprise, audiences embraced the continuous vaudeville format and found many advantages to its flexibility and, not incidentally, the low admission prices.

Two other changes in vaudeville policies became evident in early 1897. Managers like Keith and Proctor were signing legitimate actors to perform short skits at their theaters. Their salaries may have been high, but audiences crowded the theaters to see first-hand dramatic artists whom they would not have been able to see otherwise. However, Tony was not yet convinced that these players would appeal to his patrons.

More performers were uniting to form teams of sketch artists. While teaming had been more common among men doing comedy, Irish dances or song and dance routines, and women as singers and dancers, the new teams were made up of a man and a woman, often married, who performed a scripted and plotted sketch. There were three categories of sketches: entirely humorous, filled with jokes; serious with song and dance to lighten the mood; social commentary, satire, with character acting. Audiences enjoyed the change of pace, the woman performer as lead, and the social commentary as insightful glimpses of daily life. Tony saw these teams as welcome additions to his program, some of them seemingly like extensions of his own singing satires and parodies. He began to include at least one of these acts in each week's program. The format would become more important in succeeding years as male-female teams became star attractions.

Still another phenomenon was noticed in the theatrical weeklies. Performers became primary advertisers, mentioning in their ads where they had recently played to good success, and where they are about to play. This was an excellent promotional device to obtain future bookings. Many of Tony's newcomers advertised after playing at his theater since appearing at Pastor's was still an important stamp of approval. This personal advertising continued until the onset of the Syndicate, when all booking began to go through agents and a centralized system.

Celebrations filled the March calendar. The Elks celebrated their 29th anniversary with a stag social with over 600 members present. Several vaudeville performers appeared in the program and a large banquet was served. Tony was chairman of the event. A moment of silence paid respect to the charter members of the organization begun in 1868. Both Fernando and Billy Pastor had been original members of the fraternal group and were honored.

Tony was feted on his thirty-second anniversary of theater management by an all-star cast, including veteran artists like Gus Williams, Lillie Western, James F. Hoey and Bonnie Thornton. The house was packed with admirers and friends. A joyful Tony sang several new songs "with as much gusto as he ever did." A week later, Harry Sanderson was given his annual benefit, in the nineteenth year of his work as Tony's treasurer and personal counselor. Volunteers put on a long stage program, and gifts came from performers, theater associates and backstage crews.

The annual summer tour began March 29 in Philadelphia with a mixed company of familiar favorites and newcomers with none from Europe. Gus Williams, James F. Hoey, the Donovans, and Dick and Alice McAvoy represented the veterans. New to the company were Mr. and Mrs. Charles Ellis in a comedy sketch; Florence Bindley, vocalist; John and Bertha Gleeson, in a serio-comic skit; and Watson and Hutchins, comic acrobats. From Philadelphia, they jumped to Chicago for a three-week engagement, one week at each of three theaters. Each theater had "big houses." A special feature of the Chicago run was the appearance of Maud Nugent singing her new hit, "Sweet Rosie O"Grady." After Chicago, Tony took a three-week vacation at the seashore.

Nine theaters remained open during the summer in New York. Two of them, the Casino and the Olympia, introduced roof garden entertainment. These were open-air shows, with a temporary stage and tables and chairs for the audience. Their operations were problematic, with the weather determining the schedule. Still, it was a new form of entertainment and attracted good audiences.

Of the nine theaters, six were vaudeville houses, including Tony's. To combat the new outdoor theaters, Tony advertised that he had "the coolest theater in New York." How he supported that claim is unknown. Kineopticon pictures were added to Tony's summer bills only to be replaced by Lumiere's cinematographe in August.

Following his vacation, Tony called back the summer company, opening at Saratoga on August 16. Stops in cities in Connecticut, Massachusetts and New York preceded the usual weekly engagements in Cleveland, Detroit, Chicago (for another two weeks), Cincinnati, Philadelphia, Baltimore and Brooklyn. Crowds were good in these cities but very few claimed sellouts. Sanderson reported that the company was "doing a good business," but superlatives were missing from the statement.

Big features at Tony's theater during September included the Four Cohans in a skit entitled "Money to Burn," written by George M.; the first appearance of the Negro team Williams and Walker at the Pastor theater; Edward Harrigan and Company in a play, *Sergeant Hickey*; Pauline Markham, a dramatic actress in a one-act play; and J.K. Emmett, son of the original Fritz, in a character skit. They all drew full houses. But most significant to theater critics and patrons was Tony's announcement that he had signed a lease to continue at the 14th Street Theater for another ten years. After much consideration, Tony had decided to remain at his current location.

Tony missed a few weeks while on tour due to illness but he was in full voice when his theater opened its new season October 25. His songs won their usual welcome and applause. The traveling company was featured, and they entertained the full house with enthusiasm. Eleven other vaudeville theaters were open, most of them promoting high-class entertainment.

Foreign artists like Bonehill, Victoria and Tilley had been signed to tour the country and appear at rival theaters in New York. Comic opera was in full bloom with Lillian Russell, Della Fox and Louise Montague attracting large audiences with their elegantly costumed fantasies. Dramatic theater was well attended due to a coterie of stars represented by Sarah Bernhardt (on one of her several farewell tours), Richard Mansfield, Maude Adams and John Drew. New York theaters were

The Four Cohans were a featured act at Tony's theater during the 1890s. The teenager George M. was already providing material for the family act.

flourishing, and a new commercial center around Long Acre Square attracted large crowds, locals and tourists.

The fall season at Tony's presented more old favorites, fewer foreigners, more sketch teams, fewer novelties and the cinematographe. Audiences cheered the appearances of stalwarts Bonnie Thornton, George "Honey Boy" Evans, Lew Dockstater, the Elinore Sisters, Billy Carter, Frank Cushman, the Sidmans and the Four Cohans. Newcomer Charles T. Aldrich, a comic juggling sensation, was well received as were the Seven Reed Birds, a singing group. Sketch artists Sam and Kittie Morton, Bob and Kittie Emmett and Filson and Errol garnered audience approval with their comic and satirical acts. The cinematographe showed current events from around the world and short stories. Business was good and Tony was maintaining a small profit in spite of the competition. Audiences observed that his high-class shows had not been compromised. And Tony could depend on a group of loyal artists to appear at his theater often.

Personal health had now become Tony's primary concern. He had rarely been ill, missing only a few days during the previous three decades. The past six months, however, revealed a series of physical problems brought on by arthritis, rheumatism and a feeling of fatigue. For years, Tony had depended on medications to alleviate the aches, pains and stress of performance, travel and business crises. He particularly depended on an all-purpose medicine, St. John's Wort, said to be helpful for anything from "la grippe" to muscular strains. (Today, we know the product to be used for depression, anxiety and exhaustion.) Tony even appeared in ads for the product, extolling its virtues and claiming that its use every morning gave him energy throughout the day.

No one would suggest to Tony that he might be slowing down because of age, although it was apparent to those who knew him well. Reviewers and audiences were aware that his voice had become even more husky and gravelly than before. At several performances, he was forced to speak his lyrics rather than sing them because of vocal strain. And when he forgot some of the lyrics to familiar songs, Tony began to realize both his physical and mental problems.

Only Harry Sanderson and Tony's wife could recognize the actual effects of business stress and pressure that affected Tony during the previous few years. Tony had already relinquished tasks to Sanderson and summer vacations were now scheduled without dispute. Foreign trips had ceased and summer tours were less arduous. Running a theater and performing in it was no easy task, and Tony pondered his strength and ability to do both with his usual efficiency and buoyancy. He realized, with some degree of sadness, that his performing days might soon be over.

The Christmas festival for children of the stage was held December 26 at Tony's theater with the manager as host. The committee and Sanderson handled all of the arrangements, which concluded to everyone's enjoyment. But of greatest interest to New Yorkers was a special event to take place on New Year's Eve—the unification of five cities into a super city, greater New York, that would encompass Manhattan, Brooklyn, Queens, Staten Island and the Bronx. The event was one of the largest festivals of connection in U.S. history, maybe the world. The road to Consolidation Eve, as it was called, had not been an easy one.

Brooklyn's town fathers tried to halt it but failed. Tammany Hall was ambivalent even though "Boss" Croker would control the new city. Manhattan was wary of accepting the responsibilities of their sister cities. Staten Islanders wondered how they had become a part of this arrangement, being so geographically removed. But on the cold and rainy evening of December 31, 1897, the population was ready for the transformation.

William Randolph Hearst volunteered to produce the extravaganza. A committee of important business people in the city was formed to plan the festivities. Tony was selected as a member of this committee, representing the entertainment industry. Months of planning, and thousands of dollars from donors, went into the event.

An immense crowd gathered at Union Square ready to accompany a line of illuminated floats to City Hall. The entire parade filled City Hall Park, brightened by 500 magnesium lights. Bands and choral groups entertained and competed for silver cups, awarded by Tony and the committee. Near midnight, the rain turned to snow. When Trinity Church's bells tolled the hour, field artillery gave a 100-gun salute, flares were shot into the sky, the city's ferries and tugs whistled and the crowd joined in singing "Auld Lang Syne."

New York City now had a combined population of three million people and was over three hundred square miles in size, larger than Paris.

Tony, unlike many of his business colleagues, could recall when the city was in the stop-and-start throes of development, from its Bowery origins to its uptown commercial culture. The changes in popular theater that made Tony nostalgic — immigrant populations and rising social classes, enterprising managers and entrepreneurs, theater builders, and performing artists who brought amusement to the masses. Tony had been an integral part of this movement for almost fifty years.

The year 1898 brought both domestic and international events that helped to reshape and revitalize popular theater yet again. After diplomatic skirmishing for months with Spain, the U.S. demanded that Cuba be given its independence. National opinion, inflamed by the "yellow sheets" of Hearst and Pulitzer, strongly supported U.S. intervention. The battleship *Maine* was sent to Havana to protect American citizens in Cuba. On February 15, the *Maine* mysteriously exploded and killed 260 on board. The U.S. declared war on Spain on April 21. The war continued until August, when Spain was soundly defeated. While the war was going on, the country was overtaken with patriotic spirit.

In what was called the birth of Negro musical comedy, Bob Cole and Billy Johnson produced and played in *A Trip to Coon Town* (a takeoff on Hoyt's *A Trip to Chinatown*, produced in 1891). The show opened April 5 at the Third Avenue Theater and remained for almost the entire summer. It proved that there was an audience for an all–Negro production. On July 5, Will Marion Cook put on a musical sketch called "Clorindy, the Origin of the Cakewalk" at the Casino Theater roof garden. It was the first time an all–Negro show appeared at a major theater before an all-white audience. Several other all–Negro shows followed and it became more common to see Negro performers on vaudeville stages.

Buffalo Bill's Wild West Show opened in New York in April, outdoing any of its previous visits to the city. With cattle stampedes, stagecoach robberies, cowboy–Indian shoot-outs and the expert marksmanship of Annie Oakley, crowds of 5,000 spectators at every performance relived the idealized West of Bill Cody. Buffalo Bill, an impressive figure, attired in elegant Western wear, white mustached with flowing white hair, sitting erect in the saddle, was viewed as the "greatest one-man tableau that ever lived," according to one reviewer. When Buffalo Bill came to town, popular theater patrons shifted to his arena.

Dramatic theater had been sparked by the aura of Sarah Bernhardt, which translated into an increased interest in serious plays and larger-than-life artists whose fame was exploited by the press. Madam Mojeska, John Drew, Ada Rehan, Maude Adams, E.H. Southern, Julia Marlowe, Fanny Davenport, McKee Rankin, Mrs. Leslie Carter and Richard Mansfield represented the largest collection of legitimate actors and actresses at any one time in New York. Increasing numbers of the middle class found dramatic theater a pleasurable way to elevate themselves.

What had once been a continuous trail of foreign headliners traveling to the U.S. to conquer American audiences had reversed itself. Now, more American performers were going to Europe to enhance their careers and score triumphs before expectant audiences. After successes in Europe, performers returned home to lucrative bookings and personal fame. Nothing was more intriguing to an audience than an ad that declared "Now, after three years of triumph in Europe, _____ will headline the coming week's attraction."

Professional baseball had become such a popular leisure time amusement that it competed directly with theaters for attendance during the summer. Many theaters closed for the summer because of the baseball craze. Several well-known baseball players appeared on the vaudeville stage during the winter and were well received. This was equally true for boxing champions.

Tony was obviously influenced by all these events, adopting programs, artist selection and schedules to meet changing audience tastes. He promoted American performers with uniquely American acts. He signed several dramatic artists to appear at his theater in one-act plays. And he introduced a number of acts that had matured after playing in lesser vaudeville houses or on tour. Ed Latell was a banjo comedian; Joe Welch did Hebrew impersonations; Bobby Gaylor was an Irish comedian; and Florence Moore was a twelve-year-old singing comedienne. Sketch artists included Al Fields and Belle Stewart, Hallen and Fuller, Dick and Alice McAvoy and O'Brien and Havel. Tony even persuaded seventy-year-old Annie Yeamans (Lydia's mother) to perform an old skit, "A Basement Flirtation," to audiences' delight.

When the Spanish-American War began, Tony sang patriotic songs, some of them dating back to the Civil War, updating the lyrics. He reintroduced the singing of "The Star-Spangled Banner" with audiences. It was only one of many patriotic songs at the time. (Congress did not designate it the national anthem until 1931.)

Each week, moving pictures were filled with current events, particularly war-related shorts. Specific moving picture companies like Lubin, Biograph and Edison sold reels of film at twelve cents for 100 feet. They were producing dozens of new shorts each month for distribution.

Tony advertised heavily during the spring and summer, emphasizing the quality of his presentations, along with the low prices. He attracted good to excellent crowds, based on the artist's popularity or a unique program. The *Clipper,* noting Tony's continued flow of customers, observed that

> There is no diminution in the crowds which throng this old established and favorite resort for admirers of all that is good and wholesome in vaudeville.[15]

When, on March 22, Tony celebrated his thirty-third anniversary, there was no special observance except a full "to the walls" theater that cheered him each time he appeared on stage. At the evening show, after his performance, Tony gave a short speech of thanks. The *Clipper,* with a note of wonder, commented on Tony's continued stage presence.

> Still in the harness, he sings his comic songs and patriotic lays with as much gusto, with attendant applause, as of yore.[16]

Tony decided to keep his theater open for the summer, in spite of potentially smaller audiences. He also decided to put together a traveling company and begin a summer tour April 11 in Brooklyn. The cast was impressive: the Rogers Brothers; Maud Raymond; Ed Latell; Milton and Dolly Nobles, sketch artists; Harry Foy and Flo Clark, in a comic skit; Manning and Weston, Irish comedians; and the Pantzer Trio, acrobats. They played to full houses at Hyde and Behman's.

The company was on its way to Philadelphia when the Spanish-American War began. The government immediately limited all railroad travel, forcing a disappointed Tony and company to return to New York. During the first week in May, Tony was absent from his theater, no excuse given. He returned the following week and appeared on the program for five consecutive weeks. He missed two weeks in June but returned again June 18 and played to the end of July when he and his wife went on vacation visiting friends in Indiana. The press speculated on Tony's "disappearances" but were unable to question him or Sanderson. Later information, coming from

Tony's wife, indicated he was suffering from arthritis, sometimes so severe that he could hardly walk. He also suffered some depression, attributed to the aborted summer tour.

A refreshed Tony decided to form a new traveling company to tour even though the government continued its ban on non-essential train travel. The tour would be confined to cities close to New York with the railroad agreeing to accommodate Tony. The company opened in Newark on August 20. The tour was terminated September 3. Theater attendance was poor and transportation problems abounded. After thirty-two consecutive years, Tony never took out a summer touring company again.

Back at his theater, Tony missed two weeks in mid–September. He returned the third week to large crowds of cheering patrons welcoming him back.

> After a short lay off, the manager is singing again, and his host of friends find their usual delight in his round of comic ditties and well-pointed parodies, the applause which invariably follows, showing plainly that all retain a warm spot in their affections for the ever industrious warrior of song.[17]

Tony's bills continued to feature the latest in headliners: the Russell Brothers, Emma Carus, Ethel Levey, Maud Nugent, Frank McNish, Nellie Burt and "good old" Lillie Western. If Tony himself was not on the bill, he still presented a stellar program of proven artists. And Tony was gone again from the end of September to November 13, a long time for audiences not to see their favorite at the theater. No public explanation was forthcoming. The press noted that, for the first time under Tony's management, he did not put on an official fall opening event. Tony was at home bedridden, preventing him from going to the theater. Sanderson was handling all of the business affairs and performer scheduling. What was wrong with Tony? the press wondered. Is it possible he is about to retire? The queries were answered — to some degree — when Tony appeared on the program the second week of November. The *Clipper* headlined the event.

> Manager Pastor is again in stage harness after a few week's lay off and is singing a splendid round of comic ballads and parodies.[18]

He played to December 3 and was off again. This time it was announced that Sanderson was handling business affairs in Tony's absence. Tony reappeared for the holiday season. The theater was crowded with well wishers. However, Tony did not attend the annual Christmas festival for stage children. His absence was conspicuous.

Press speculation was rampant with questions about Tony's health and his future. Since August, Tony had performed for only six weeks. Tony himself was weighing the alternatives about carrying on his responsibilities both on and backstage.

At the same time, the question of Tony's financial stability flared in the press when it was discovered that he had recently sold a property on 94th Street.

14

Tony Retires from the Stage

Tony astonished everyone by returning to his theater at the beginning of January 1899. An ad in the *Kennebec Journal* provided a reason for his quick recovery. Hyomei was a recently produced patent medicine.

> Dear Sirs:
> One may live without "Hyomei" but one cannot live truly happy without it. So far as I know, it is the only remedy that positively cures catarrh and kindred diseases. It has been invaluable to me, for in my work much depends on my freedom from illness.
> Tony Pastor

For years, Tony had been known to depend on daily doses of St. John's Wort to sustain his energy level and motivation. Ads boasting of his use of the product appeared occasionally in the *New York Clipper*. The switch in use and endorsement of a new medicine at this particular time seems more than coincidental.

Whether Tony was really be helped by this elixir is unknown. What is known is that he was back performing "as of yore." Audiences crowded the theater to see the only Tony and cheered his performances. Theater attendance improved dramatically. Invigorated by the response, Tony vowed to continue as long as he was able.

When one theatrical weekly discovered that Tony was about to return, they declared there would be "a continuation of prosperity for the genial actor/manager." In bold letters, his ads shouted, "Tony Pastor Will Sing!" The theater was filled every day to see "the old warrior," as the *Dramatic Mirror* called him, at his place on the stage. It was as if Tony and his audiences had been suddenly rejuvenated. When Tony performed, his loyal followers rushed to see their idol.

Tony played through all of January, two appearances a day, the matinee and evening shows. Dramatic actresses in one-act skits were on the bill with him. They were drifting into vaudeville because of the easy hours and high salaries. The bill also included a group of sketch teams and some newcomers, namely Elfie Fay, a petite, pretty vocalist; the Maude Detty Trio, in song and dances; the Garnellas, acrobats; and Emma Carus, a bright new star, made a reappearance, and William T. Carleton, a singer of Irish songs who had debuted at Tony's two decades earlier, now sang operatic solos. For the entire month, tremendous crowds filled the house.

One sour note claimed Tony's attention during this time. He had to lean on his lawyer, Abe Hummel, to deal with a breach of contract against the Rogers Brothers. They were to appear in January but E.A. Albee gave them a more lucrative deal to appear on the Keith circuit, disrupting Tony's plans. Tony had paid the Rogers Brothers for two weeks in advance. Hummel took the brothers and Keith to court but, to avoid any negative publicity, they returned the salaries. The Rogers Brothers never appeared at Tony's theater again; a few years later, they were hired by Keith to compete against Weber and Fields. Keith and Albee were gaining a reputation for stealing headliners from other managers, a practice that had previously been rare. Such tactics were an early indication of their aggressive business practices.

Tony did not perform for the entire month of February. He was seen at the theater but not during the performances. In his place were familiars like Ed Latell, Filson and Errol, Elfie Fay, in a return engagement, and Mr. and Mrs. Harry Budworth, new, in a dramatic sketch. Business fell off.

Tony reappeared on the Washington's Birthday program with new comic songs. "Profitable patronage was a remarkable feature this week," reported the *Clipper* reviewer. Tony continued his daily appearances through the middle of May. During this time, he was supported by the services of Emma Carus, Gus Williams, Dick and Alice McAvoy, the Seven Reed Birds, Elfie Fay (again), Ella Wesner (out of retirement), Pat Rooney, Jess Dandy in Jewish parodies and a startling newcomer, Billy Van, a mimic and impersonator. A full complement of sketch artists completed the program. Good business returned to the theater.

Tony was on the committee and performed at the annual Actors' Fund benefit on April 3. Thanks to the participation of more than fifty performers and crowds of people willing to pay one or two dollars for seats, more than $10,000 was collected. The fund manager reported that in the past year they had assisted 779 people and buried another sixty-two.

In May, actor Dan Sully, an old Pastor favorite, declared bankruptcy, owing several thousand dollars to a host of lenders, one of whom was Tony. Tony not only forgave Sully's debt but also paid off some of the bills. Sully was ill and it appeared unlikely that he would return to the stage.

March 22 was Tony's thirty-fourth anniversary as manager, but little attention was paid to the event. A few floral arrangements were in the lobby and telegrams were delivered to the theater. Tony sang his usual budget of songs, but deferred the audience's attention to the rest of the program, a mixed group of new sketch artists—Joseph Palmer and Company, Greene and Friend, Matthews and Harris (soon to be frequent visitors to the theater), and Fostelle and Emmett, a male-female song and dance team gaining recognition for their fine work. Another newcomer to the vaudeville stage was a young, handsome singer and dancer named Jack Norworth, destined for headliner status as a composer and oft-married entertainer. One week in April featured Edward Harrigan in a comic skit. (David Braham, Jr., son of Harrigan's musical conductor at the old Theater Comique, was in the skit.) Children of previous performers were appearing frequently on the vaudeville stage.

Tony was missing from the program for a week in the middle of May, "resting" said Harry Sanderson. He returned the following week and performed until early June, when a personal appointment of importance took him from New York to Elmhurst, Long Island. The press believed they had discovered why Tony had sold a property the previous year. He announced the purchase of a home in Elmhurst, in a colony of homes owned by various business people and performers. While his theater remained open during the summer, Tony did not perform.

Elmhurst was an extensive tract, subdivided into 1,700 lots. Plot size was limited to two city lots or 50 × 100 feet. Most of the city dwellers bought more than two lots, greatly reducing the actual number of dwellings. Elmhurst's population consisted of Manhattan and Brooklyn businessmen who wanted to combine the comfort and luxury of a country villa with proximity to their offices in town. Edgar Smith, playwright for Weber and Fields; Amelia Summerville, actress; Frank Bush and J.W. Kelly joined such personages as the chief inspector of the New York Board of Health, a Manhattan restaurant owner, the clerk of the Supreme Court, several manufacturers and professional people.

Pat Rooney, Sr., was an outstanding Irish song and dance man who affected an intimate touch with his audiences. When Tony needed a headliner, Rooney was always available for his old friend (Harry Ransom Humanities Research Center).

Tony purchased a Queen Anne mansion on the corner of Whitney Avenue and Ninth Street, on a spacious lot, for $7,200. After the Pastors moved in, Mrs. Pastor put on a formal housewarming, attended by locals of all ages.

The housewarming, held on July 13, Mrs. Pastor's birthday, began early in the morning. She had invited all the children of Elmhurst to take part. More than 200 children came to the

Pastor residence, where a decorated barn was open to them. Tony served as host, telling the children stories and leading them in songs. Ransome, the magician, entertained the children and was followed by a Punch and Judy show. Tony sat in the midst of the children and enjoyed the show as much as his little friends. A donkey party started, each child receiving a tail to pin on the tailless animal. Lunch and refreshments, with Mrs. Pastor as hostess, included a wide assortment of sandwiches and desserts.

The same evening, a gathering for the adults took place. A barn dance was held, the property decorated with Chinese lanterns, bunting and plants. An orchestra played until midnight. A cakewalk contest was put on, with Tony and John T. Kelly as judges. Mrs. Kelly and John Russell won honors. At the end of the evening festivities, Tony presented his wife with a deed conveying the entire property to her, the crowd cheering their assent. He also gave her a diamond and pearl belt and diamond ring. Among the guests present were the Russells, Bonnie Thornton, the Hallens, the Kellys, the Slavins, Augusta de Forrest, Beatrice Moreland, and the Angelis Sisters.

To get to the theater each day, Tony had to rise early and catch a train to Manhattan, a forty-five minute ride, in order to be at his desk at 9:30 A.M. In the evening, he left the theater at 9 or 9:30 P.M. and returned home, finishing the day with a dessert and coffee with his wife.

Summer audiences were good to average, depending on the bill. Even with the occasional favorite headliner, the theater was never full. Several stars returned to Tony's during their time-off from the Syndicate circuits to supplement his program, their loyalty to the manager more important than the salary they received. Irene Franklin, now a star, put on a child's dress which she had worn during the early Christmas festivals for stage children and sang some catchy tunes. Blanche Ring, on the vaudeville stage for five years, interpolated several hit songs. The Four Cohans entertained with George's skit, "Running for Office." And Charles "Honey Boy" Evans, a decided favorite of the audience, sang and danced to tremendous applause.

But the star of the summer was a machine. In June, Tony acquired the American Vitagraph, a moving picture machine vastly improved over existing models, along with a dictionary of films covering a wide variety of topics. Audiences saw Jim Jefferies training for his fight, Spanish-American War films, parades of foreign royalty, Admiral Dewey's return, and assorted short subjects. Tony featured the Vitagraph in his ads and bill postings.

When Tony returned to performing in early October, the results were predictable.

> Manager Pastor returned to stage activity and was welcomed by an overflowing house. His repertory of new songs pleased immensely.[1]

The program for the week was attractive: playing along with Tony were Hilda Thomas, Ed Latell, Fred Niblo, Nellie Burt, the Pantzer Trio, Ward and Curran and Harry Thomson. The Vitagraph concluded the bill. Ads declared "Tony will sing every evening." He appeared on the evening programs only.

Tony performed for four weeks and his appearance spurred attendance. When he left the stage this time, it was not because of illness but rather money. Tony had negotiated an engagement in Chicago for three weeks, one week each at the Olympic Theater, Haymarket Theater and the Grand Opera House. His salary of $600 a week was more than his theater would have made in profit for the same period. Chicago was one of Tony's favorite cities, and he had not appeared there for several seasons. Patrons waited in anticipation for his return. Tickets for performances were sold out a week in advance. A house company of fifteen artists was made up mostly of unknowns, at least unknown to New Yorkers. The three-week engagement generated full houses and many accolades for Tony.

After the highly successful trip to Chicago, Tony returned to his theater in time for the Thanksgiving program.

Manager Pastor is in harness again after his Western trip, and his songs and parodies were as abundantly applauded and as much appreciated as ever.[2]

But Tony was tired, and audiences could see it in his step and hear it in his voice. He persevered for two weeks, then left the stage and did not perform for the remainder of the year, including the holiday program. When the thirteenth annual Christmas festival for children of the stage took place on December 24, Tony was not in attendance. Harry Sanderson took over his duties as host.

The last few weeks of the year did produce some firsts at the theater, however. Artie Hall, a petite vocalist with a strong voice, appeared in New York for the first time with a rendition of songs soon to be labeled coon-shouting. She was so well received by patrons that she appeared for two more weeks. A new comedy team to locals, Mr. and Mrs. Joe Keaton, knockabout dancers and kickers, enthused the crowds with their antics. Their child, Buster, watched them from the wings.

Early in January, 1900, the Actors' Fund staged a memorial benefit in honor of performers who had passed on. It was another fund-raising event in which artists impersonated some of the past headliners. Tony had had quite a few of them and as their names were mentioned to the audience, he reminisced some episode about each one of them. The list included Billy Birch, the great minstrel man; Nels Seymour, a versatile artist; Frank Kerns, a stalwart in the many skits the stock company performed each week; Tony Hart; Charley White; Billy Emmet; Kitty O'Neil and the talented but tormented Harry Kernall. The event reportedly had a somber effect on Tony, as these former headliners were recalled and their accomplishments reviewed.

Tony rejoined the company at the beginning of the year with the knowledge that his presence on the stage meant larger crowds. At the same time, he featured the American Vitagraph even more in his ads and on the program. One week, he led off the bill with Vitagraph films and the event was duly noted by the press. It was the story of Cinderella and "scored one of the most distinct successes within our knowledge of animated views," said the *Clipper*. Cinderella played for three weeks, leading off the bill with another assortment of moving pictures at the end, as well. The format continued until Cinderella was removed. Three other vaudeville theaters showed moving pictures—Koster & Bial's, Keith's Union Square and the Theater Comique—but all three used the films as chasers.

The winter and spring programs featured a mixture of familiar headliners and new acts. Emma Carus, James Richmond Glenroy, Nellie Burt, George Evans, Blanche Ring and Fred Niblo were joined by new sketch artists and the recent successes Artie Hall and Hilda Thomas, whom Tony touted as a successor to Lillian Russell. Also on the bill were Billy and Mildred Jackson, a Negro couple, who performed an eccentric song and dance. Tony performed through early February and then left the entertaining to others. This time, he admitted to hoarseness and fatigue. Attendance dropped when Tony was not on the bill.

On March 22, Tony returned to the theater to celebrate his thirty-fifth anniversary, appearing at both the matinee and evening programs. Audiences cheered his presence and his comic songs. He received many floral offerings and congratulatory messages. Tony continued performing until the middle of May. Packed houses ensued as long as Tony and his excellent programs were maintained.

Tony left the theater to appear at a meeting of vaudeville managers and owners in Boston. B.F. Keith and E.A. Albee had brought everyone together for a discussion about new policies to run vaudeville theaters. The group included F.F. Proctor, Hyde and Behman, Kohl and Castle, J.D. Hopkins, Martin Beck and Morris Meyerfield. Combined, these managers controlled more than sixty first-class vaudeville theaters across the country. Tony and Weber and Fields were also invited to attend. Weber and Fields were there because of their popular touring companies

A poster of the outstanding women artists who played at Tony's theater during the 1890s. Tilley, Bellwood and Victoria were from the English music halls. Havel and Huth represented the "new American women" in vaudeville (Harry Ransom Humanities Research center).

and leases on theaters in Boston and Chicago. Tony only owned one theater and had no interest in expanding, yet he had been asked to attend the meetings. It is likely that Keith and the others viewed Tony's reputation and long-time prestige as important factors in selling their new ideas to the theatrical community.[3]

The Boston meetings ended with no decisions. Managers voiced their own opinions about the Keith-Albee recommendation for them to operate a centralized booking agency. The meeting moved to New York where, after three days of negotiations, the Association of Vaudeville Managers (A.V.M.) was formed. Both Tony and Weber and Fields were suspicious of Keith's intent and signed the agreement reluctantly. Tony visualized only problems for himself. His access to the best headliners would be limited. The number of available performers for his theater would be reduced. He would be unable to sign them for the times he wanted them to appear. And he would be unable to pay the salaries that the new booking agency would demand. But, if he did not sign, he would be left out of the planning and operational structure of the new group.

Albee had persuaded managers that a centralized and efficiently run organization was essential for the continual growth of vaudeville. To offset a performer's possible loss of income, the centrally controlled booking agency could guarantee four or more weeks of continuous work. Performers would no longer need agents. For its services, the A.V.M. would be entitled to a 5 percent commission from performers. The new system would eliminate the competition that enabled performers to negotiate contracts. Albee assured the managers that this was in no way a monopoly, no individual manager would put his own interests above that of the general benefit of the organization.

While most managers were not fooled by Albee's assertions, they could not compete against the power of Keith in the East and the Orpheum circuit (Beck and Meyerfield) in the West, so they had little choice but to join. In effect, Keith-Albee had laid the groundwork for a directorate that would dominate vaudeville for the next decade. Vaudeville performers, antagonized by the new arrangements, derogatorily referred to the new organization as the Syndicate.

Simultaneously with the forming of the A.V.M., Tony retired from the stage as a performer, with only periodic appearances for special occasions. At the age of nearly sixty-eight, his playing days were over. Yet, for months, audiences did not seem to recognize this decision. There had been no fanfares, no announcements, no benefits or testimonials to reveal Tony's decision. At no point did the press mention his retirement; he just was not performing anymore. The entire episode was conducted in Tony's characteristic quiet style, the same way he handled all of his private affairs. It would seem that the managers' decision to form the A.V.M. was the signal for Tony to terminate his long performing career. If the A.V.M. was successful in its intent, Tony's future in vaudeville would be problematic.

The performers, taken unawares by the A.V.M.'s policies, argued against them, claiming that they would lose income. They balked at being forced to join the A.V.M. in order to get forty weeks' work. Nor did they like the requirement of paying a 5 percent fee for every booking they obtained. Performers found that they were also required to accept whatever routing that might be assigned during the forty week season. They would be required to pay out of their own pocket for unexpected, revised schedules, which were common occurrences on the road. In addition, managers could cancel performers during any given week, thus undermining the value of a forty week agreement.

As the A.V.M was detailing its policies, a group of vaudevillians, led by George Fuller Golden, were meeting to form an organization of their own to fight the Syndicate. They were not about to acquiesce quietly.

Golden, an American actor working in England, had fallen on hard times and was stranded in London. A group of London music hall actors, who called themselves the Water Rats ("star" spelled backwards), organized benefits for destitute performers and helped Golden and his wife return to the U.S. Golden arrived in New York just as the A.V.M. announced its agenda. He wondered why performers in America could not organize a protective society like the Water Rats.

Golden contacted eight fellow actors, explaining his intentions. In July, the eight formed what was to become the first actors union in America. They would object, fight the Syndicate and protect the performer. They agreed on the need to recruit one hundred members, the top headliners in the profession. When Golden told the story of his London rescue by the Water Rats, the word Rats was used in their name.

At the second meeting, sixteen performers attended; a third meeting attracted fifty people, including George M. Cohan, Eddie Foy, Nat Wills, Charles T. Aldrich, James J. Corbett, George Evans, Bobby Gaylor, Fred Niblo, Pat Rooney and others.

For Weber and Fields, becoming a part of the A.V.M. was distasteful. They disliked both Keith and Albee. At the same time, they shared sympathies for the White Rats; while now managers, they were still performers. A photo of the White Rats Star Cabinet featured Lew Fields. Weber and Fields attended Rats meetings. In September, at the White Rats' first testimonial dinner, Weber and Fields gave $300. They also resigned from the A.V.M.

Tony could not sit on the sidelines and view the coming confrontation of business interests. Nor did he feel comfortable about his name being identified with the A.V.M. At first, he secretly gave money to the Rats. After all, most of the members were people who had played and still appeared at his theater. They were friends, colleagues and favorites who had so beautifully entertained his audiences. When the *New York Clipper* printed an ad for the White Rats, spelling out their intentions and listing the names of sixty-five theatrical people, Tony's name was among them. Within days, Tony resigned from the A.V.M. and became a primary donor to the Rats. No question now who supported the Rats. The war had begun.[4]

The White Rats' first benefit collected $2,000, enough to open offices on 23rd Street and purchase ads in the *Clipper*. The A.V.M., after initially regarding the Rats with indifference, took immediate action. They published an ad in the *Clipper* threatening that no member of the White Rats would obtain a booking from them for the coming season. The Rats ad became a blacklist sent to every manager belonging to the A.V.M.

More top headliners joined the Rats, including Lew Dockstater, McIntyre and Heath and Gus Williams. The A.V.M. responded with a threat of reduced salaries for the coming season. The move persuaded more actors to join the Rats.

The dispute was a boon for Tony during the summer and fall, as top headliners made themselves available to appear at his theater. Even though Tony himself was not on the bill, the theater was continually crowded. That the performers were fighting the Syndicate was also in their favor. Tony took advantage of the situation by signing these people to frequent appearances in the future.

New members to the A.V.M. were Percy Williams, Hurtig and Seamon and S.Z. Poli, thus adding several dozen more theaters to their control. The White Rats' membership passed 300. The A.V.M., realizing the increasing threat to their organization, ordered all managers not to sign White Rats members to any bill, starting immediately. Stage performance had now become the battlefield.

Performers like the Keatons, Emma Carus, Harry and Sadie Fields, Gus Williams, Pat Rooney and the Pantzer Trio appeared often at Tony's theater during this period of uncertainty for actors. The second annual benefit for the White Rats took place at the New York Theater on September 2 to an SRO audience. During the early days of the confrontation, the general public had paid little attention to the struggle. When the new season began, however, when audiences realized they might not see their favorites, theatergoers supported the Rats. Both the *Clipper* and *New York Times* reported on the confrontation but tended to side with the Rats. In retaliation, some managers pulled advertising out of the *Times*.

The benefit netted $7,000, which included donations and receipts from the selling of flowers and programs by actresses even though they were not yet inducted as members. Tony paid $100 for a box to watch many of his friends perform.

For the rest of 1900, there was a stalemate between managers and performers. The Syndicate had signed performers to appear at their theaters, but only a few of them were headliners. White Rats' members appeared at independent theaters but their bookings were spotty and salaries irregular. Tony continued to feature White Rats members at his theater — Montgomery and Stone, among the original founders; Emma Carus; Julian Rose; Fostelle and Emmett; Nay Wills, whose impersonations included one of Keith; Jess Dandy; the Brownings; Harry Thomson with monologues that pled the case for the Rats; Joe Welch; the Russell Brothers and Lydia Yeamans-Titus. Audiences filled the theater each week to cheer these artists on.

One program was designated as "minstrel week" and all the performers wore blackface. Another week was devoted to the circus and the bill was filled with acrobats, jugglers, wire walkers, magicians, contortionists and animal acts. On December 8th the Keatons began a week's engagement, for the first time in New York featuring their little son, Buster. Attired in a tramp outfit, with a beard from head to chin, Buster did some tumbling and danced a number with his parents. He was well received and took several bows.

The American Vitagraph remained on each week's program, showing films of the Galveston flood, the Hoboken fire, ship burnings, boxing bouts and short stories. Attendance during this period was excellent, according to Sanderson, who bragged that receipts were even better than at Keith's Union Square Theater.

With Tony gone, it became obvious that Sanderson was in charge of selecting acts and scheduling programs. Tony was sometimes seen backstage and in the wings watching performances. A few saw him in the morning in his office or mentoring some of the newcomers. Tony occasionally stopped in the White Rats' office to see about signing acts from their membership roster.

As usual, the annual Christmas festival took place at Tony's theater but, this year, "Aunt" Louisa Eldredge did not lead the festivities. She had recently retired from the committee for health reasons, and Mrs. Pastor had taken over her responsibilities. Tony served as host. Over 400 children attended, and thirty-two of them performed. After the performance, a banquet was served and gifts distributed. Later, Mrs. Pastor and her committee distributed clothing to eighty children of stage people.

The holiday program included acts designed to appeal to ladies and children: comic singing; jugglers; marionettes; trained dogs; and a Negro comedy team, Herbert and Willing, in "coonology." The Vitagraph showed children's fairy tales.

At the beginning of 1901, a strike against the A.V.M. seemed inevitable. The White Rats had begun formulating a plan to strike at the heart of the A.V.M. — its box office receipts. The A.V.M. wished to prevent such action, since a walkout of any kind would mean financial losses for their theaters. They suggested a meeting with Golden and his board of directors, at which time they promised to rescind the 5 percent commission at their next meeting, its date unspecified. Moreover, the A.V.M. did not notify its members of any future meeting.

In February, due to A.V.M.'s delaying tactics, the White Rats struck, its members refusing to appear for a Thursday matinee at Keith theaters in all the eastern cities. The strike caused these theaters to close. The A.V.M., livid because of the Rats' action, fired all performers who had participated in the strike and refused them entry into the theaters, except to pick up their personal belongings. A *Times* article about the strike noted that Tony's theater was the only one that remained open.

The Rats had met that evening to initiate seventy-five performers who had struck that day. Twenty were women, the first to become members of the organization. They included Lillian Russell, Marie Dressler, Dorothy Morton and Annie Yeamans.

Albee quickly met with Golden and worked out a temporary truce, agreeing to abolish the 5 percent commission immediately. The Rats were jubilant and returned to work. However, nothing changed in the A.V.M. organization. By March, the commission was still being collected. At the same time, in a surreptitious move, representatives of the A.V.M. were meeting with individual performers offering them lucrative, long-term contracts if they booked through them.

The Rats responded with a series of sickouts at Syndicate theaters. They also staged a number of benefits, collecting money to pay performers who were laid off. Then, the A.V.M. used the press to raise resentment against the performers for disrupting theater programs. They claimed to have done away with the commission. Albee even suggested that the White Rats were political agitators. The Rats responded with an ad that described the real issues, signed by their most popular headliners.

The following day, Albee threatened the Rats' financial backers, including Tony, declaring, "We will make them pay dearly." Sickouts continued for another week, when the A.V.M. met to officially abolish the commissions. The Rats claimed victory. But the A.V.M.'s move to entice performers to sign with them was highly successful, targeting those who were in financial trouble or frightened about being blacklisted. The new contracts included the 5 percent commission for booking.

By May, the A.V.M. maneuvering had reduced the White Rats to token opposition. Membership was declining. Fund-raising events were not sufficient to assist out-of-work performers. Headliners found other work and were unable to participate in Rats activities. The rebellion was over and performers had gained nothing. Instead, they lost a great deal of freedom choosing engagements and negotiating salaries. The failure of the White Rats had a profound effect on Tony.

For the first time in his career, Tony's managerial colleagues had become adversaries. Tony's avowed association with the White Rats and theirs with the A.V.M. had severed any cooperative efforts between the managers. They would not even say hello to one another when meeting on the street. The separation carried over to the usually nonpartisan activities for the Actors' Fund and other similar benefits. Tony withdrew from participation in these events. There was no sharing of performers or new acts. With few independent booking agents available, Tony had few sources to call on to obtain artists for his theater. Only those current managers who had formerly appeared at Tony's, like Edward Harrigan, continued to befriend him.

In the old days, Tony went it alone because there were few others whom he might collaborate. Now, because of the new business policies initiated by the A.V.M., Tony was forced to go it alone, a decided disadvantage in the current vaudeville environment. The question of whether he could do it, whether he even wanted to do it, was debated by the press and Tony's friends. Tony was viewed as having lost a battle by supporting the losing side. The White Rats were now an ineffectual, disjointed group; it would take them seven years to recover their energy. This left Tony as the only businessman facing the powerful, controlled juggernaut of the A.V.M.

Because the A.V.M. forced a large majority of top vaudevillians into their booking orbit, Tony had no more than a few hundred artists who were free to appear at his theater. His long list, compiled during years of booking, scheduling and evaluating performers, had dwindled.

Many headliners were lost. Many old favorites had sought other venues. Others had retired. Tony's only compensation came when headliners would return to his theater when they had a few weeks free during the off-season or between assignments.

Tony was forced to rely on new performers not yet affiliated with the A.V.M. or so new as to not even be recognized as legitimate vaudeville talent. This would create situations when less than top-notch acts appeared on Tony's stage, subject to criticism by reviewers and audiences. It was unlike anything Tony had ever experienced.

Tony thought that by renewing the summer tour he could sign high-class talent and make some money. But the A.V.M. pledged not to book road shows that year, barring Tony from playing at principal theaters throughout the country.

The spring of 1901 saw an altered list of performers appearing at Tony's theater. Sketch artists, newcomers and an assortment of circus acts filled the programs. Several headliners who had refused to join the A.V.M. were welcomed by Tony's audiences. Nat Wills appeared three times, as did James Richard Glenroy and Bonnie Thornton. Post and Clinton, Ford and Dot West, Mr. and Mrs. Litchfield, Harry Thomson and Lillie Western appeared twice. The Russell Brothers gave a skit that included John's wife and child. The Keatons—Myra, Joe and Buster—did grotesque comedy. Near the end of the spring season, when vaudeville circuits were winding down, Artie Hall, Hilda Thomas, Julian Rose, Joe Welch, Jess Dandy and Billy Carter were on Tony's bills. In spite of the limitations, Tony was still able to put together good programs by repeating his regular favorites. Audiences seemed pleased with the arrangement, and box office receipts were good to excellent.

On March 21, Tony's thirty-sixth year as manager was celebrated. He was on hand to sing a number of familiar songs to a crowded house. The *Clipper* acknowledged his rare appearance.

> Genial, great-hearted and well-beloved Tony Pastor celebrated at his theater the close of his 35th year as a theatrical manager. He was greeted by a house full of friends who gave him a rousing reception, and to whom he sang his songs as blithely and with as much vigor and unction as ever before. He has now entered upon the 36th year of his managerial career, having the esteem of all men, occupying a rank among local managers second to none, known and respected throughout the land, and worthy of all the good wishes which in the sincerity of regard we now tender him.[5]

The *Clipper* had always been an enthusiastic supporter of Tony and his accomplishments. Now he was being recognized as one of the few theater managers who retained his original business policies to protect the interests of performers. Tony was deeply gratified by being recognized, if only for one evening.

In April, F.F. Proctor changed the format at his theaters. He employed a stock company at each to perform sketches and short plays. In between the acts, vaudeville artists performed. At the same time, Proctor withdrew from the A.V.M. due to disagreements with Keith and Albee. After the announcement, Proctor and Pastor were seen dining together. The Shubert Brothers, who recently moved to New York, leased their first theater, the Casino. They chose to join the A.V.M. In a few years, they would become the A.V.M.'s biggest and stiffest competition.

The beginning of the summer season in New York saw six vaudeville houses open for business, one of which was Tony's. As in the spring programs, Tony repeated the headliners and other acts that had performed well. The rest of the programs were made up of newcomers, none of whom made big hits with the audience. Tony planned to spend the summer in Elmhurst, coming into the city occasionally to confer with Harry Sanderson. Sanderson was handling the selection and scheduling of bills. But business fell off in July and early August. Besides the usual excuse of the summer heat, the press attributed the decline to the opening of four roof gardens, all presenting vaudeville, and the recent openings of vaudeville theaters in resorts like Brighton Beach, Rockaway Beach and Bergen Beach.

Tony felt compelled to reappear at his theater August 12. Announcement of his return created SRO conditions, with many people left on the street.

> A great shout of greeting when Tony Pastor appeared to unfold his budget of comic songs and he was then reluctantly permitted to withdraw.[6]

Tony also took over handling the bill's introductions, shouting his enthusiastic superlatives for each performer. Audiences cheered every time he walked on stage. He played a second week to full houses. When he failed to appear on the bill the following week, attendance declined.

When the new season opened in late August and early September, there were a total of thirty-six theaters in Manhattan, twenty-four dramatic houses and twelve devoted to vaudeville. A slight interruption to the season occurred in September when President McKinley was shot and his subsequent funeral closed all theaters on September 19. It took several weeks for theaters to fill again.

Another interruption of theater business was the Gerry Society's renewed attack on theaters allowing children under sixteen to perform. The city council had passed a bill giving the society new impetus to press their evangelism. Instead of warning managers about possible transgressions, groups of society members would storm a performance, stop the show, and remove the "offending" performers. Managers would be brought to court the next day. After several weeks, and a good deal of lobbying, theater managers were able to persuade the court to reign in the society's aggressive tactics. Tony suffered one encounter when he featured Master Alfred, a singer of coon songs. The society dragged the unfortunate youngster from the stage, claiming he was underage. The court later found he was sixteen, but the young performer's career was ended.

During the fall season, Tony appeared only once, on October 24, to celebrate the twentieth anniversary of the occupancy of his theater on 14th Street. For the program, he brought back a host of old favorites, including May Irwin, Frank McNish, the French Twin Sisters, Jacques Kruger and Dan Collyer. Along with performing their specialties, they put on an old skit. Juxtaposed against the appearance of "old-timers" was a program of newcomers in serio-comic sketches, a Hebrew comedian, acrobats, and an animal act. The Vitagraph showed royal funerals and coronations, and short stories. In the ad for the event, the Vitagraph was as conspicuous as the names of the old entertainers.

Tony did not appear at either the Thanksgiving or Christmas shows. But he was again host for the stage children's annual Christmas festival. The children featured on this year's program were Louise Allen, Willie Howard, Anita Heckler, Harry Le Van and Musical Jones, all of whom later became popular theater headliners. The almost 400 children in attendance received horns, drums, dolls and other presents along with the usual sumptuous banquet. The artists present to serve the children were Anna Held, Edna Wallace Hopper, Nina Farrington, Millie Thorne, May Robson, John T. Kelly and Lee Harrison. The festival was in its sixteenth year under a committee now headed by Mrs. Pastor and Mrs. Fernandez. Major contributors to the event were reported to be J. Pierpont Morgan, William C. Whitney, Elbridge T. Gerry and Abe Hummel.[7]

On New Year's Eve, Tony and his wife hosted a late dinner for a few old friends and relatives at their home in Elmhurst. It was a quiet meal filled with toasts and reminiscences. His wife and guests could not help but notice the past year's effect on Tony's physical and mental health. They celebrated the New Year with the traditional singing of "Auld Lang Syne."

15

Struggling to Stay Open

In 1902, Tony found that New York's theatrical environment had rushed past his doors and planted itself around the new "crossroads of the world," Broadway and 42nd Street. Department stores, hotels, restaurants, and theaters had moved uptown. The once thriving commercial and theatrical center around Union Square had succumbed to age and obsolescence. Once fine residential neighborhoods had been taken over by immigrants who wished to make the city their home.

Recent inventions made New York into a vital city for manufacturing, consumerism and building. Electric lights brightened streets, stores and homes. Telephones were now available to those who could afford them. The typewriter improved record-keeping and business operations. New bridges and highways united the boroughs, and improved and speeded up accessibility. Increasingly tall buildings on small lots were being erected at a rapid pace. The tallest building was 612 feet high with plans for even taller structures already committed. Elevators deposited people at their respective levels of business. Subway construction had begun in 1900; in 1904 the first trains would rapidly move passengers from City Hall to 42nd Street and Times Square.

It was the automobile, though, that made New York "on the go," busy, bustling, hectic, and frenetic if you were a visitor. Streets had to be reconfigured to accommodate them. Motorized taxis changed the way people moved around town. Trucks replaced horses and wagons. Meanwhile, to accommodate the railroad's entry into the suburbs, Pennsylvania Station was under construction.

Once a dilapidated section made up of old factories, part of the Bowery now housed the business and financial center of the country. Wall Street was a symbol of financial power. Fine department stores, retail shops and restaurants were now spread from 34th Street to Central Park South. The city's most famous restaurants—Hoffman House, Delmonico's, Rector's, Shanley's, Gilsey House and the Metropole bar—catered to the elite, the theatrical crowd and their followers. Fifth Avenue was lined with the mansions of the rich. Since Theodore Roosevelt's inaugural as president of the United States in 1901, the general public was in an optimistic and expansive mood. New York was the trendsetter.

New York was also the country's entertainment center. The top artists lived and worked in the city. New performers came to the city to be discovered. Popular songs were written and published in the city and distributed countrywide. Touring companies had their origin in the city. Plays that were performed across the country were those that first enjoyed success in New York. Popular books and magazines were published in the city. New York had more than forty theaters, catering to all social and ethnic classes. An unknown number of beer gardens, concert halls and saloons, and neighborhood amusement centers gave ambitious performers the opportunity for future stardom.

Twelve theaters were built and opened between 1902 and 1907, all in the vicinity of Times Square. The New Amsterdam Theater possessed the most beautiful interior of any playhouse to date. Oscar Hammerstein contributed three magnificent structures for patrons' pleasure—the Olympia Music Hall, Victoria Theater and the Lew Fields Theater. When the Majestic Theater was erected at 59th Street and 8th Avenue, some felt it was too far from patrons to be successful. The theater opened with *The Wizard of Oz* in 1903 and quickly dispelled these doubts. The Hippodrome, opened in 1905, covered an entire city block and was claimed to be the largest theater in the world, seating 6,000 people. Unfortunately, it never generated a profit. Going to the theater, whether dramatic or musical, was a delight for locals and visitors, the city's most popular leisure time activity.

As theaters were moving uptown, Tony made the decision to remain at the 14th Street location he had long occupied. When the vaudeville format was changed, Tony was forced to follow or lose business. While he enjoyed good to excellent box office receipts, artist salaries and his low admission prices made it difficult for him to make a reasonable profit. He was too old and physically unable to perform or tour the country. A new generation of managers, using his model in their business enterprises, became successful. Business combinations, like the A.V.M., marginalized the small, independent entrepreneurs so that they were no more than neighborhood theaters.

Tony's theater was located in the 18th Ward. The area contained more than 1,300 tenements, housing 40,700 residents. Businesses were found in storefronts, apartment living rooms and street pushcarts. Just south of the theater were Jewish enclaves, where the recent wave of eastern European Jews had settled. East of the theater was an Italian neighborhood, also filled with recent immigrants. Within walking distance was the garment district, noted for its notorious sweat shops.

Tony's fashionable audience had given way to patrons with a great interest in popular theater but with modest incomes and unsophisticated tastes. Tony's theater was the brightest, most enjoyable place in an environment that featured the daily trials and stresses of an assimilating working class. When reviewers spoke of Tony's "loyal legions," they were serious. These were the people who now kept Tony in business.

Vaudeville, too, had matured. Every city in the country with over 5,000 people had at least one vaudeville theater. Most were open all year long. The "continuous vaudeville" format was common. Year-round touring companies had become moneymakers for managers and local theaters. Performers found touring to be secure, offering work for forty or more weeks and with little need to change a routine. Top headliners were now earning $1,000 a week and were covered by the press as the general public devoured the latest news of their activities. Moving pictures had become an important element in the vaudeville program. Audiences came to expect new picture experiences each week, and producing companies rushed to satisfy their desires. Moving pictures also changed the way patrons behaved in the theaters, making them quiet and passive.

The A.V.M. (Syndicate) grew and spread to control at least one first-class theater in each city. They owned touring routes, companies and performers. They had the power to dictate scheduling and salaries. Any performer who refused to sign with them risked being out of work or blacklisted. Only top headliners were independent enough to obtain engagements. Many top performers would turn toward the developing musical theater as a lucrative outlet for their talent.

Musical theater, as a new presentation form, was coming of age. In its infancy, it was no more than vaudeville olios with a wisp of plot. *Sally in Our Alley*, starring Marie Cahill, was one of the first plotted shows. *The Wizard of Oz* was the first highly successful play that put plot before song. In another year, musical comedy—a play with music—would become the new entertainment through the works of George M. Cohan and Lew Fields. In 1907, Flo Ziegfeld introduced a new format, filled with music, comedy and beautiful girls. He called it "the Follies."

Called the "poor man's amusement," the nickelodeon gave a customer five minutes of moving pictures for five cents. Begun on the lower East Side, these novelty film experiences prospered to the extent that they spread north to more refined commercial districts. Small entrepreneurs like William Fox, Marcus Loew and Adolph Zukor owned many of these outlets and grew rich from them.

The power of the A.V.M. had greatly reduced Tony's ability to sign top headliners. Performers with a fond feeling for Tony occasionally returned, some at their former salaries. Tony only had to glance at theater ads to see the names of his old favorites—Montgomery and Stone, Weber and Fields, George M. Cohan, Pat Rooney, the Rogers Brothers, May Irwin, Charles Evans, Lew Dockstater, Nat Wills and Irene Franklin. They were appearing on the major vaudeville circuits or in musicals.

Some of Tony's favorites had died or retired. Great headliners from his halcyon days who had passed on included Billy Birch, Nels Seymour, Ella Wesner, Frank Kerns, Tony Hart, Charley White, Billy Emmet, Kitty O'Neil and Harry Kernell. Those who had retired read like a list of variety and vaudeville's major contributors—Maggie Cline, Gus Williams, Jenny Engel, Lizzie B. Raymond, James F. Hoey, Dan Collyer, the St. Felix Sisters, Frank and Lillian White, the Worrell Sisters and countless others.

The winter and spring of 1902 were, however, surprisingly good times at Tony's theater. In spite of featuring a score of nervous newcomers and a mixture of sketch teams, the theater drew steady crowds and box office receipts swelled beyond his expectations. Hundreds of loyal customers came to the theater each week to see fresh programs. Featured acts on the bill included Hebrew comedians (gaining in popularity each year), ballad singers and the usual assortment of circus-style acts that audiences continued to enjoy. The only familiar favorites that Tony was able to obtain were the Russell Brothers, Elinor Sisters, Nat Wills and Blanche Ring. The spring program also introduced the comedy sketch team of Duffy, Sawtelle and Duffy, Eddie Leonard singing coon songs in blackface, and Harding and Ah Sid, a comedy acrobatic act that elicited much laughter.

Listed in the real estate section of the *New York Times* was a small notice which reported on the sale of two of Tony's properties, the amount unrecorded. These were homes that Tony had inherited a few years earlier when his older sister Caroline died. Those close to Tony knew that he needed the funds to continue running his theater. Although box office receipts were good, it was difficult to maintain profitability.

When the summer season officially opened in June, there were seven vaudeville houses open, two roof gardens offering vaudeville acts and four resorts, also featuring vaudeville. Since many of the headlining performers typically had down time during the summer months, they appeared at these houses, including visits to Tony's. The Three Keatons, Nat Wills, Hilda Thomas, Ed Latell, Julian Rose, Irene Franklin, Joe Welch and Billy Carter attracted good audiences, even in the summer heat. There were also new Irish and Dutch comedians and blackface teams.

Tony was reported to be back at the theater when the fall season began, selecting performers and scheduling programs. Sanderson told a reporter that Tony arrived every morning at 10

The Russell Brothers, John and James, the "foremost delineators of Irish Chambermaids," were immediate hits at Tony's theater and appeared there often. They helped out Tony when he needed headliners for his programs.

to work in his little office backstage. For the rest of the morning, he was on stage, reviewing new acts and helping others to improve their routines. Mondays were especially busy as Tony readied performers for their first appearance of the week.

When the show began, Tony was often seen in the wings in shirtsleeves, waving a fan, observing the performers and cheering them on. On several occasions, he would come on stage to introduce a new act not seen before in New York. But each time he appeared, the audience applauded him and shouted for songs, taking attention away from the performers. He abandoned the practice.

Tony ate lunch and dinner in his office while conducting business with Sanderson and other employees. He remained at the theater until the second show had concluded, about 7:00

P.M. and then left for home. Sanderson reported that Tony was in good spirits and able to perform, but chose not to. Tony enjoyed time at the theater, being around performers, orchestra members and backstage people.

Several times during the fall, the *Clipper* reported "capacity business" and mentioned Tony's "carefully prepared programs with diverse entertainments." The regular clientele that filled the theater each week were "one big happy family," especially on Mondays.

> Unless one came early to this cozy theater, his only satisfaction would be to find a small sign in the box office window that read "all seats sold." The regular patrons, however, are familiar with this order of things so they came early, and one is reasonably sure to see the same faces in the audience on each succeeding Monday.[1]

Yet even with the reports of "capacity business," Sanderson's ledgers showed minimally profitable weeks, losing weeks, generous salaries and sizable advertising expenditures. The end result was a break-even status for the season.

The fall season was marred by a report from England that Bessie Bonehill had died after being ill for three months with cancer. A dozen years ago Tony had introduced her to American audiences. The press recalled her prominence and popularity while in this country. Upon hearing of her death, Tony planned an evening performance in her honor. Vocalists on the program sang some of her signature songs.

On December 28, the annual Christmas festival for stage children was held with Tony acting as host and master of ceremonies. He announced to the children that while Santa had already returned North, he and Abe Hummel as appointed deputies, would pass out the gifts for the evening. More than $2,300 had been collected from such notables as Joseph Jefferson, Eldridge T. Gerry, Mrs. Cornelius Vanderbilt, and Richard Mansfield. Mrs. Fernandez and Mrs. Pastor had planned the event and helped to serve the children at the banquet.

In early 1903, Keith's Union Square Theater changed its continuous vaudeville format to two complete shows a day instead of three. Shows now began at 1:30 P.M., went to 5:45 P.M., and then repeated, closing at 10:00 P.M. Keith hired core performers but they only had to appear only twice on the program daily. Top headliners would appear only once, during the evening performance.

Tony had little choice but to duplicate the same format. But, instead of hiring more performers to fill the bill, he gave each act a longer time on stage. This worked well with sketch teams but proved difficult for vocalists and comedians. By spring, fewer of the latter were appearing. During some weeks, the program consisted of five or six sketches, some running as long as twenty minutes. Audiences often lost interest in such long pieces, especially if they presented serious material.

The spring also saw repeated returns for selected performers. Gardner and Vincent, in comic sketches, appeared three times; John and Bertha Gleeson, twice; Cook and Sonora, twice; and a newcomer, the Carter De Haven Trio, a song and dance team, twice. Another newcomer was a pretty, petite, knockabout comedienne, Polly Moran, who later found fame in silent movies. The ever-present Vitagraph showed the story of Rip Van Winkle, and short subjects produced by Melius, Lubin, Edison and Biograph.

By June, when the majority of circuit tours had terminated for the season, Tony got several of the old favorites to feature a week's bill: the Three Keatons; Irene Franklin; Annie Hart; Bonnie Thornton; the Elinore Sisters and Jess Dandy. When any of these loyal-to-Tony headliners had a free week, they appeared at Tony's theater.

In March, Tony celebrated his thirty-eighth anniversary as manager by appearing on stage to thank his patrons for their support. He apologized for not performing. In early April, the

15. Struggling to Stay Open

Elks gave their first ladies' social, with Tony as host. A week later, Tony served as chairman for the Actors' Fund testimonial. Tony attended the May opening of George M. Cohan's farce *Running for Office*, a skit he had expanded into a full-length play. At the end of the opening night performance, Cohan recognized Tony as the person who gave him the opportunity to put on skits.

Also in May, the twenty-second annual Actors' Fund show was put on at the Savoy Theater; $11,000 was collected. Tony was among the more than fifty performers who appeared. When he broke out in song, the audience stood up and applauded. His fellow performers came on stage to shake his hand.

Amidst these events, Tony celebrated his seventieth birthday, the evening of April 26. He and his wife, Harry Sanderson and his wife, and a few close friends enjoyed a quiet dinner at the Pastor home. There was no mention of Tony's birthday in the press although many knew of the date. The press had an unwritten law never to mention personal items publicly unless the person in question agreed.

In June, Tony returned to the three-a-day format. Audiences had slimmed out with the two-a-day version instituted by Keith in January. Tony could not afford an arrangement that tended to reduce daily attendance. He could return to employing more comedians, vocalists and circus acts, whom audiences enjoyed most. Box office receipts improved almost immediately.

But Tony was further reminded of the influence of the A.V.M. when the Orpheum circuit announced that they had expanded across the country and had moved their offices to New York City from San Francisco. In combination with the Keith circuit, they controlled more than 200 theaters, six in Manhattan alone.

When Tony officially opened the new season in mid–September, there were forty-two theaters in New York, the most ever, including twelve vaudeville houses. Harlem had four vaudeville theaters and Brooklyn now had five. This represented the largest number of vaudeville theaters ever in the New York area. With the advent of musical theater, the number would gradually decline over the next decade. All classes of audiences were attracted to musicals, and many of vaudeville's headliners matriculated to the musical stage.

On November 2, Coney Island, its Luna Park amusement center open only six months, was struck by a fierce fire that destroyed most of the buildings. The fire displaced more than 600 people who worked and lived there and destroyed 264 buildings with an estimate of damage close to one million dollars. Two men were detained on suspicion of starting the fires. During the preceding months, vaudeville managers had complained that Luna Park was taking away customers. Allegations of arson filled the press, who noted that, for the time being, the public would have to return to theaters for their entertainment. An investigation determined that there was no arson but blame was put on the local fire department for its inadequacy. Alerted to the accusations, New York fire authorities proposed to examine all theaters.

Proposals were still being debated when, on December 30, the Iroquois Theater in Chicago caught fire, during a matinee filled with women and children. The fire spread so rapidly that close to 600 people perished; it was the most devastating fire in theater history. Chicago officials closed all theaters for a month to examine their fire-fighting capabilities. Fire departments across the country followed.

The New York fire commission shut down six theaters, four of them vaudeville houses, and gave out warnings to six others to repair deficiencies or be closed. Weber and Fields closed their theater in February and went on tour. Tony was given a warning and had to make some costly repairs, amounting to several thousand dollars. He was forced to get rid of the calcium lights backstage and to limit his standing room areas (again), which affected box office receipts.

In December, another favorite performer passed away. John Kernell, one of the last of the Irish knockabout comedians, with his brother, Harry, died after a performance in Detroit. The team had instituted their act of "sidewalk comedy" at Tony's theater in the late 1870s. John Kernell had a wife and three children. Tony put on a benefit for him, honoring the Kernell brothers for their contributions to popular theater.

Tony again played Santa Claus at the annual Christmas festival for stage children at his theater.

> Tony Pastor, who refuses to grow old because every Sunday following Christmas he seizes the chance to appear in his own theater as Santa Claus, minus the gray beard, was the master of ceremonies at a performance, billed as a "sacred concert" and Christmas festival of the little children of the stage.[2]

Tony was everywhere on stage assisting the little performers. One young girl started singing with the orchestra an octave too low. She began to cry. Tony rushed from the wings and silenced the orchestra. He caught the girl in his arms and told her it was not her fault. The orchestra moved to a different key and the little girl finished her song while holding Tony's hand. A pianist was unable to reach the pedals; Tony had her sit on his lap and she played her piece. An umbrella refused to open for a dancer and Tony came to her rescue.

More than 1000 people attended, of whom 400 were children. After a banquet, Tony, his wife, Mrs. Fernandez and other members of the committee passed out gifts to all the children. Among those who contributed to the evening's enjoyment were Mrs. Vanderbilt, Abe Hummel, Eldridge T. Gerry and Helen and George Gould. A resolution was passed that, for next year's event, special attention would be paid to crippled children.

The Christmas edition of the *New York Clipper* featured a full-page photograph of Tony. They called him "The Dean of the Vaudeville Stage." There was certainly no dispute to the title. Tony proudly added the photo to the wall in his office.

Throughout 1904, the weekly programs at Tony's theater remained much the same as before. A mixture of sketches filled the bill. There were many repeaters. Circus acts continued to appeal to neighborhood audiences. Tony brought El Nino Eddie out of retirement to perform his highwire act for two weeks. He featured Polly Moran once more. He put on an entire minstrel show. A Hebrew comedienne, Annie Bernstein, was introduced and brought back several times during the year. He also introduced the Avon Comedy Four (Coleman, Lester, Smith and Dale). The latter two later formed a comedy team that quickly became a vaudeville favorite. In a gesture to their old friend Tony, the Three Keatons returned for a week's appearances.

Tony sang again! Not once, but twice. The Green Room held a benefit at the New York Theater the evening of February 14. Among a group of well-known performers—Dan Daly, Emma Carus, Marie Dressler and Gus Hill—was Tony. To the surprise of everyone, Tony sang two of his old favorites. His voice was a little scratchy but it made no difference to the crowd; they cheered him for several minutes. Three months later, at the Green Room Club show, Tony sang again, this time offering renditions of "Down in a Coal Mine" and "Lucy Lu." The press was astonished, pointing out that Tony had not performed publicly for four years.

Like every year preceding, at the March 22nd show Tony was celebrated for his thirty-ninth year as a manager. Tony did not appear. However, the theatrical weeklies noted the anniversary, commenting on his longevity and contributions to vaudeville.

> The legions of friends and patrons of the veteran manager evidenced their loyalty and appreciation of his sterling worth as an amusement caterer by crowding the theater to its capacity, which marked Pastor's 39th anniversary as a vaudeville manager in this city. It was a popular and well deserved tribute to the "Dean of American Vaudeville managers."[3]

Several important theater business activities highlighted the summer months. Oscar Hammerstein announced that he was changing the Victoria Theater into a vaudeville house. Weber and Fields dissolved their life-long partnership amid cheers and tears at the end of their last show at the New Amsterdam Theater. It is ironic that they played this show at a Klaw and Erlanger theater, the very people they had been battling against for several years. A short while later, Weber disclosed his partnership with Flo Ziegfeld to continue the Weber-Fields–style shows. Fields, in turn, made a deal with Oscar Hammerstein, Julian Mitchell and Fred Hamlin to star in a new musical at his own theater. Klaw and Erlanger opened the Liberty Theater featuring the Rogers Brothers. And two more vaudeville theaters were scheduled to open in September.

Good-sized audiences made summer business at Tony's respectable. His advertising during this period emphasized the "diversity of acts designed to please all tastes." Among old favorites appearing were J. Bernard Dyllyn, Lottie Gilson and O'Brien and Havel. Repeaters included Harry Thomson, Avon Comedy Four, Belle Hathaway's monkeys, and Annie Bernstein. A special feature was the American debut of Jewell's Automatic Electric Manikin Theater, a troupe of performers from European music halls who presented a miniature production with elaborate design and effect.

The fall season was no less popular with patrons. Most acts were well received and appropriately encored, but a few were quite amateurish. Audiences were quite vocal about this lack of professionalism. Lottie Gilson returned, as did Harding and Ah Sid, Ward and Curran, Tascott, Ed Latell, Bobby Gaylor and Mr. and Mrs. Harry Thorne. Several authentic Negro acts were introduced; a Mexican singing and dancing trio pleased audiences; but a Japanese musical act obtained average reactions.

The star theater attractions for the fall came from the creative minds of George M. Cohan and Lew Fields. Cohan's *Little Johnny Jones* offered a mixture of vaudeville, Edward Harrigan and melodrama but it was Cohan's songs that captivated audiences. The show was a revelation: a musical of dramatic shape with songs in a vernacular that mimicked everyday speech.

The show also revealed what were to become Cohan trademarks—a blend of patriotism and sentimentality that captured the public's psyche. Fields combined the music of Victor Herbert and his own theatrical instincts to put on a show with a flowing plot, brisk staging, dazzling spectacle, pretty girls and catchy tunes. The two shows launched the development of musical theater for the next decade.

Tony had been invited to attend the openings of both shows. Backstage after Cohan's show, Tony found himself surrounded by the Cohan family (minus Josie), Ethel Levey (Cohan's wife) and David Brian, all graduates of his theater. At the Fields opening, Tony and Fields reminisced about the early days of variety.

December 25 was the annual Christmas festival for stage children at Tony's theater. Tony again played Santa Claus, emceed the program, served as host for the banquet and gift giving. Mrs. Pastor, Mrs. Fernandez, Mabel Talliaferro, Marguerite St. John, Truly Shattuck, Bijou Fernandez and the ever-present Abe Hummel served the children. A little-noticed episode proved embarrassing to Tony but his wife quickly stepped in to solve the mix-up. He mistakenly gave stickpins to the girls and brooches to the boys. Mrs. Pastor intervened and made the proper exchanges before anyone took notice of her husband's error.

Tony seemed fit enough to continue first-hand management of his theater through early 1905. Programs for the winter and spring were similar to those gone before but with very few old favorites appearing on the bill. The press praised a few notable programs. In late January, Ernest Hogan, a Negro in blackface, known as "the unbleached American," sang his signature song, "All Coons Look Alike to Me," to great success. Coon songs were very popular and Negroes were the chief purveyors of these tunes. Audiences of the day delighted in these songs; they would remain popular for another two decades. On the same bill was a pretty young singer named Nora Bayes, who had recently appeared in New York for the first time in a Rogers Brothers show in a bit part. Tony gave her the opportunity to sing a full repertoire of songs, including one that gained her attention, "Down Where the Wurzburger Flows." One of her other renditions, "Meet Me in St. Louis, Louis," would soon become a hit for her.

In February, Polly Moran's early success at Tony's gained her a repeat engagement and the comedienne made the most of heading the bill with a very laughable comedy act. Victor Moore and his wife, Emma Littlefield, performed a skit, "Change Your Act, or Back to the Woods," that included some refined toe and acrobatic dancing. Cohan, seeing Moore act, signed him to appear in *Forty-Five Minutes from Broadway*, that opened in January 1906.

Tony celebrated his fortieth anniversary as a manager during the March 22 evening program but, considering the importance of the event, it was handled in a modest way. Tony appeared on stage, talked briefly about his early days, accepted floral tributes and telegrams of congratulations and thanked the audience for their years of loyalty. He did not sing although the audience shouted for him to render a few old favorites. After several minutes of applause, Tony left the stage. A reporter noted tears in Tony's eyes as he departed.

A few weeks later, Tony appeared as part of a vaudeville benefit for the Actors' Home, held at the Metropolitan Opera House. Tony was scheduled to appear at the end of the program. The *Times* reported that he "concluded in one of his old-time songs assisted by the entire company, this being Mr. Pastor's only appearance and probably his farewell to the stage."[4]

During the summer months, for the first time in his association with the *New York Clipper*, Tony did not advertise during July and August. Tony was said to be conserving his funds for the new season.

With the fall season in full force, forty-six theaters were operating in Manhattan, fifteen of them vaudeville houses. Six of the vaudeville theaters showed moving pictures on the bill. The big debate at the beginning of the new season dealt with performing on Sundays, with theater managers against religious organizations. The latter group had many supporters in city government, and Sunday performances were again banned. Actually, several theaters gave Sunday "concerts," but could not legally charge admission. Instead, donations to the performers were allowed.

For the fall, Tony worked hard to present old favorites at his theater. Frank Bush, Irene Franklin (who would never turn down a Pastor request) and the Three Keatons attracted good audiences. He persuaded the St. Felix Sisters to come out of retirement. But the remainder of the acts were of mixed value. Reviewers mentioned the increasing number of mediocre performers appearing at Tony's theater. Lesser coverage of Tony's theater and reduced advertising space may have contributed to smaller audiences. Because of the many vaudeville theaters in operation, the *Clipper* reduced the space given for each. Tony's program was confined to a short paragraph and no mention was made of attendance. Tony also bought smaller advertising space in the press, just enough space to list the acts.

Deaths marred theater news in December. Two weeks before the annual Christmas festival, "Aunt" Louisa Eldredge died. A huge funeral was held at St. Patrick's Cathedral which thousands of people attended, including hundreds of performers and managers. Tony served as pallbearer. Of less grandeur was the funeral of Lillie Western, who died on December 19 from cancer. She made her professional debut on Tony's stage in 1878 playing thirteen instruments and appeared often in succeeding years. She was one of Tony's favorites and they were close friends for a quarter of a century. She never failed to play at Tony's when he asked her.

At the annual Christmas festival for the children, "Aunt" Louisa Eldredge was missed for the first time since 1887, when the event was inaugurated. Mrs. Pastor and Mrs. Fernandez handled the arrangements with Harry Sanderson, who also served as master of ceremonies. Tony was not in attendance. He had again disappeared from the theater.

Throughout most of 1906, Harry Sanderson managed the theater, its finances, artist selection, scheduling and advertising. Tony was occasionally seen in the wings watching the acts and encouraging performers. Attendance, when it was mentioned by the *Clipper,* was described in terms like "crowded houses," "the usual business," and "fine audience." Capacity houses usually occurred on Mondays, the opening of a new week's program, and at holiday special programs. Unfortunately, ledgers are no longer available to reveal true box office receipts and expenses. In May, a brief note in the *Clipper* reported that Tony had sold another property, this one on 94th Street.

Tony reappeared on the stage for his forty-first anniversary. The theater was filled with floral arrangements and the audience was excited. The veteran manager entertained the crowd with some old-fashioned capers. The *Times* reviewer covered this rare event.

> "House Full" was the sign on the box office at Pastor's Theater shortly after 8 PM last night. The occasion was the appearance of Tony Pastor himself in celebration of his 41st anniversary as a manager. Tony did a jig-step and sang "Sarah's Young Man" and "Down in a Coal Mine," and many of his old-time admirers said they enjoyed the performance as much as when he sang these songs forty years ago.[5]

An ovation lasted five minutes, after which fifteen floral pieces were presented to the veteran actor-manager by friends and organizations, including the White Rats, an association of theatrical performers, and Lodge No. 1 of the Elks.

"I'm glad to see here tonight many eminent people who, forty years ago, sat in my galleries," said Tony Pastor in response. "And they needn't be ashamed of it because they have all done something to be proud of and can buy box seats now."

Just the fact that Tony came on stage and performed, although briefly, was all the audience needed to make the event a memorable experience.

The only old-timers who appeared at the theater during the year were Billy Carter (three times), Irene Franklin (three times), Tascott (twice), Gus Williams and Frank Bush. Pat Rooney, Jr., appeared with his new wife, Marion Bent, with an Irish song and dance routine. It was Junior's first appearance at Tony's. Rooney and Bent played together for 28 years, longer than any other team in vaudeville. An increasing number of novelty acts appeared on the bill principally because their salaries were lower and their availability greater. One August program was entirely made up of circus acts.

The 1906 edition of the Christmas festival took place December 23. For this event, Tony appeared as host and master of ceremonies. Close to 1,000 children attended. A variety performance was given by a number of the children, a banquet followed and gift-giving around a giant tree concluded the happy event. Tony was seen to be helping those children who were nervous about playing before such a large crowd. To all concerned, Tony appeared in good spirits.

The *Dramatic Mirror's* Christmas issue devoted several pages to Tony, including a group of photographs of Tony as he appeared in costume during his early appearances in variety.

> These portraits were made in 1864, some years before Mr. Pastor adapted the famous dress suit and crush hat that were his trade-mark until a few years ago, when he discontinued his regular public appearances. The picture in the center shows Mr. Pastor in his prime. Even today, he has a jaunty appearance, and "age cannot wither nor custom stale" his interest in the variety brand of the profession of which he is the acknowledged dean.[6]

Many testimonials followed the article's publication, all of them attesting to Tony's exalted position in popular theater.

Shortly after the New Year began, Mrs. Pastor gave a luncheon to celebrate the Pastors' thirty-second wedding anniversary. The Hotel Carleton laid out a sumptuous banquet for the friends, relatives and performers who attended, close to 150 people. An orchestra entertained the guests. And when the Pastors took the floor to dance, others followed. The report of the party by the *Dramatic Mirror* revealed that Tony and his wife were staying at the Carleton for the winter months, eliminating Tony's need to travel.

On March 9, the White Rats put on their first annual ball at the Grand Central Palace (a non–Syndicate theater). More than 3000 people attended, and with 5000 tickets sold, the Rats reaped a sizable profit for operations. With new management, the Rats were attempting to regroup the organization and attract new members. George Fuller Golden, the founder of the White Rats, gave a rousing speech about their potential to combat the forces of the Syndicate. A grand march preceded a vaudeville show. Tony, who was to have led the grand march, was present during the early part of the evening, but had to leave the ball because of illness. Tony had given $100 to the Rats' fund, demonstrating his continued affiliation and support for the group.

But health problems did not deter Tony from appearing, and performing, during the forty-second anniversary evening at his theater. The theater was not large enough to hold the crowd of well-wishers, old friends and loyal patrons, all of them determined to offer congratulations to their favorite manager. When the card boy came out and placed cards on either side of the stage reading "Tony Pastor," the noise caused the walls of the theater to tremble. Tony sang "Down in a Coal Mine" with the audience joining in the choruses. For an encore, he rendered "Sarah's Young Man" and had to make a speech before the crowd allowed him to leave. The lobby was filled with floral offerings, and in the boxes were artists who had played for Tony over the past forty years. The stage was covered with telegrams and congratulatory letters from across the country. Tony expressed delight with the way his friends had remembered him.

One floral piece in particular attracted Tony's attention. A letter attached to the flowers read:

> Dear Mr. Pastor:
> We, the undersigned, representing practically every vaudeville theater in America, extend greetings and congratulations to you on this, the anniversary of your forty-second year as a vaudeville manager. Your career and example have made it possible for many of us to follow in your footsteps. Loved by every one in all branches of our profession, you have been a help and guide to many who have reached the highest pinnacle of success. We extend the hand of friendship and the sincere wish that you may be spared many years in the position which you now occupy as "Dean of Vaudeville."[7]

The letter was signed by B.F. Keith, F.F. Proctor, Percy Williams, E.F. Albee, Oscar Hammerstein, S.Z. Poli, Martin Beck, Morris Meyerfield, Hyde and Behman and others. The letter and floral offering was the first positive interaction between Tony and the A.V.M. since he quit the organization. While the sincerity of the gift could not be denied, one reporter wondered why it was given to Tony at the very moment when he was laboring to keep his "lone little theater" open. How Tony felt about the honor was unreported.

In April, Tony gave a rare interview to a theater critic from the *New York Times*. "I'm no good at the interview game," were Tony's first words to the interviewer.[8] Once he began, however, he reminisced about the past, his beginnings in variety at 444 Broadway, his three theaters, the performers he introduced and the changes in the theater business. "Still, Pastor's is doing business at the old stand," he said. "The public has never lost its love of variety shows, and I don't think it ever will," he concluded. The title of the article was "The Father of Vaudeville."

Weekly programs for the spring and summer duplicated previous seasons, mostly made up of newcomers and those establishing themselves as viable entertainers. Attendance fluctuated with the nature of performers playing. Sketch artists were popular, as were vocalists and comedians, but Tony's patrons especially enjoyed novelty acts. Old-timers had disappeared from the bills. Harry Sanderson ran the house with Tony dropping in occasionally to watch the acts and go over the books.

In July, the roof garden at the New York Theater, renamed "Jardin de Paris," saw the opening of Flo Ziegfeld's "Follies of 1907." The show would become a national institution and add an exciting new element of enjoyment to popular theater. The headliner in the show was Nora Bayes. The production had cost $13,000.

The economy was to suffer through one more convulsion before Congress created the Federal Reserve System in 1914. Tony had survived the panics of 1873, 1884 and 1893, but the October Panic of 1907 convinced him that his management days were coming to an end.

16

The Venerable Showman's Decline

The Panic of 1907 was the last and most severe of the bank panics that affected the American economy. Unlike previous panics, this episode focused on New York City trust companies.[1]

On October 16, Augustus Heinze's scheme to corner the stock of the United Copper Company failed. The failure exposed an intricate network of interlocking directorates among banks, trust companies and Wall Street brokerage houses. The revelation made depositors anxious.

Over the past few years, the economy had been slowing. The stock market began declining early in the year, and interest rates were rising. With tight credit markets, the U.S. was unable to expand its money supply. On October 21, the National Bank of Commerce announced that it would stop clearing checks from the Knickerbocker Trust Company, the largest trust in the city. The next day, a run at Knickerbocker occurred as hundreds of depositors wished to withdraw their deposits. Knickerbocker paid out more than eight million in cash.

The following day, the press reported excitedly about the bank run, causing depositors to rush out to other trust companies to recover their deposits. The run, which lasted for two weeks, forced withdrawals of more than forty-seven million dollars in deposits. The Knickerbocker and several other trust companies were forced to close their doors. Those depositors who had been slow to retrieve their funds lost their money.

Lillian Russell and the Professional Women's League had their deposits at the Knickerbocker and lost their savings. But the Panic had an even greater effect on theater attendance. Immediately after the bank run, attendance declined dramatically. A wave of apprehension swept across entrepreneurs and workers who feared for their businesses and jobs. These concerns were particularly felt in the working class neighborhoods.

Tony saw attendance at his theater fall precipitously. During the next two months, even as recovery gradually replaced anxiety, crowds at Tony's theater were slim. It was not until the holiday season that theatergoers returned to their favorite pastime.

The fall programs at Tony's theater were attractive, and up until the onset of the Panic he garnered good crowds. Three new acts featured performers who later became stars in their respective specialties. Isabelle Patricola and her brother Tom opened their New York careers with an appearance at Tony's. Isabelle sang and played the violin; Tom danced and played the ukulele. Le Maire and Le Maire were brothers adept at song and dance. They would go on to produce and act in musicals. Ned Wayburn's Nightingales were female graduates from his dance school. He would soon become one of the most popular dance directors for musical comedies. Wayburn also had the distinction of inventing tap dancing.

On December 22, Tony appeared as host and master of ceremonies for the annual Christmas festival for stage children. The *Times* reported that two thousand people attended the event (although the theater seated only 948). Four hundred of the attendees were children; twenty of them performed, ranging in age from four to twelve. Several were the children of well-known artists. Mrs. Pastor and Mrs. Fernandez and their committee handled the arrangements, which featured the usual banquet and gift distribution. Everyone agreed that it was the best festival they had ever attended.

The accumulated changes in vaudeville management and Tony's own health helped to convince him to make 1908 his final year as a theater proprietor. His theater lease ended in September. Tammany Hall administrators were discussing refurbishing their quarters, including Tony's theater. Tony's time at the theater had been restricted due to his deteriorating health. His movements were limited by the pain of arthritis and rheumatism, and his mental state showed the early signs of depression and senility.

The winter and spring of 1908 began well enough to be encouraging to Tony. Business had improved, and patrons were returning to the theater with their usual frequency. New acts were plentiful and salaries reasonable. However, competition among vaudeville entrepreneurs remained fierce and the tactics were viewed by some as illicit if not illegal. The fact that vaudeville audiences were becoming attracted to other leisure time activities made the business even more tense and anxiety-producing. Still, a good vaudeville program drew patrons, and one that catered to the desires of a particular neighborhood solicited crowds.

Tony's programs featured both acts that had appeared successfully during the past few years and newcomers to the stage. Tony introduced Friday amateur nights, which were well received by patrons. This also gave him the opportunity to audition possible new acts. Sketch teams dominated the bill. Every bill included a coon singer and a Hebrew act, and the Vitagraph films were as eagerly anticipated as favorite performers, showing the latest in natural disasters, fires and short specialties ("College Chum," "Midnight Ride of Paul Revere," "Jack the Kisser," and "Rescue from an Eagle's Nest.")

The spring program introduced several new performers to New York audiences. A child act, the Two Pucks, in a humorous sketch, displayed the acting potential of the young Eva. A group of Negro children did an intricate song and dance and were favorably received by patrons. A Lilliputian Circus, made up of performing ponies and dogs, was especially enjoyed. In April, a young blackface performer by the name of Sophie Tucker belted out coon songs, to everyone's delight. And at his forty-third anniversary as theater manager, Tony appeared on stage and sang for his enthusiastic audience. The *Clipper* reported the gay celebration in detail.

> The many friends of Tony Pastor, managers, actors, and theatergoers, crowded the theater on the 43rd anniversary of his career as a manager on Monday, March 23. The news of the day where Mr. Pastor started his first vaudeville theater downtown, was that he was to sing some of his old, popular songs, attracted so many people that it was impossible to get a seat in the house an hour before the performance began.[2]

According to the *Clipper,* cheering began the moment Tony stepped on the stage. The audience stood up and enthusiastically applauded him. It was some minutes before he was able to sing his first song, "Sarah's Young Man." The first bar had hardly been sung when the applause began again. Tony was finally allowed to finish his song. During the applause many floral pieces were passed over the footlights. The New York Lodge of Elks occupied the boxes and contributed many of the floral gifts.

After the floral contributions, Tony sang "Down in a Coal Mine," a song that aroused pleasant recollections of Tony's early days. After the song, Tony made a brief speech saying, "I feelingly thank the public for its interest, and I feel that I'll be able to go through many more anniversaries." The nostalgic event proved to be Tony's last performing appearance.

Discussing Tony's special day, the *Clipper* went on to say:

> During the day, Mr. Pastor was almost overwhelmed with letters and telegrams of congratulation from old friends, many of whom, though now theatrical stars, made their first appearance on his stage. Mr. Pastor has been the starter of many professional careers that have interested and charmed the American theatergoing public. He has been of service to many theatrical people, has earned the right to be proud of and think of them with satisfaction. The many experiences have equipped him with materials for pleasant reflection.[3]

On May 12, Tammany Hall executives held a meeting to discuss the future of their building. A proposition was presented to move the hall farther uptown, after having been at the current location for forty-one years. Neighboring property owners in the vicinity were all too happy to accommodate the building's removal. The space represented lucrative commercial property. Instead, the idea was overwritten by a proposal to improve the existing building. In either case, Tony's theater would be affected; he would either be forced to move or to close. Results of the meeting were published the next day: Tammany Hall (and Tony's Theater) would remain where it was. The entire building would be modernized. A date for reconstruction was not set. Tony would be expected to close his theater at the appointed time.

On June 23, Tony received a business-like letter from Tammany Hall that he must vacate the premises by September 1. Tammany expressed a concern about Tony's theater, believing it to be old and attracting the "wrong people." Older members of the Tammany committee attempted to block the demand, but failed. Tony himself had little desire to fight the decision; he and Sanderson were said to be diverting their attention to moving to an uptown site. The decision was reported to be anything but cordial, a situation that Tony found disillusioning.

In early July, the press reported that Tony did not plan to renew his lease for his theater. The story suggested that the owners had wanted Tony to sign a five-year lease and Tony wished to lease on a year-by-year basis. The public announcement served to cover up the letter to Tony and allowed him to save face. The *Times* indicated that "relations between the holders of the property and Mr. Pastor are very cordial, but they are unable to come to terms." Tony was reported to be giving up the house by September 1 and was looking for another theater. Little in the press release was true. In fact, Tony had given up any thought of continuing in the theater business.

The June 6 week was the last showing of a Pastor vaudeville program, although no one was aware of this. The following week, to the surprise of patrons, the theater was given over entirely to vitagraph moving pictures. The American Vitagraph Company had subleased the theater from Tony "for the summer months" although Tony's name remained on the marquee. Pictures would be changed daily; admission prices were the same, twenty and thirty cents. The show would run continuously, from 1 P.M. to 11 P.M., Monday through Saturday.

On July 17, a benefit for the Home of Destitute and Crippled Children was held at the Polo Grounds. Theater performers were out in force, playing baseball, running races and putting on three-round sparring bouts. Tony was in attendance, refereeing a sparring bout. It was his last appearance in public. A photo revealed an old, thin, tired-looking man, a shadow of his former self.

On the evening of August 9, Tony's name was removed from his theater. The next morning, a force of laborers came in and tore the lobby out to begin remodeling the entrance for a reopening. A new lessee planned to feature a burlesque format and call the remodeled house the Olympic Theater. Tony was unable to witness the unceremonious closing of his theater, even if he actually wanted to, because he was already bedridden, too weak to leave home. A doctor and nurse were visiting him daily.

The fact that Tony was ailing could no longer be kept from the press. On August 14, the newspapers revealed that Tony was seriously ill. According to the report in the *Times*, "as his old house passed, so did his career end." They attributed Tony's illness to a general breakdown, brought on by his advanced age and worry during the last two years. "Tony Pastor's old variety theater in 14th Street has been losing money of late," the *Times* declared.

The newspaper went on to report that Tony was forced to bed "and at one time was believed to be dying." He had been unconscious for two days but awoke and talked to those around him, seemingly recovered. The *Times* spoke about Tony's recent troubles.

In July 1908, at a benefit for destitute and crippled children, a visibly ailing Tony Pastor appeared in public for the last time. He died a month later (Harry Ransom Humanities Research Center).

> The story of the illness of the old manager comes to the public with special pathos at this particular time. Early in the summer it was announced that he had given up the lease of his theater, and it seems as if the old man's life were ebbing away with the passing of his famous amusement resort. Tony, though he stubbornly denied that he was going to retire from business, admitted frankly that the neighborhood and the patronage was not what it used to be.[4]

The article talked about Tony's last days at his theater. After he had lost control and had taken down all the photographs and old playbills from the walls of his office, he still returned each day. "He could not give up haunting the old place," wrote the *Times* reporter.

> "I have come here everyday to get my mail and look after business matters," Tony explained. "I simply can't drop out of line and leave the theater business. I must have something to do to keep me going. I must always be busy."
>
> Then he sat down to chat and tell stories of other days. But his memory failed him from time to time, and he ended the conversation with a weary apology for his own forgetfulness.[5]

A week later, the press reported that Tony had suffered a relapse. Dr. G.D. Farwell, the family physician, said Tony's condition was very serious. The next day, the doctor reported that Tony had a slight rally and was able to take nourishment. Mrs. Pastor was said to be caring for Tony and she herself was near exhaustion. A nurse was called in. Hundreds of letters and telegrams were being received every day at the Pastor house but no one was prepared to sort or read them. When Harry Sanderson was questioned about Tony's illness, he wanted to contradict any report that Tony's condition had been hastened by financial worries or that he had had a stroke. Some of the newspapers speculated that Tony was dying of a broken heart as the result of the closing of his theater and the termination of a long and glorious career.

Epilogue

Tony Pastor died in his sleep on August 26, 1908. He was seventy-five years old. At his bedside were his wife, her cousin, Dr. Farwell and Harry Sanderson. The official death certificate said that Tony had died of senility and inanition (exhaustion from lack of food or inability to assimilate it).

Three days later, Tony's body was taken from his home in Elmhurst to the Brooklyn Lodge of Elks for display. The funeral was held with a solemn mass at St. Bartholomew's Roman Catholic Church. More than four thousand friends and acquaintances were in attendance, most of them attached to the theater. Pallbearers were Harry Sanderson; John T. Kelly; Ralph Delmore, of the Actor's Order of Friendship; Clay M. Greene, from the Actors' Club; James J. Morton, from the Comedy Club; Timothy Cronin, of the White Rats; Gus Williams; Tom Russell and Sam Collyer.

Among those who attended the funeral and burial in Evergreens Cemetery were William Harris, F.F. Proctor, Frank Russell, Charles J. Ross, Maggie Cline, Lew Dockstater, George Considine, Amy de Angelis, Miss Kernell, Mr. and Mrs. Henry Pastor and representatives from Tammany Hall.

Also attending the burial were William Morris, Joe Weber, Billy Carter, Lillian Russell, Jerry Cohan and members of the Actors' Fund, Theatrical Men's Association, Theatrical Mechanic's Association and the White Rats. Lillian laid a white carnation on Tony's casket. It was the flower he had always worn in his lapel when on stage.

Tony's will was made public several weeks later. The will, with codicils, was dated January 21, 1899. Ironically, Abe Hummel, who had been disbarred and was living in Paris after serving a year on Blackwell's Island, was named executor and Bertha Hummel, his sister, was named executrix.

To Abe Hummel, Tony left the gold watch presented to him on the twentieth anniversary of his career as a manager and a diamond-studded medal presented to him on his twenty-fifth anniversary. Bertha Hummel received the album given Tony by theatrical managers as well as all the mementos of his first wife.

To Henry Pastor, son of William Pastor, Tony left $2,000. To Harry Sanderson, he gave $500 and a gold watch "in appreciation of said Sanderson's friendship and loyal attention to me." All of Tony's wearing apparel went to William Kennedy, doorman of the theater. To Adele Pastor, Frank Pastor's widow, he left $1,000 and all the medals that Frank had received during his career. The executors of the estate were authorized to sell at auction all of Tony's dramatic and musical manuscripts, wardrobe and name as a trademark.

The Pastor family plot at Evergreens Cemetery. The statue was erected at the time of Anna's death. Besides Tony, his mother, Cornelia, Fernando, William and Frank, Caroline, Tony's sister, and the husbands of Tony's two sisters were buried there. Tony's second wife, Josephine, buried there in 1923, was the last member of the Pastor family.

Ten thousand dollars was paid to the Actors' Fund of America. All other funds and property went to Josephine Pastor, Tony's wife. It amounted to $68,559. In an interview several months after Tony's death, Mrs. Pastor revealed that Tony had spent more than $100,000 during the last five years he owned the theater just to keep it open and pay performers' salaries. She also suggested that her husband's death was due directly to the worry and troubles of his last years as a manager.

Newspapers across the country reported on Tony's death, his long career and his vast contributions to popular theater. They spoke in glowing terms of his long journey through theater, and called him a hero whose sense of duty, honor, courage, righteousness and justice was unequalled.

The *Clipper* critic wrote of an incident that occurred a few years before Tony's death. One night, as he was leaving the theater, Tony accidentally fell to the sidewalk. In the process, he knocked down a well-dressed man. The man reacted with an outburst of profanity. As Tony was about to apologize, the man recognized him. "Oh," he exclaimed apologetically, "I didn't know it was you, Mr. Pastor. You can fall over me at any time."

"The happiest moments of my life," Tony once said, "have been those when I was on stage before a large audience and felt that I was amusing the people. It is a satisfactory feeling to have when you are conscious that you are interesting your auditors so that they forget themselves, their unhappiness, their troubles and their disappointments."

Charles Heckler, one of Tony's booking agents, wrote: "Tony lived a life of kindness and charity. He had friends by the score in every walk of life who loved and respected him, for they knew that whatever he said or whatever he did was the honest judgement of his heart."

Chapter Notes

Chapter 1

1. New York Genealogical Records, 1675–1920.
2. Ibid.
3. New York City Directories, 1824–26.
4. Geneology.com. "Pastor as a Sephardic name," Holy Office of the Catholic Church of Spain.
5. New York City Deed Book 288, p.570 FHC 0888448
6. Eric Hornberger, *The Historical Atlas of New York City* (New York: Holt, 1994).
7. All information on birth dates, store and residence locations can be found in the New York Genealogical Records, 1675–1920, and the Census Reports for 1830, 1840, 1850 and 1860.
8. Information on early theaters in New York can be found in Mary Henderson, *The City and the Theater* (New York: Back Stage Books, 2004).
9. Baptism certificate, Church of the Transfiguration, New York, August 28, 1836. Tony's birth was recorded on that certificate as April 26, 1833. It was common practice to wait several years before baptizing a child because of frequent early childhood deaths.
10. New York City Directories, 1833–41.
11. Tony Pastor, "The Life of Tony Pastor," *Tony Pastor's Songs* (New York, Frank Harding, 1862).
12. Ibid.
13. New York City Directories, 1843–47.
14. For a detailed biography of John Nathans, his family and circus career, see Thayer, Stuart, *American Circus Anthology, Essays of the Early Years*, arranged and edited by William L. Stout, Circus Historical Society, 2005; and John H. Glenroy, *Ins and Outs of Circus Life* (Boston: Wing, 1885).
15. New York City Directories, 1848–52.

Chapter 2

1. Glenroy, Chapter 5.
2. John Dingess manuscript in the Harry Hertzberg Collection of the Public Library of San Antonio, Texas. Born in 1829, died in New York, April 15, 1901. Dingess was the advance agent for several circuses, including Spalding & Rogers and Raymond & Waring. p. 149.
3. Glenroy, Chapter 5.
4. Stuart Thayer, "The Nathans, A Circus Family," in *Annals of the American Circus*, vol. 3, 1848–1860 (Seattle: Dauven and Thayer, 1992).
5. Dingess, p. 150.
6. Circus Historical Society, *Olympians of the Sawdust Circle*, http: //www.circushistory.org/Olympians/olympiansN.htm
7. *Huron Reflector*, Norwalk, Ohio, July 3, 1849; Dingess, p. 305.
8. Thayer, vol. 3, 1848–1860.
9. Ibid., p.150.
10. Ibid., p. 182.
11. Dingess, p.150.
12. *New York Clipper*, March 11, 1876.
13. *Olympians of the Sawdust Circle*, biographies; *New York Clipper*, August 10, 1863.
14. *Olympians of the Sawdust Circle*, biographies; *Clipper*, October 24, 1868.
15. Thayer, vol. 3, 1848–1860.
16. *The Ohio Repository*, Canton, Ohio, July 29, 1857.
17. *Clipper*, March 27, 1875.
18. Thayer, vol. 3, p. 214.
19. Palace Garden, www.circusinamerica.org/public/essays/frick
20. *Clipper*, February 6, 1876.
21. Thayer, vol. 3, p. 233.

Chapter 3

1. *New York Clipper*, January 17, 1860.
2. *Clipper*, January 5, 1861.
3. *Philadelphia Ledger*, February 15, 1861.
4. For a biography of Robert Butler, see the *New York Clipper* obituary, June 19, 1885.
5. *Philadelphia Ledger*, April 12, 1861.
6. New York Directory, 1862.
7. *Clipper*, May 11, 1861.
8. *Clipper*, June 1, 1861.
9. *Clipper*, July 6, 1861.
10. *Clipper*, October 12, 1861.
11. *Clipper*, November 2, 1861.
12. *New York Times*, January 5, 1862, January 26, 1862, March 29, 1862.

Chapter 4

1. *New York Times,* April 22, 1862.
2. *New York Clipper,* April 19, 1862.
3. Copies of the Pastor songsters can be found at the Harvard Theater Library. They contain lyrics to the songs as well as references for the original music source.
4. "The Bill-Poster's Dream," *Tony Pastor's Bowery Songster* (New York: Dick and Fitzgerald, 1862).
5. "The Upper and Lower Ten Thousand," *Tony Pastor's Bowery Songster.*
6. "Miles O'Reilly's Love Letter," *Tony Pastor's Complete Budget of Comic Songs* (New York: Dick and Fitzgerald, 1865).
7. *Clipper,* November 8, 1862.
8. *Clipper,* November 29, 1862.
9. Advertisement, *Clipper,* April 11, 1863.
10. *Clipper,* July 25, 1863.
11. *Times,* August 2, 1863.
12. *Clipper,* September 5, 1863.
13. *Chicago Tribune,* January 7, 1864.
14. *Tribune,* February 25, 1864.
15. *Clipper,* September 17, 1864.
16. *Clipper,* October 1, 1864.
17. *Washington Post,* January 7, 1865.
18. *Clipper,* March 11, 1865.

Chapter 5

1. *New York Clipper,* July 30, 1865.
2. *Tony Pastor's Complete Budget of Comic Songs* (New York: Dick and Fitzgerald, 1865).
3. "The Streets of New York," *Tony Pastor's 201 Bowery Songster* (New York: Dick and Fitzgerald, 1867).
4. *Clipper,* February 3, 1866.
5. For a biography of John F. Poole, see C.E. Ellis, *An Authentic History of the Benevolent and Protective Order of Elks* (Chicago: Ellis, 1910), pp. 308–9.
6. *New York Times,* December 19, 1865.
7. *Clipper,* February 17, 1866.
8. *Clipper,* May 5, 1866.
9. *Clipper,* August 11, 1866.
10. *Times,* December 22, 1866.
11. *Clipper,* January 19, 1867.
12. *New York Herald,* February 23, 1867.
13. Advertisement, *Clipper,* June 15, 1867,
14. *Clipper,* November 16, 1867.

Chapter 6

1. For a complete story of Charles Vivian, the Jolly Corks and the Elks, see Ellis, *An Authentic History of the Benevolent and Protective Order of Elks.* The book also includes short biographies of the organization's original members, including Tony, Billy and Fernando Pastor.
2. *New York Clipper,* January 18, 1868.
3. *Clipper,* September 26, 1868.
4. *New York Times,* January 2, 1869.
5. *Clipper,* January 30, 1869.
6. The original manuscript of "Broadway and the Bowery" can be found at the Harvard Theater Library.
7. Advertisement, *Clipper,* September-October 1869.
8. *Clipper,* January 29, 1870.
9. The original manuscript of "Romeo and Juliet" can be found at the Harry Ransom Humanities Research Center, the University of Texas at Austin. An analysis of the burlesque is contained in Susan Kattwinkel, *Tony Pastor Presents: Afterpieces From the Vaudeville Stage* (Westport, CT: Greenwood Press, 1998).
10. *New York Herald,* October 1, 1870.
11. *Clipper,* March 4, 1871.
12. *Clipper,* July 29, 1871.

Chapter 7

1. *New York Clipper,* November 25, 1871.
2. For a detailed analysis of tuberculosis in the 19th century, see G.N. Meachen, *A Short History of Tuberculosis* (New York: AMS Press, 1978); and R.M. Burke, *A Historical Chronology of Tuberculosis* (Springfield, IL.: Thomas, 1955).
3. See R. Moody, *Ned Harrigan From Corlear's Hook to Herald Square* (Chicago: Nelson-Hall, 1980), particularly Chapters 4 and 5.
4. Ibid.
5. *Clipper,* May 25, 1872.
6. *New York Times,* June 18, 1872.
7. *Clipper,* August 17, 1872.
8. Ellis, pp. 179–180.
9. Sanderson's financial ledgers are located at the Harry Ransom Humanities Research Center at the University of Texas at Austin. They include daily receipts, weekly expenditures including performer salaries, competition, weather, audience response and even itemization of money Tony loaned out.
10. Biographies of Harry Kernell and John T. Kelly can be found in A. Fields and L.M. Fields, *From the Bowery to Broadway* (New York: Oxford University Press, 1993), pp. 84–87 and 126–130.
11. *Chicago Tribune,* July 21, 1873.
12. *Clipper,* August 30, 1873.
13. September 20, 1873.
14. Panic of 1873, Lower East Side Tenement Museum, New York.
15. *Times,* November 17, 1873.
16. *Clipper,* April 18, 1874.
17. *Clipper,* July 18, 1874.
18. *Clipper,* July 25, 1874; *Dramatic Mirror,* July 25, 1874.
19. *Clipper,* September 12, 1874.
20. *Times,* September 30, 1874.
21. *Times,* January 31, 1875.

Chapter 8

1. *New York Clipper,* January 29, 1876.
2. *Clipper,* March 4, 1876.
3. *Clipper,* October 7, 1876.
4. *New York Times,* November 4, 1876.
5. *Clipper,* March 17, 1877.
6. For biographies of May Irwin, see A. Slide, *The Vaudevillians* (Westport, CT: Arlington House, 1981), p.

77; and A. Fields, *Women Vaudeville Stars* (Jefferson, NC: McFarland, 2006), pp. 147–151.
7. *Clipper,* January-February, 1878.
8. *Baltimore Gazette,* April 25, 1878.
9. *Brooklyn Eagle,* May 25, 1878,
10. *Clipper,* May 27, 1878.
11. *San Francisco Sunday Chronicle,* July 21, 1878.
12. *San Francisco Evening Post,* July 20, 1878.
13. *Clipper,* March 8, 1879.
14. *Clipper,* March 15, 1879.
15. *Clipper,* May 17, 1879.
16. *Tony Pastor's Almanac,* 1880.
17. Biographical information about Jacques Kruger was obtained from the New York City Directory, Italian Genealogical Group and the *New York Times.*
18. See Kattwinkle, *Tony Pastor Presents: Afterpieces From the Vaudeville Stage.*
19. For a biography of Lillian Russell, see A. Fields, *Lillian Russell, a Biography of America's Beauty* (Jefferson, NC: McFarland, 1999).
20. See Kattwinkle.
21. *Times,* February 19, 1881.

Chapter 9

1. *Tony Pastor's Songs* (New York: Frank Harding, 1862).
2. *Dramatic Mirror,* October 29, 1881.
3. A biography of Maggie Cline can be found in Fields, *Women Vaudeville Stars,* pp. 13–16.
4. *New York Clipper,* April 8, 1882.
5. *Clipper,* October 28, 1882.
6. *Clipper,* November 25, 1882.
7. 14th Street Theater financial ledgers, Harry Ransom Humanities Research Center.
8. Advertisement, *Clipper,* May 5, 1883.
9. Advertisement, *Clipper,* June 9, 1883.
10. *Clipper,* May 3, 1884.
11. *Clipper,* May 10, 1884.
12. Fields, *Women Vaudeville Stars,* pp. 151–154.
13. *Clipper,* January 24, 1885.
14. *Clipper,* April 11, 1885.

Chapter 10

1. *New York World,* February 12, 1885.
2. *Daily Democratic Times,* Lima, Ohio, July 11, 1885.
3. *Chicago Times-Star,* August 23, 1885.
4. *Philadelphia Times,* October 4, 1885.
5. *New York Clipper,* July 3, 1886.
6. *New York Times,* October 29, 1886.
7. *Boston Daily Globe,* April 23, 1887.
8. *Times,* June 29, 1887.
9. *Clipper,* August 13, 1887.
10. *Clipper,* October 29, 1887.

Chapter 11

1. *New York Clipper,* October 6, 1888.
2. *Boston Globe,* August 19, 1888.
3. *Clipper,* November 10, 1888.
4. *New York Sunday Dispatch,* March 3, 1889.
5. *New York Times,* February 5, 1889.
6. *Clipper,* December 7, 1889.
7. *Clipper,* February 15, 1890.
8. *Clipper,* March 29, 1890.
9. *Times,* March 22, 1890.

Chapter 12

1. *New York Clipper,* June 14, 1890.
2. *Clipper,* June 14, 1890.
3. *The Era,* August 2, 1890.
4. *Clipper,* October 25, 1890.
5. *Clipper,* November 1, 1890.
6. *Clipper,* November 1, 1890.
7. *Clipper,* November 1, 1890.
8. *Clipper,* February 28, 1891.
9. *New York Times,* October 27, 1891.
10. *Clipper,* December 12, 1891.
11. *Clipper,* February 20, 1892.
12. *Clipper,* November 5, 1892.
13. *Clipper,* November 5, 1892.
14. *Times,* December 7, 1892.
15. *Clipper,* January 7, 1893.
16. *Times,* January 1, 1893.
17. For details about the Panic of 1893 and its effect on the New York City economy, see E.G. Burrows and M. Wallace, *Gotham: A History of New York City to 1898* (New York: Oxford University Press, 1999).
18. *Clipper,* September 23, 1893.
19. *Clipper,* October 28, 1893.
20. *Clipper,* November 4, 1893.

Chapter 13

1. *New York Clipper,* April 21, 1894.
2. *Clipper,* April 28, 1894.
3. *Chicago Tribune,* May 15, 1894.
4. Burrows and Wallace, *Gotham,* p. 1146.
5. For a detailed story of Tin Pan Alley, see D.A. Jasen, *Tin Pan Alley* (New York: Donald I. Fine, 1988).
6. *New York Times,* October 30, 1894.
7. *Clipper,* December 29, 1894.
8. H. Kellocks, *Houdini: His Life Story* (New York: Harcourt, Brace, 1928), pp. 66–71.
9. *Times,* January 19, 1896.
10. *Clipper,* January 18, 1896.
11. *Clipper,* February 1, 1896.
12. *Clipper,* February 8, 1896.
13. *Clipper,* October 31, 1896.
14. *Times,* January 9, 1897.
15. *Clipper,* March 19, 1898.
16. *Clipper,* March 26, 1898.
17. *Clipper,* September 24, 1898.
18. *Clipper,* November 19, 1898.

Chapter 14

1. *New York Clipper,* October 7, 1899.
2. *Clipper,* December 9, 1899.

3. For a detailed story of the A.V.M. (Syndicate), see F. Wertheim, *Vaudeville Wars: How the Keith-Albee and Orpheum Circuit Controlled the Big-time and its Performers* (New York: Palgrave Macmillan, 2006).
4. The story of the White Rats can be found in G.F. Golden, *My Lady Vaudeville and Her White Rats* (New York: The Board of Directors of the White Rats of America, 1909); and for a history of the White Rats' battle with the Syndicate see A. Fields, "Actors Strike," *Vaudeville Times* 3, 4, and 4, 2, 2001–2002.
5. *Clipper,* March 30, 1901.
6. *Clipper,* August 17, 1901.
7. *New York Times,* December 30, 1901.

Chapter 15

1. *New York Clipper,* November 8, 1902.
2. *New York Times,* December 28, 1903.
3. *Clipper,* April 2, 1904.
4. *Times,* May 9, 1905.
5. *Times,* March 26, 1906.
6. *Dramatic Mirror,* December 29, 1906.
7. *Dramatic Mirror,* April 6, 1907.
8. *Times,* April 21, 1907.

Chapter 16

1. J. Moen and E. Tallman, "Lessons from the Panic of 1907," *Federal Reserve Bank of Atlanta Economic Review* 75 (May–June 1990): 2–13.
2. *New York Clipper,* March 28, 1908.
3. *Clipper,* March 28, 1908.
4. *New York Times,* August 14, 1908.
5. *Times,* August 16, 1908.

Bibliography

Archives, Collections, Libraries

Circus Historical Society
Circus World Museum
Columbia University
Harry Ransom Humanities Research Center, University of Texas
Houghton Library, Harvard University
Museum of the City of New York
New York Census
New York City Directory
New York Historical Society
New York Public Library, Billy Rose Theater Collection
University of Southern California, Special Collections

Newspapers, Theatrical Weeklies

New York Clipper, January 1855 to December 1910
New York Dramatic Mirror, January 1880 to December 1910
Variety, December 1905 to December 1915
ProQuest Internet file for all newspaper articles on Tony Pastor in the *New York Times, Boston Globe, Washington Post, Chicago Tribune* and *Los Angeles Times*. Other newspapers for selected dates include *New York Herald, Philadelphia Ledger, San Francisco Chronicle*.

Genealogical and Historical Sources

Ancestry.com for census and newspapers: www.ancestry.com
Godfrey Memorial Library for historical newspapers: www.godfrey.com
Rootsweb for general information and queries: www.rootsweb.com
Heritage Quest census database: www.kslc.org
Films of deeds and vital records ordered from Family History Center, The Church of Jesus Christ of Latter-day Saints
Historical New York City information and data: http://www.bklyn-genealogy-info.com/Manhattan/Broadway/Union.html
Evergreens Cemetery information: The Evergreens Cemetery, 1629 Bushwick Ave. Brooklyn, NY 11207-1849
New York City maps: http://maps.infospace.com
Maps in New York Public Library Digital Collection: http://digitalgallery.nypl.org
Library of Congress Digital Collection: http://memory.loc.gov
Civil War Draft Records in *Prologue Magazine*: http://www.archives.gov/publications/prologue

Books

Bordman, G. *American Musical Theater*. New York: Oxford University Press, 1978.
Brown, T. Allston. *A History of the New York Stage From the First Performance in 1732–1901*. New York: Dodd, Mead, 1903.
Burrows, E.G., and M. Wallace. *Gotham: A History of New York City to 1898*. New York: Oxford University Press, 1999.
Circus Historical Society. *Olympians of the Sawdust Circle*. http://www.circushistory.org/Olympians/olympiansN.htm.
Coffin, C. *Vaudeville*. New York: Mitchell Kennerly, 1914.
Culhane, J. *The American Circus*. New York: Holt, 1990.
Dingess, J. Manuscript on circus life in the Harry Heryzberg Collection of the Public Library of San Antonio, Texas.

Ellis, C.E. *An Authentic History of the Benevolent and Protective Order of Elks.* Chicago: Ellis, 1910.

Erdman, A.L. *Blue Vaudeville,* Jefferson, NC: McFarland, 2004.

Fields, A. *Lillian Russell,* Jefferson, NC: McFarland, 1999.

_____. *James J. Corbett,* Jefferson, NC: McFarland, 2001.

_____. *Fred Stone,* Jefferson, NC: McFarland, 2002.

_____. *Women Vaudeville Stars,* Jefferson, NC: McFarland, 2006.

_____, and L.M. Fields. *From the Bowery to Broadway.* New York: Oxford University Press, 1993.

Gilbert, D. *American Vaudeville, Its Life and Times.* New York: Whittlesey House, 1940.

Glenroy, J.H. *Ins and Outs of Circus Life.* Boston: Wing, 1885.

Golden, G.F. *My Lady Vaudeville and Her White Rats.* New York: The Board of Directors of the White Rats of America, 1909.

Grau, R. *Forty Years of Observation of Music and the Drama.* New York: Broadway, 1909.

_____. *The Business Man in the Amusement World.* New York: Broadway, 1910.

Green, A., and J. Laurie Jr. *Show Biz From Vaude to Video.* New York: Holt, 1951.

Harlow, A. *Old Bowery Days: The Chronicle of a Famous Street.* New York: Appleton, 1931.

Henderson, M. *The City and the Theater.* New York: Back Stage Books, 2004.

Homberger, E. *The Historical Atlas of New York City.* New York: Holt, 1994.

Jasen, D.A. *Tin Pan Alley.* New York: Donald I. Fine, 1988.

Kattwinkle, S. *Tony Pastor Presents: Afterpieces From the Vaudeville Stage.* Westport: Greenwood Press, 1998.

Kellocks, H. *Houdini: His Life Story.* New York: Harcourt, Brace, 1928.

Leavitt, M.B. *Fifty Years in Theatrical Management.* New York: Broadway, 1912.

Lewis, R.M. *From Traveling Show to Vaudeville.* Baltimore: Johns Hopkins University Press, 2003.

Malone, D., ed. *Dictionary of American Biography.* New York: Scribners, 1934.

Marks, E.B. *They All Sang: From Tony Pastor to Rudy Vallee.* New York: Viking Press, 1935.

Marston, W.M., and J.H. Feller. *F.F. Proctor, Vaudeville Pioneer.* New York: Richard R. Smith, 1943.

McCabe, J.D. Jr. *New York by Gaslight.* Reprint. New York: Greenwich House, 1984.

Meachen, G.N. *A Short History of Tuberculosis.* New York: AMS Press, 1978.

Moody, R. *Ned Harrigan: From Corlear's Hook to Herald Square.* Chicago: Nelson-Hall, 1980.

Morris, L. *Incredible New York.* New York: Random House, 1951.

Nasaw, D. *Going Out: The Rise and Fall of Public Amusements.* New York: Basic Books, 1993.

Odell, G. *Annals of the New York Stage 1883–1889.* Reprint. New York: Columbia University Press, 1949.

Pastor, T. *Tony Pastor's Bowery Songster.* New York: Dick and Fitzgerald, 1862.

_____. *Tony Pastor's Complete Budget of Comic Songs.* New York: Dick and Fitzgerald, 1865.

_____. *Tony Pastor's Songs.* New York: Frank Harding, 1862.

_____. *Tony Pastor's Stories and Jokes.* New York: Small, 1872.

_____. *Tony Pastor's 201 Bowery Songster.* New York: Dick and Fitzgerald, 1867.

Rovere, R.H. *Howe and Hummel.* London: Arlington Books, 1947.

Samuels, C., and L. Samuels. *Once Upon a Stage.* New York: Dodd, Mead, 1974.

Sanders, R. *The Lower East Side.* New York: Dover, 1979.

Scherzer, K.A. *The Unbounded Community: Neighborhood Life and Social Structure in New York City.* Duke University Press, 1992.

Sheean, V. *Oscar Hammerstein I: The Life and Exploits of an Impresario.* New York: Simon and Schuster, 1956.

Slide, A. *The Vaudevillians.* Westport: Arlington House, 1981.

Stein, C., ed. *American Vaudeville As Seen by Its Contemporaries.* New York: Knopf, 1984.

Thayer, S. *Annals of the American Circus.* Seattle: Dauven and Thayer, 1976.

_____. *Traveling Showmen.* Detroit: Astley & Ricketts, 1997.

_____. *The Performers: A History of Circus Acts.* Seattle: Dauven and Thayer, 2005.

Toll. R.C. *On with the Show: The First Century of Show Business in America.* New York: Oxford University Press, 1976.

Trav, S.D. *No Applause—Just Throw Money.* New York: Faber and Faber, 2005.

Wertheim, F. *Vaudeville Wars: How the Keith-Albee and Orpheum Circuit Controlled the Big-time and its Performers.* New York: Palgrave Macmillan, 2006.

Zellers, P. *Tony Pastor: Dean of the Vaudeville Stage.* Ypsilanti, MI: Eastern University Press, 1971.

Periodicals, Articles

Barry, E. "Tony Pastor—A Strictly Personal Showman." *Variety,* January 27, 1926.

"Dean of Vaudeville Celebrities." *Variety,* March 24, 1906.

Eaton, W.P. "The Wizards of Vaudeville." *McClure,* September 1923.

"The Father of Vaudeville." *New York Times,* April 21, 1907.

Fostelle, A. "The Days of Tony Pastor." *New York Clipper,* December 19, 1914.

Golwey, E.A. "Tony Pastor, the Starmaker." *The Dance Magazine,* August 1929.

Heckler, C. Jr. "The Tony Pastor Collection." *Music Journal,* July-August 1956.

Bibliography

Isaacs, E., and R. Gilder. "American Musical Comedy." *Theater Arts,* August 1945.

Matlaw, M. "Tony the Trouper; Pastor's Early Years." *The Theater Annual* 24, 1968: 70–90.

Moses, M. "Tony Pastor, Father of Vaudeville." *Theater Guild Magazine,* April 1931.

"The Passing of Tony Pastor." *Green Book Album,* January 1909.

"Recollections of Pastor's." *Variety,* December 12, 1908.

Sanderson, H. "Reminiscences of Tony Pastor, Vaudeville's Dean." *Variety,* December 12, 1908.

"Tony Pastor's Fortune." *Billboard,* October 22, 1910.

"Tony Pastor — the Father of Vaudeville." *Harper's Weekly,* September 5, 1908.

Traber, J.M. "Pen Sketch of Tony Pastor, the Father of Modern Variety." *Billboard,* February 18, 1911.

"The Variety Stage." *Harper's Weekly,* March 22, 1902.

Index

Academy of Music (New Orleans) 45
Academy of Music (New York) 1, 79, 100, 104, 107, 109, 112, 116–118
Actor's Fund 92, 110, 129, 139, 144, 167, 170, 175, 182, 194
Adams, Casey 122
Adams, Howard 122
Albee, E.A. 149, 155, 166–167, 170, 172–173, 175–176, 188
Aldrich, Charles T. 162
Alexander Musee (New York) 123
All Men Are Liars 33
Allen, Louise 177
American Four 112
American Music Hall (New York) 21–22, 30, 33, 37
American Vitagraph 169–170, 174, 177, 182, 191, 192
Angelis Sisters 169
Arch Street Theater (Philadelphia) 85
Armstrong, Willis 42, 47–49, 60
Arthur, Julia 141
Austin, Carrie 42
Avon Comedy Four 184–185

Barnum, P.T. 8–9
Barnum's American Museum 8, 34, 44, 49, 57
Barrett, Tom 128
Barry, Billy 2, 64, 73, 77, 79–80, 90–92
Barry and Fay 112
Bayes, Nora 186, 188
Beauchamps, George 141
Beck, Martin 170, 188
Belle Hathaway's monkeys 185
Bellwood, Bessie 2, 156, 171
Bennett, James Gordon 42
Bennett and Gardner 107
Benson, "Baby" 59–60, 72, 76
Benson, Jenny 59–60, 72, 76
Bernhardt, Sarah 161, 163
Bernstein, Annie 184–185
Bertha, Mlle. 42, 47
Beverly, Maud 117
Bibb and Bob 128

Bijou Theater (New York) 102
Billee Taylor 104
The Billposters Dream 31
Billy Barlow 22
Bindley, Florence 160
Biograph 159, 164, 182
Birch, Billy 26, 28, 111, 125, 130, 134
Board of Managers of Vaudeville Theaters 122
Bonehill, Bessie 2, 131–133, 137–140, 144, 146, 148–149, 152–153, 161, 182
Boston Globe 128
Boston Museum (Boston) 35–36
Bowery Amphitheater (New York) 6
Bowery Theater (New York) 6, 38, 47, 50, 72, 119
Braham, David 38
Braham, Harry 85, 121
Braham, John 112
Braham, Joseph 61, 66, 71
The Brantfords 123
Brian, David 185
Brimmer, Lew 47–48
Broadway Magazine 34
Broadway Music Hall (New York) 25–28
Broadway Theater (New York) 14, 17, 118
Brooklyn Eagle 90, 177
Brothers Ali 140
Brown, Celia 49
Brown, T. Allston 63
The Brownings 174
Bryant, Dan 1, 34
Bryant, Lulu 117
Bryant and Hoey 92–93, 96
Bryant's Opera House 34
Budworth, Frank 105
Budworth, Mr. and Mrs. Henry 167
Buffalo Bills Wild West Show 163
Burch, Billy 26, 28, 111, 125, 125, 134
Burt, Nellie 165, 169–170
Bush, Frank 90, 119, 121, 129, 131, 133, 135, 151–152, 167, 186

Bush Street Theater (San Francisco) 85, 95, 163
Butler, Robert 17, 21–22, 24–28, 30–31, 33–36, 38–42, 47, 52, 59, 63, 66
Byrnes and Helene 119

Cahill, Marie 179
Caicedo, Juan 116
Caldwell, Walter 42
Canterbury Theater (Washington, D.C.) 40
Captain Slingsby 140
Carleton, William 47–48, 54, 64, 66, 96
Carroll, William 104–105, 107, 112, 116
Carte de Visite Songster 31
Carter, Billy 61–62, 64, 72, 74, 151, 162, 176, 180, 194
Carter De Haven Trio 182
Carus, Emma 165–167, 170, 173–174, 184
Casino Theater (New York) 161, 176; roof garden 163
Cawthorne, Herbert 72
Cazman, Henry 135
Central Park 23, 36
Charley Shea's Opera House (New York) 72–73
Chateau Mobille Varieties (New York) 87
Chatham Theater (New York) 19
Chicago Tribune 38, 74, 79, 90, 136, 152
Cholera epidemic 5, 13
Christmas party for children 130–131, 138–139, 141, 147, 153, 156, 159, 162, 165, 174, 177, 182–183, 185–186, 190
Church of the Tranfiguration (Little Church Around the Corner) 7, 89
Cinematographe 159, 161–162
Clifford and Huth 154, 158
Clifton Sisters 130–131
Cline, Maggie 2, 103, 125, 129–130, 133, 135, 137–141, 146, 153, 155

Index

Clinton and Post 176
Clipper Quartet 122
Clive, Alfred 123
Clorindy 163
Cohan, George M. 180, 183, 185–186
Cohan, Jerry 52,194
Cole, Bob 163
Collene, Ellen 42
Collier, John W. 50, 66
Collins, Lizzie 131
Collyer, Dan 50, 79, 95, 97–98, 103, 105–106, 177
Collyer, Sam 50, 52, 59, 79, 106, 194
Columbia Opera House (New York) 87
Comic Irish Songster 31
Comic Songster 31
Concert Saloon Law 28–29
Conroy and Fox 140
Consumption/TB 68–69
Continental Theater (Philadelphia) 21, 31, 34–35
Continuous vaudeville 143, 149, 157, 160, 179, 182
Cook, Will Marion 163
Cook and Sonora 182
Costello, Tom 128
Cotton, Ben 26, 28
Coulson Sisters 123
Cushman, Frank 85, 162

Daily Democratic Times 115
Daly, Dan 184
Daly, Polly 62
Daly Brothers 87, 105–106
Daly Sisters 140, 146–147
Daly's Theater (New York) 99
Dan Bryant's Minstrels 100
Dan Rice's Great Show 20
Dan Sully's Company 118, 125
Dandy, Jess 167, 174, 176, 182
Dearan, Sam 140–141
Delahanty and Hengler 59, 72, 74, 88
Devere, Sam 66, 68–69, 85, 90, 111
Dixey, Henry E. 112
Dockstater, Lew 118–119, 159, 162, 180, 194
Dockstater's Theater (New York) 123
Donaldson, James 121
The Donnelles 123, 126
Donnelly, Dan 109
The Donovans 158–160
Down in a Coal Mine 101, 184, 188, 191
Dramatic Mirror 77,100, 103–104, 112, 139, 154–155, 166, 187–188
Dressler, Marie 175, 184
Drew, John E. 140
Duffy, Duffy 180
Duffy, Sawtelle 180
Dumont, Frank 122
Dyllyn, J. Bernard 158, 185
Dyring, H.T. 92, 103

Eagan, Jennie 66
Eden Musee (New York)-123

Edison 164, 182
Edward Harrigan's Compnay 140, 161
Edwin Booth Theater (New York) 34, 41, 108
1863 draft riots 22, 35–36
8th Avenue Theater (New York) 119
El Nino Eddie 42, 47, 183
Eldredge, "Aunt" Louisa 130–131, 138, 141, 156, 159, 174
The Elevated Railroad 92
Elinore Sisters 158, 162, 180, 182
The Elks 54–55, 68, 85, 92, 160, 183, 191
Elmhurst, Long Island 167–169, 176–177
Emerson, Billy 49
Emmet, Billy 47–48, 52, 57, 73
Emmett, J.K. 164
Emmett, Kitty 162
Engle, Jennie 47–48, 52, 56, 62, 69, 70, 72–74, 85
Eureka Dramatic Agency 63
Evans, George "Honey Boy" 2, 162, 158–159, 169–170, 180
Evans and Hoey 135
Evans and Livermore 140

Faiber, Constantine de 42
The Famous East Side of Town 50
Farrell and Wilmont 126
Farwell, Dr. G.D. 193–194
Fay, Elfie 166–167
Federal Street Theater (Boston) 13
Female at Ease 26
The Female M.D. 22
Ferguson and Mack 97–98
Fernandez, Mrs. 130, 177, 182–183, 185, 187, 190
The Fieldings 59, 61, 74, 77, 80
Fields, Harry 173
Fields, Sadie 173
Fields and Hanson 2
Fields & Hoey 87–88
Fields & Wooley 158
Fifth Avenue Hotel 23
Fifth Avenue Theater (New York) 98
Filson and Errol 162, 167
Fish, Marguerite 138, 140
Fisher and Caswell 156
585 Broadway (New York) 26, 80–82, 85–90, 92, 95–99, 113
Foley, Josephine 77–78, 80
The Follies 180, 188
Forrest, Capitola 119, 143
Fortesque Sisters 154
Fostelle, Charles 96, 107, 109, 117
Fostelle and Emmett 167, 174
Four Cohans 161–162, 169
444 Broadway (New York) 1, 17, 21–22, 24–38, 40, 44, 47, 127, 188
444 Combination Songster 31
14th Street Theater (New York) 101, 104–105, 107–108, 110–111, 116, 118–119, 121–124, 125, 128, 139–131, 137–138, 141, 143, 149, 151, 161–162, 179, 193

Fox, Charley 40
Fox, Della 161
Fox, Will H. 154, 156
Fox, William 180
Fox's American Theater (Philadelphia) 61
Foy, Dave 125
Foy and Clark 164
Foy Sisters 80
Francini's Traveling Hippodrome 14
Franklin, Irene 1, 130–131, 169, 180, 182, 186
Franklin Theater (New York) 6
Franks, Sydney 69
Freeman Sisters 74, 77
French, Edwin 92–93, 130, 139, 141
French Twin Sisters 69, 92–93, 96–97, 104, 177
Front Street Theater (Philadelphia) 11

Gardner and Vincent 182
Garnella Bros. 77, 80, 166
Gaylor, Bobby 164, 185
Gaynor, James 42,49
George Thatcher's Minstrels 140
Germania Theater (New York) 100–101
Gilbert and Sullivan 92–93, 97–98, 101
Gilmer, Jennie 66
Gilmore, William 122
Gilmore Sisters 117
Gilson, Lottie 1, 133–134, 136, 151–153, 185
Girard, Frank 64, 66, 69, 72, 74, 77, 79–81, 88, 90–91, 97–98, 103–105, 117
Gleeson, Bertha 160, 182
Gleeson, John 160, 182
Glenroy, James Richard 170, 176
Glenroy Bros. 146
Globe Museum (New York) 119, 133
Globe Theater (New York) 62–63, 82, 85
Golden, George Fuller 172–175, 188
Good Bye Jack, Till You Get Back 2
Goodwin, Nat C. 2, 85
Gorenflo Sisters 47, 57, 59, 61, 66, 72
Graham Sisters 131
Grand Opera House (Chicago) 116, 169
Grand Opera House (New York) 87, 90, 95, 194, 119
Grau, Robert 157
Graver, J.A. 61, 66, 69
Great Sensation Songster 31
Grenier, Thomas 122, 152
Gur, Harry 60, 62

Hall, Artie 170, 176
Hall, Nathans and Tufts Circus 9
Hallen and Fuller 164
Hallen and Hart 95
The Hallens 169

Index

Hamlin, Fred 185
Hammerstein, Oscar 154, 179, 185, 188
Hammerstein's Victoria (New York) 156, 179, 184
Harbecks 154
Harding and Ah Sid 180, 185
Harlem Pavilion (New York) 123
Harrigan, Edward 1, 135, 138, 167, 175, 185
Harrigan and Hart 68–74, 105, 108, 111
Harrigan's Theater (New York) 139–143
Harris, Nellie 152
Harris, Sam 118
Harris, William 121
Harris and Carroll 88
Harry Williams Company 134
Hart, Annie 111, 151, 154, 182
Hart, Joe 119, 121–122
Hart, Josh 68, 73
Hart, Tony 70, 72, 170
Harvey Bros. 119
Has Anybody Seen My Sister 17
Hasker and Lester 152
Haymarket Theater (Chicago) 169
Haytors 138, 140
Hearst, William R. 162
Hector & Lorraine 140
Hengler Sisters 154
Herald Square Theater (New York) 144
Herbert, Victor 185
Herbert and Albini 140
Herr Grais 144
Herring, Fannie 72
He's a Grand Old Has-Been 33
"Hey, Rube" 13, 19
Hill, Jenny 2, 128,138–140
Hindle, Annie 72
Hines and Remington 116
The Hippodrome (New York) 179
H.M.S. Pinafore 92–93
Hoey, James F. 2, 133, 147, 152, 159–160
Hogan, Ernest 185
Hooley's Opera House (Brooklyn) 72
Hooley's Theater (Chicago) 79
Hopkins, J.D. 170
Hopper, De Wolf 135
Houdini 155, 159
Howard, May 121
Howard, Willie 177
Howard Athenaeum (Boston) 58–59, 74, 79, 107, 110,122, 125, 128, 140
Howell, Ida 146
Huber and Allyn 124
Huber's Museum (New York) 155
Huber's Prospect Theater (New York) 119
Hummel, A.H. 135, 157, 166, 188, 194
Hummel, Bertha 194
Hurtig and Seaman 173
Hyde and Behman's Theater (Brooklyn) 104, 107, 110, 112, 131, 135, 137, 139–140, 164, 170, 188
Hylton, Millie 131
Hylton, Prof. 68

I Am a Bowery Boy 52
Iferd, Celia 72
Immigrants 6, 23, 41, 57, 63, 76, 82, 105, 133, 178–179
Inman Sisters 130–131
Irma, Mlle. 62
Iroquois Theater (Chicago) 183
Irwin, Flora 98, 109–110
Irwin, May 1, 89, 98, 109
Irwin Sisters 88, 91–94, 98, 103–105, 107

Jackson, Billy 170
Jackson, Mildred 170
Jerome, Wiliam 143
Jewell's Automatic Electric Manikin Theater 185
Joe Pentland's Circus 14
John Poole's Theater (New York) 119, 123
Johnson, Billy 163
"Jolly Corks" 54
Joseph Osburn and Company 167
The Julians 119, 121–123, 130–131, 133, 135–136

Kamochi 138
Keaton, Buster 170, 174, 176
Keaton, Mr. and Mrs. Joe 170, 173–174, 176
Keene, Laura 34, 41
Keith, B.F. 139, 143, 149–150, 155, 157, 160, 166–167, 170, 172–174, 176, 182–183, 188
Keith circuit 183
Kelly, John T. 69, 72, 92–93, 117–118, 123–124, 129, 139, 152, 194
Kelly, John W. 146–148, 152–154, 167, 169
Kelly and Ashby 138
Kelly and Murphy 109
Kelly and O'Brien 107
Kennebec Journal 166
Kennedy, Harry 92, 130
Kernan, James 121
Kernell, Harry 2, 72, 80, 85–86, 88, 91–92, 96–97, 107, 111–112, 116, 118, 122–123, 130, 135, 139, 140, 170, 182
Kernell, John 2, 88, 91–92, 96–97, 107, 112, 122–123, 131, 182
Kernell's Company 125
Kerns, Frank 57–64, 66, 69, 73, 170
Kincade, William 11–12
Kineopticon 159, 161
Klaw and Erlanger 185
Knight, George S. 75, 111
Kohl and Castle 170
Koster & Bial's Theater (New York) 119, 123, 157, 159, 170
Kruger, Jacques 96, 103–105, 107, 109, 177

Lafayette Theater (New York) 6
La Rose, Harry 116–117, 121, 123, 129–130,139
La Strange, Nellie 148–149
Latell, Ed 164,167, 169, 189, 185
The Law Won't Allow Me to Do It 146
Lawrence, Katie 146, 148
Leavitt, M.B. 80–82, 89, 104, 107–108, 112, 122, 128
Leavitt and Pastor Combination 104
Le Brun, Addie 57, 59, 61
Le Maire and Le Maire 190
Leonard, Eddie 180
The Leonards 140
Lester and Allen 96, 98, 104, 109, 129–130, 133
Levey, Ethel 165, 185
Levi J. North's Circus 15–16
Lew Fields Theater (New York) 179
Liberty Theater (New York) 185
Lilliputian Circus 191
Lina and Vani 140
Lingard, Nellie 140
Little Johnny Jones 185
Little Nell 57
Little Tich 108, 123, 126
Loew, Marcus 180
Loftus, Cissie 2, 111
London Theater (New York) 86, 119, 123, 133
Long Acre Square (Times Square) 154, 162, 178–179
Lord Lovell 26
Lubin 164, 182
Lucy Long 13, 184

Mack, Johnny 47–48
Madison Square Garden (New York) 144
Maguire, Nellie 143
Majestic Theater (New York) 179
Manning and Weston 164
The March of the Union 26
Markham, Lillian 116, 121
Markham, Pauline 161
Mason, Hen 68–69, 72–73
Master Barry 43
Mayo, Frank 85
McAvoy, Dan 152, 154, 160, 164, 167
McAvoy, May 152, 154, 160, 164, 167
McCarthy, John 156
McCarthy, Nellie 156
McCaull, Col. 102
McDonald, G.F. 47–49, 54, 60
McIntyre and Heath 2, 110, 117
McNish, Frank 98, 141, 165, 177
McVicker's Theater (Chicago) 88
Mechanic's Hall (New York) 21
Melius 182
Melodeon Music Hall (Philadelphia) 20–22, 25, 33, 40
Mephisto Electriic Orchestra 119
Merton, Florence 97–98
Metropolitan Hotel 23

Metropolitan Opera House (New York) 108, 119, 186
Meyerfield, Morris 170, 188
Miles O'Reilly's Love-Letters 33
Miner, Harry 86, 108, 118–119, 121
Miner's Bowery Theater (New York) 123, 133
Miner's 8th Avenue Theater (New York) 123
Minstrelsy 9, 23, 28, 40, 59, 69, 72
Mitchell, Julian 185
Mitchell, Kitty 158
Mlle. Duclerc 149
Mlle. Langtree 148, 150
The Monitor and the Merrimack 26
Monroe & Mack 144, 146
Montague, Harry 85, 90
Montague, Louise 92, 161
Montgomery and Stone 174, 180
Moore, Clara 88
Moore, Flora 92, 96, 117, 133
Moore, Florence 164
Moore, "Pony" 128, 135, 137
Moore, Victor 186
Mora, Helen 150
Moran, Frank 105, 111, 116–117, 130, 134, 152, 157
Moran, Polly 182, 184, 186
Morgan, Jennie 80, 85
Morris, D.L. 62
Morris, Harry 118
Morris Bros. Opera House (Boston) 42, 48, 56
Morton, Dorothy 175
Morton, Kittie 162
Morton, Sam 162
Musical Dale 152, 154
Musical Lindsey's 126
My Grandfather Was a Most Wonderful Man 17

Nash, Jolly 119, 121
Nathans, Emma 9, 15, 17
Nathans, John 8–12, 14–15, 17–20, 25
National Theater (Philadelphia) 11, 116
Ned Wayburn's Nightingales 190
New Amsterdam Theater (New York) 179, 185
New York Clipper 24, 26–27, 30, 33, 36–38, 40, 42–44, 47, 51–52, 57, 63, 65, 68, 70–71, 74, 77, 79, 88, 92, 96–97, 99, 104–105, 197, 112, 118–119, 123, 128–129, 132, 134, 136, 141, 146, 149, 151, 154–155, 157–159, 164–167, 170, 173–174, 176, 182–183, 186–187, 191–192, 195
New York Herald 5, 42, 50, 62
New York Ledger 42
New York Temperance Society 8
New York Theater (New York) 6, 173
New York Times 29–30, 50, 57, 70, 76, 80, 83, 99, 122, 130, 135, 140, 157, 159–160, 174–175, 180, 186, 188, 192–193
New York World 115

Newall, Major 144
Newland, Bobby 87
Niblo, Fred 169–170
Niblo's Garden (New York) 23
Nixon's Amphitheater (Chicago) 70, 74
Nobles, Dolly 164
Nobles, Martin 164
North's Amphitheater (Chicago) 15
Norworth, Jack 167
Nugent, Maud 160, 165

Oakland Garden (Oakland) 108
Oakley, Annie 126, 147, 163
O'Brien, Tim 42
O'Brien and Havel 141, 157–158, 164, 185, 170
Olcott, Chauncey 112
Old Bowery Theater (New York) 21
Olivette 99
Olympia Music Hall (New York) 179
Olympia Theater (New York) 161
Olympic Theater (Chicago) 169
Olympic Theater (New York) 57, 71, 77, 82, 85, 87, 108
O'Neil, Kitty 61, 64, 66, 69–70, 90–92, 97, 105, 107, 111, 116–117, 170
Open House Songster 31
Orpheum circuit 183
Owens, John E. 34
Own Comic Songster 31

Pacquerette 147, 156
Palace Garden (New York) 16
Panic of 1837 6–9, 12
Panic of 1857 16
Panic of 1873 75
Panic of 1893 147–150, 153–154
Panic of 1907 189–190
Pantzer Trio 164, 169, 173
Parisian Varieties (New York) 96
Park Row 3–6
Park Theater (New York) 6, 11
Pastor, Adele 123, 194, 195
Pastor, Amelia 8, 11
Pastor, Anna 39, 52, 194
Pastor, Antony 3–10, 123
Pastor, Caroline 5, 7, 9–10, 123, 180, 195
Pastor, Cornelia (Buckley) 3–5, 7–8, 10, 21–22, 48, 61, 122–123, 195
Pastor, Dolores 5, 7, 9, 123
Pastor, Dora 73
Pastor, Fernando 8–10, 21–22, 48, 51–52, 54–55, 59, 61–62, 66, 68–69, 71, 73, 85, 115, 160, 195
Pastor, Fernando, Jr. 73
Pastor, Frank 7–12, 14, 22, 37, 61, 90, 93, 96, 104, 107–108, 114–115, 194–195
Pastor, Mr. and Mrs. Henry 123, 194
Pastor, Josephine 130–131, 139, 152, 156, 158, 162, 164–165, 168–169, 174, 177, 182–183, 185, 187–190, 193–195
Pastor, Willian "Billy" 7, 9, 10–12, 14–15, 17, 22, 37, 45, 47–51, 54, 59–60, 64, 66, 68–69, 74, 81, 85, 88–89, 115, 160, 194–195
Patience 102–104
Patricola, Isabel 190
Patricola, Tom 190
The People's Theater (New York) 108, 123
Pettingill, Max 126, 130
Phantos 144
Philadelphia Press 116
Pikes Opera House (New York) 57
Piper's Opera House (Virginia City) 85
Pirates of Penzance 98
Pitrot, Herr 124
Poli, S.Z. 173, 188
Poole, John F. 43–45, 47, 49, 51–52, 57–59, 61–62, 73, 75–77, 82, 93, 95–96, 98, 109, 118
Proctor, F.F. 139, 143, 156, 160, 170, 176, 188, 194
Proctor's 23rd Street Theater (New York) 143, 154
Proctor's 58th Street Theater (New York) 156
Prof. Abt 130–131, 133, 139
Prof. Richards 76
Prof. Warner 108
Professional baseball 164
Pryde, Peggy 128
Puck, Eva 191

Queen, Johnny 66

Ragged Coat 26
Ray, Charlotte 158
Raymond, Maud 158–159, 164
Raymond and Waring Menagerie 12
Regan, H.W. 66
Revene and Athos 126, 131
Rice, Dan 20
Rice, E.E. 112
Rice & Barton 123
Richmond, Harry 109
Riggs, T.G. 34, 47–49, 52, 54, 57–62, 64
Riggs and Fitzgerald 63
Riley, William 121
Ring, Blanche 1, 169–170, 180
Rivers, Frank 17, 20–22
Robinson, Hall 8
Rogers Bros. 150, 152–154, 158–159, 164, 180, 185–186
Roof garden shows 161, 176
Rooney, Katie 158
Rooney, Pat 2, 77, 80, 119, 167–168, 173, 180
Rosa, Patti 77
Rose, Julian 174, 176, 180
Routt, Cora 158
Ruin High or Die 16
Runnells, Bonnie 95–96, 108, 110
Russell, Lillian 1, 97–99, 101, 103–104, 109, 112, 148, 161, 175, 190, 194

Index

Russell, Susie 131
Russell Bros. 110, 133, 137–140, 144, 147–148, 151–152, 154, 156, 158, 165, 169, 174, 176, 180–181, 194
Ryan and Richfield 129
Ryman, Ad 96, 133, 157

Sabel, Josephine 158–159
St. Felix Ballet Troupe 74
St. Felix Sisters 95–96, 110, 116, 122, 139, 186
St. James Theater (New York) 68
St. John's Wort 162, 166
St. Nicholas Hotel 23
Sanderson, Harry 71–72, 90, 93, 95–97, 104, 107, 110, 116, 118, 123, 125, 127, 129, 139–140, 143–144, 146, 149, 152, 155, 157–161, 164–165, 167, 174, 176, 181–183, 187, 189, 192–194
Sand's Circus 20
Sands, Nathans and Quick Circus 14, 17, 19, 22
Sanford, S.S. 40, 73
Sanford and Weston 80
Sarah's Young Man 188, 191
Savoy Theater (New York) 183
The Schallers 140
Schrode Bros. 111
Schubert Bros. 176
Scully, Dan 2, 167
Seabert, Charles F. 62, 64, 66, 68, 72–73
Seeley and West 138, 146
The Seven Ages of Women 33
Seven Reed Birds 162, 167
Seymour, Nels 38, 60–62, 64, 170
Sharpley, Sam 26, 38, 40, 42–45, 47–48
Sheppard, Billy 54, 57, 62
Sheridan and Flynn 135
Sheridan and Mack 42
Siddons, Mrs. Sarah 34
Sidman, Arthur 159, 162
Simms, Lizzie 104, 111
Sisters Coleman 138
Sisters Flexmore 144
Sisters Hartwicke 138
Sisters le Blanche 140
Sisters Preston 148, 154
Smith, Edgar 167
Smith, Helene 61,63
Somers, Alice 61
Southern, Georgia 90
Spanish-American war 163–165, 169
Staats Zeitung 29
Standard Theater (New York) 92–93, 102
Star Spangled Banner 26, 64, 164
Steele, Harry 107
Stereopticon 77, 157
The Streets of New York 43–44
Sullivan, J.L. 114
Sullivan, Rose 135
Summerville, Amelia 1, 167
Sunday Dispatch 130
Sweatnam, William 159

Syndicate (A.V.M.) 160, 169–170, 172–176, 178, 180, 183, 188

Tammany Hall 1–2, 8, 57–60, 100, 103, 111, 125–127, 139, 162, 190, 192, 194
Tammany Society 100, 127
Tascott 185
Taylor, Laura 42
Temperance groups 8
Temple, Rose 107
Tettenborn, Lina 95–96
Thatcher, George 93
That's What's the Matter 26
Theater Comique (New York) 57–58, 60, 62, 68–69, 72, 74, 82, 87–88, 108, 111, 148, 167, 170
Theater fires 6, 55–56, 68, 87, 111, 125–126, 137, 183
Things I Don't Like to See 13
3rd Street Theater (New York) 112, 114
Thomas, Hilda 111–112, 116, 119, 169–170, 176, 180
Thompson, Denman 2, 87, 135
Thomson, G.W. 54,56, 59
Thomson, Harry 169, 174, 176, 185
Thornberg, Prof. 144
Thorne, Harry 76, 116, 185
Thorne, Mrs. Harry 185
Thornton, Bonnie 147, 150, 153, 156, 160, 162, 169, 176, 182
The Three Keatons 180, 182, 184, 186
The Three Phoites 121–122
Tilley, Vesta 2, 148, 151–153, 155–156, 161, 171
Till's Marionettes 110, 118
Tivoli Theater (New York) 85
Tony Pastor's Almanac 95
Tony Pastor's Bowery Songster 31
Tony Pastor's Opera House (New York) 43–52, 54–64, 66, 68–69, 71–76, 79, 81
Tony Pastor's Union Songster 26
Tony's Choice for Mayor 92
Tooley, Larry 64, 77, 79–80
Travelle 156
A Trip to Coontown 163
T'row Him Down McClusky 146
Tucker, Sophie 191
Turles 138
Turner and Lester 66
201 Bowery (New York) 42, 46, 52, 58, 63, 81–82

Unification of five cities 162–163
Union Forever 26
Union Square 41,63, 66, 98, 100–101, 133, 143–144, 151, 153, 163, 178
Union Square Theater (New York) 100, 125, 149–150, 155–156, 158, 170, 174, 182
The Union Train 26
The Upper and Lower Ten Thousand 31

Valarez, Juniori 141, 150
Valmore, Jennie 131

Van, Billy 167
Varieties Theater (Chicago) 19, 38
Varieties Theater (New York) 40, 44, 59, 60
Vassar, Queen 116, 121, 141
Victoria, Vesta 2, 144, 146–147, 156, 161, 171
Vincent, Edith 138
Vivian, Charles 52, 54
The Vivians 112
Vonare 135

Waldman, Fred 122
Wallack's Theater (New York) 25
Walters, Charles 66
Wambold, James 38–40
Ward, Isabel 119, 121, 135
Ward and Curran 169, 185
Ward and Vokes 146, 149, 152
Washburn's Circus 14
Washington Post 40
Waterfall Sonster 31
Watson and Ellis 88,92
Watson Bros. 104, 112
Waverly Theater (New York) 59, 66
Wayburn, Ned 191
Weber, Joe 152, 185, 194
Weber & Fields 2, 122, 140, 144–145, 148, 152, 167, 170, 172–173, 180, 183, 185
Weber & Fields Music Hall (New York) 180, 185
Wedlock Is a Tickish Thing 17
Welch, Joe 164, 174, 176, 180
Welch and Mann's Circus 11
Welch and Nathans Circus 9
Welch, Delevan and Nathan's Circus 13
Welch, Mann and Delevan Circus 12
Welch, Nathans, Bancker and Christy Circus 13–14
Wells, Amelia 42
Wesner, Ella 1, 22, 60–62, 64, 69–70, 74, 77, 96, 110, 129, 167
West, Dot 176
West, Ford 176
Western, Lilly 1,105, 107,110–111, 116–117, 130–131, 133, 141, 146, 157, 159–160, 165, 176, 186
Weston Sisters 85
When the Band Begins to Play 69
Where Was Moses When the Lights Went Out? 92
White, Charley 8, 26, 30–31, 33, 38, 40, 49, 52, 55, 170
White, Frank 105, 107, 116, 117, 121, 131, 133
White, Lillian 105, 107, 116, 121, 131, 133
The White Rats 173–175, 188, 194
White's Athenaeum (New York) 72–73
Whitlock, Billy 8
The Wife That Wears the Breeches 33
Wild, Johnny 30, 40, 42, 48, 62, 64
Williams, Gus 1, 55, 60, 72–74, 80, 85, 88, 90, 135, 160, 167, 173, 194
Williams, H.W. 121

Williams, Percy 173, 188
Williams and Griffin 140
Williams and Walker 154–155, 161
Wills, Nat 2, 174, 176, 180
Wilson, Francis 2
Witmark and Sons 153
Witmark Bros. 130–131
Woodruff, Christian B. 8
Wood's Minstrel Hall (New York) 34

Wood's Museum (New York) 57, 62, 87
Wray, Ada 64

A Yankee Boy Is Trim and Tall 26
Yeamans, Annie 1, 85, 164, 17
Yeamans, Lydia 1, 85, 121, 133, 139, 141, 143–144, 148, 157, 174
Yeamans, Titus, F.J. 143–144, 148, 157, 174

You'll Never Miss the Water Til the Well Runs Dry 81

Ziegfeld, Flo 180, 185, 188
Zukor, Adolphe 180

www.ingramcontent.com/pod-product-compliance
Ingram Content Group UK Ltd.
Pitfield, Milton Keynes, MK11 3LW, UK
UKHW050527150426
5217IPUK00026B/1832